The European Monetary System and European Monetary Union

The Political Economy of Global Interdependence
Thomas D. Willett, Series Editor

The European Monetary System and European Monetary Union,
Michele Fratianni and Jürgen von Hagen

Speculation and the Dollar: The Political Economy of Exchange Rates,
Laurence A. Krause

Profit-Making Speculation in Foreign Exchange Markets,
Patchara Surajaras and Richard J. Sweeney

The Political Economy of International Organizations:
A Public Choice Approach, edited by Roland Vaubel and
Thomas D. Willett

Crossing Frontiers: Explorations in International
Political Economy, Benjamin J. Cohen

FORTHCOMING

Growth, Debt, and Politics: The Political Performance
of Governments and the Third World Debt Crisis,
Lewis W. Snider

International Economic Sanctions,
William H. Kaempfer and Anton D. Lowenberg

The European Monetary System and European Monetary Union

Michele Fratianni and
Jürgen von Hagen

Westview Press

BOULDER • SAN FRANCISCO • OXFORD

The Political Economy of Global Interdependence

Copyright © 1992 by Westview Press, Inc.

Published in 1992 in the United States of America by Westview Press, Inc., 5500 Central Avenue, Boulder, Colorado 80301-2847, and in the United Kingdom by Westview Press, 36 Lonsdale Road, Summertown, Oxford OX2 7EW

Library of Congress Cataloging-in-Publication Data
Fratianni, Michele.
  The European monetary system and European monetary union / by Michele Fratianni and Jürgen von Hagen.
    p. cm. — (Political economy of global interdependence)
  Includes bibliographical references and index.
  ISBN 0-8133-7995-4
  1. European Monetary System (Organization) 2. Monetary policy—European Economic Community countries. I. Hagen, Jürgen von. II. Title. III. Series.
HG930.5.F735 1992
332.4'5'094—dc20   92-1348
                                                                                CIP

Printed and bound in the United States of America

     The paper used in this publication meets the requirements
(∞) of the American National Standard for Permanence of Paper
     for Printed Library Materials Z39.48-1984.

10   9   8   7   6   5   4   3   2   1

For Linda and Ilse

Contents

Tables and Figures

Tables

Figures

Acronyms

ARCH	Autoregressive Conditional Heteroskedasticity
BFR	Belgian/Luxemborg Franc
CAP	Common Agricultural Policy
DKR	Danish Kroner
DM	Deutsche Mark
EC	European Community
ECB	European Central Bank
ECU	European Currency Unit
EEMU	European Economic and Monetary Union
EMCF	European Monetary Cooperation Fund
EMS	European Monetary System
EMU	Economic and Monetary Union
ERM	Exchange-Rate Mechanism
ESCB	European System of Central Banks
EU	Economic Union
FF	French Franc
GDH	German-Dominance Hypothesis
HECU	Hard European Currency Unit
HFL	Dutch Guilder
IRL	Irish Punt
LIT	Italian Lira
MCA	Monetary Compensatory Amount
MU	Monetary Union
OECD	Organization for Economic Cooperation and Development
PST	Spanish Peseta
VSTF	Very Short Term Facility

Preface

This book summarizes much of our individual and joint work on various aspects of the European Monetary System (EMS) developed over the last few years. We offer it to our readers as a comprehensive research report, encompassing the enumeration of the critical issues, the development of the analytical framework to discuss the issues, the empirical strategy to sort out the relevance of competing views, and the policy conclusions we draw from our entire research. The organizational principle of the book is the juxtaposition of two rival interpretations of the EMS: One views it as a system to enhance monetary discipline, the other as a framework for coordinating monetary policies. This juxtaposition serves us well also in discussing the monetary future of Europe, namely the prospects and strategies for achieving monetary union.

Methodologically, the book pursues two approaches, largely complementary. The first one is the strategic analysis of central bank policies in the open economy using international macroeconomics models and basic concepts of game theory. The other is the public choice reasoning to monetary policy and central banking. In either case, we have tried to balance theoretical arguments with empirical analysis and have used both to draw policy conclusions.

It is our hope that our methodologies make our work appealing and interesting to different types of readers: the international economist, the political economist, the political scientist, and the student of foreign affairs. The book is organized to suit the interests of these various groups. Chapters 1 and 2 present the historical and institutional background relevant for all students of European monetary integration. The rest of the book is addressed to readers who have some knowledge of international monetary economics and game theory. The main arguments and results of the EMS are laid out in Chapter 3. Chapters 4 through 7 are more analytical than the other chapters. However, we have written summaries with a view to help the political scientist, the less technically inclined scholar, and the reader who wishes to focus on the political economy of the European Monetary System and European Monetary Union.

This book would not have been possible without the support of many individuals and institutions. We thank Tom Willett for encouraging us to pursue our project and for his guidance during the realization; Richard Burdekin for careful refereeing; Paul de Grauwe, Patrick Minford, Manfred J.M. Neumann, Roland Vaubel, and Lorenzo Bini-Smaghi for valuable comments; and Shelley Arnold and Shelley Pepmeier for competent typing. The Indiana University Center for Global Business provided much appreciated financial assistance. During the time of writing this book, the authors enjoyed the hospitality and stimulating environments of the Federal Reserve Bank of St. Louis, the Sonder-forschungsbereich 303 at the University of Bonn, the Italian International Economic Center, and the Centrum voor Economische Studien at the Catholic University of Leuven. We thank these institutions and the colleagues therein for raising many interesting questions and providing insights.

Research is like a pudding: The pleasure is in the eating. These pleasures, alas, are hard to externalize. It is for this that we wish to dedicate this book to our wives, Linda and Ilse, and thank them for enduring our enjoyment nevertheless.

Michele Fratianni
Jürgen von Hagen
Bloomington, Indiana

1

Principles and Issues of European Monetary Unification

In 1978, the European Community (EC) created the European Monetary System (EMS) in an effort to strengthen the coordination of monetary and economic policies among the members of the Community, to stabilize exchange rates, and to take a new step on the road of monetary unification in Europe. The treaties establishing the EC in 1958 mentioned monetary policies and their coordination only briefly and did not talk about the creation of a monetary union in Europe at all. Yet since its foundation, the EC has spent considerable energy and political effort on these very issues. The EMS followed several unsuccessful attempts to stabilize exchange rates among the Community members. Its charter describes the goals of the EMS as "a greater measure of monetary stability," "growth with stability," and "convergence of economic development." The new system was not generally well-received. The majority of the economics profession on both sides of the Atlantic predicted its inevitable and early failure. Arguing on the strength of conventional open-economy macroeconomics, these economists concluded that an arrangement forcing high-inflation countries, like France and Italy, and low-inflation countries, like Germany, to coexist under the constraint of fixed nominal exchange rates could not last long. Others predicted that the EMS would survive for political reasons but at the cost of generally higher inflation rates in Europe.

Fourteen years later, the EMS is thriving and generally is regarded as a success. In fact, it has remained the only functioning multilateral exchange rate arrangement among industrial countries since the breakdown of the Bretton Woods system. What is more, the EMS is now about to serve as the launching pad for comprehensive monetary union in Europe.

1

This book deals with three aspects of the EMS: how it came into being, how it has worked so far, and how it may evolve into a full-fledged monetary union.

1.1 Theoretical Issues and Competing Hypotheses

The book addresses several issues in the broader areas of international economics and political economy. The first is the operation of a system like the EMS that, in principle, is based on fixed rates of exchange but seeks to retain flexibility by allowing periodic changes in the central parities. The key question is why high-inflation and low-inflation countries give up their monetary independence and join in an arrangement to maintain fixed but adjustable exchange rates.

The second issue is the operation of a monetary union, in which exchange rates are permanently fixed. The arrangement raises an important question: Under what conditions is a monetary union in Europe preferable to a system that preserves at least some exchange-rate flexibility? Furthermore, what determines the long-run inflation rate in a monetary union, and how should the union be structured to guarantee price stability? Finally, one must consider the choice between a currency union, in which the member countries adopt the same money, and an exchange-rate union, in which countries link their national monies to one another through permanently fixed exchange rates: Once the EC has decided to lock exchange rates permanently, should all the members adopt the same currency or should they retain their individual ones?

The third issue is the adjustment process from the current EMS to the future monetary union. The critical questions concern the optimal speed of the transition process and how the institutional framework of the new monetary union should be built. The fundamental choice is between superimposing a European central bank (ECB) on the existing monetary arrangements and a process of national monetary reforms leading gradually to the creation of an ECB.

The European Monetary System

Despite voluminous literature on the subject, there is still no consensus about the relative importance of two different views of the EMS. Both are based on long traditions of economic thought in Europe. The first regards the EMS as an arrangement conducive to the strategic coordination of monetary policies in the EMS countries. We call this the "cooperative interpretation" of the EMS. The second sees the EMS primarily as an instrument to reduce the inflation trends in the region. This is the "disciplinary interpretation" of the EMS.

The cooperative interpretation stresses the fixed exchange-rate mechanism of the EMS as a substitute for more complete, welfare-improving monetary policy coordination. Policy coordination in the EMS improves the EC's response to shocks originating outside the region, such as oil price shocks and swings in U.S. monetary and fiscal policy. From this perspective, there is no reason to expect that changing the trend inflation rate in the member countries is, or ought to be, the main purpose of the EMS. So long as realignments are permitted, inflation trends can be chosen in accordance with national preferences. The early literature in support of the EMS shared this view and emphasized two structural characteristics that made the EMS a new kind of exchange-rate arrangement: *symmetry*, meaning that all member countries had to share equally the burden of adjustment implied by a return to balance-of-payments equilibria; and *flexibility*, meaning that no country had to adopt an inflation trend other than its own most preferred one. Symmetry and flexibility are clearly recognized in the institutional design of the EMS.

More recently, the disciplinary interpretation of the EMS has gained popularity. It builds on the theory of central bank credibility, which holds that equilibrium inflation rates are determined by the credibility of a central bank's commitment to price stability. From this perspective, the large inflation differentials in the EMS of the late 1970s suggest that central banks in the region had widely different degrees of credibility. The German Bundesbank in particular appears to have a comparative advantage in credibility over its counterparts, like the Banque de France and the Banca d'Italia, in the more inflation-prone countries. Based on its proven commitment to price stability in the past and its relatively large degree of political independence, the Bundesbank is able to pursue a credible low-inflation monetary policy. Other central banks, in contrast, are unable to convince the private sector of their determination to carry out a disinflation program and consequently are locked into unfavorable, high-inflation equilibria. The disciplinary view contends that the high-inflation countries have used the fixed exchange-rate mechanism of the EMS to delegate the conduct of their monetary policies to the Bundesbank, thereby signaling to their own private sectors that they are serious about their newly found commitment to price stability. In return for giving up their monetary policy autonomy, these central banks enjoy the benefit of the Bundesbank's greater credibility, which allows them to reduce inflation rates and, perhaps more important, to lower the output and employment cost of disinflation relative to an independent domestic monetary strategy.

The disciplinary interpretation implies that the principles of symmetry and flexibility have failed in the EMS. In fact, it requires that the system be asymmetric in the sense that monetary policy is dominated by the rigid, low inflation rule of the Bundesbank. On the other hand, it suggests an explanation for why the larger countries in the EMS, France and Italy, have sought membership in a system in which Germany appears to be the hegemonic country.

Monetary Union

There is no categorical or unconditional reason to conclude that a monetary union is preferable to a flexible exchange regime. On the one hand, a monetary union eliminates exchange-rate flexibility and the attendant degrees of freedom economies enjoy in coping with supply and demand shocks. Because certain shocks are better handled with a common monetary policy but others are better handled with independent monetary policies, the preferability of the union depends critically on the nature and the mix of the shocks to which the participating countries are exposed. On the other hand, a common monetary policy—which is a direct implication of a monetary union—can be seen as a collusive agreement among central banks with the intent of raising the benefits of inflation. Collusion by central banks damages the discipline imposed on them by competitive monetary policies and leads to higher inflation. But one cannot exclude the prospect that monetary union could lower inflation rates. This favorable outcome will materialize if the union enables central banks, which are otherwise highly dependent on their national governments, to commit credibly to a policy of price stability.

Fixed exchange-rate regimes and monetary unions are often treated as equivalent in academic and policy discussions. However, there are reasons to distinguish carefully between these two arrangements. A regime of fixed exchange rates implies the existence of several national monies. Even though governments can engage in a formal agreement to fix irrevocably their exchange rates, the fact that national currencies remain cannot rule out that exchange rates may change in the future (perhaps under dire circumstances). Hence, an irrevocably fixed exchange-rate system has less credibility than a system in which the countries share a common currency—that is, a full-fledged monetary union.

The Adjustment Process

Governments can accept the goal of monetary union and yet hold different views and preferences on how to reach it. We identify two main camps on this issue. One group, led by the Bundesbank, argues that monetary union should be the "coronation" of a long process of economic integration and macroeconomic convergence gradually aligning the countries with high inflation and profligate fiscal policies to the countries with low inflation and prudent fiscal policies. The other group, led by the French government, argues instead that monetary union is an instrument for achieving convergence, and that therefore a monetary union can be created before convergence has been achieved. Furthermore, this group regards monetary union and economic integration as interactive processes that should proceed in parallel.[1] At the heart of this conflict, which has a long tradition in EC monetary matters, stand two critical questions: Who adjusts to whom, that is, what will be the long-run inflation rate in the monetary union, and who carries the burden of correcting balance-of-payments disequilibria?

1.2 Structure and Main Findings of the Book

Chapter 2 describes the EMS with the broadest brush. We set the stage by reviewing the antecedents of the EMS. Our intent is to underscore the long political commitment of European leaders to the idea of monetary union, a commitment that is not an end in itself but subservient to the larger objective of political union. After describing the essential elements of the EMS, we present evidence showing that its greatest achievement has been to reduce exchange-rate and inflation uncertainty. In contrast, its success in promoting disinflation is much less convincing. Indeed, the reduction of inflation rates in the EMS, praised by those who favor the disciplinary hypothesis, turns out to be no different from the inflation rate reduction achieved by countries outside the EMS, but the loss of output growth and employment associated with disinflation has been larger and more persistent in the EMS than outside it.

Chapter 3 lays out the cooperative and the disciplinary interpretations of the EMS. The first two sections of this chapter present the two views in a general way and discuss their origins and merits in the context of the historical and political events leading to the EMS and of monetary policymaking in the early 1980s. This portion of Chapter 3 is complemented with nontechnical empirical evidence presented in Section 4.2 and Chapters 5 and 7. The third part of Chapter 3 develops a model of strategic monetary policymaking in the EMS that is the basis for the theoretical discussion in Chapters 4 and 6.

Chapter 4 considers the disciplinary interpretation of the EMS. Borrowing credibility from the Bundesbank requires that the high-inflation country peg its currency to the deutsche mark; the Bundesbank chooses the monetary policy course for the whole system. The analysis of the model reveals several flaws of the hypothesis. First, the credibility gain for the high-inflation country is not unambiguous. Second, why do the same people who have little faith in the central bank's willingness to stick to a low inflation domestic monetary target believe in its commitment to a low-inflation exchange-rate target? Something special about an exchange-rate commitment must be added to the model to make it more credible than a monetary target. One possibility is that breaking an exchange-rate target carries an extra cost, such as a loss of political support, large enough to prevent the monetary policy maker from succumbing to the temptation of breaking the arrangement for the benefit of a temporary increase in output and employment.

Furthermore, the Bundesbank's incentives to supply credibility to the high-inflation central bank are unclear. Germany unambiguously loses credibility in the EMS. Consequently, its payoff from being in the EMS must come in some other form, and one must resort again to some generic political or other unspecified gains to explain German membership in the EMS.

Turning to the empirical evidence, we find that the inflation performance of the EMS during the 1980s was no different from the performance of non-EMS countries. In fact, the two empirical characteristics of the 1980s—the general reduction of inflation rates and the international convergence of inflation rates at low levels—can be observed both in the EMS and outside it. Thus, the inflation data are consistent with two alternative hypotheses that give no credit at all to the EMS: (1) namely that all industrial countries were exposed to similar macroeconomic shocks favoring disinflation during the 1980s or (2) that policymakers in all industrial countries simply became dissatisfied with the inflation consequences of the "aggressive" demand management of the 1970s and were willing to adopt policies more compatible with price stability. Therefore, the merits and achievements of the EMS cannot be inferred by looking at inflation rates alone.

An alternative way to assess the disciplinary view is to test its main structural implication, namely that Germany dominates the EMS in the sense that the Bundesbank determines the system's monetary policy independently of the other monetary authorities and that the other central banks passively follow all Bundesbank actions. Our evidence presented in Chapter 5 does not confirm the alleged hegemonic role of the Bundesbank. It suggests instead that the EMS is a largely interactive arrangement. The Bundesbank has not completely constrained the actions of the other central banks in the system, nor does it act altogether independently of other EMS countries. In other words, the EMS has created an environment in which central banks cooperate rather than submit to a hegemony.

Yet, French and Italian policymakers have claimed repeatedly that the system works asymmetrically. Our evidence indeed reveals significant asymmetries. First, there is a core group in the EMS, consisting of Germany and its smaller neighbors, acting more homogeneously than the remaining EMS countries. Second, Germany appears to be the most independent country in the EMS in the long run. In contrast, France and Italy have relatively weak positions in the system in the sense that they contribute less to EMS monetary policy making than their relative sizes would lead one to expect. However, these asymmetries are not the same as Bundesbank dominance in the EMS.

In Chapters 6 and 7 we discuss the cooperative interpretation of the EMS. Central bank cooperation can be superior to independent policies because it can incorporate the externalities generated by international spillovers of monetary policy. Interesting questions have vexed advocates of policy cooperation: Why don't we observe more cooperation in the world, and what is the relationship between optimal policy coordination and fixing exchange rates? One answer to the first question lies in the incentive structure of cooperative arrangements. There is an inherent conflict between the collective interest of a group of countries and the interest of the individual member. Once an agreement has been reached by the group, individual members gain by deviating from the joint strategy, just as a member of a cartel gains by secretly undercutting the cartel price. Therefore, successful cooperation requires relatively easy monitoring of individual members in order to make "cheating" difficult.

The agreement to peg exchange rates in the EMS can be regarded as an attempt at cooperation that fits this requirement because exchange rates can be monitored continuously. However, fixed exchange rates imply some loss of freedom and therefore yield only a suboptimal form of cooperation. The question of whether policy coordination with fixed exchange rates is better than independent monetary policies and flexible exchange rates depends critically on the nature of the shocks and the extent of structural asymmetries. The EMS is preferable if common shocks affecting all members alike dominate distributional shocks. This point is consistent with traditional open-economy macroeconomics, whose adherents see economic integration and structural similarity as preconditions for a successful exchange-rate union. Furthermore, the desirability of a system like the EMS depends on the reaction of the nonmember countries, like the United States. In general, an outsider's optimal policy response to coordinated monetary policies in the EMS is different from its response to independent monetary policies of the EMS countries. Simulation results presented in Chapter 6 indicate that an increasing degree of economic and financial integration among the members tends to alleviate the tensions created by structural asymmetries and distributional shocks. In this sense, the EC's efforts to complete the internal market are likely to strengthen the EMS and the case for a monetary union.

Individual members may gain or lose from EMS membership—even though the arrangement is beneficial to the group as a whole—because the distribution of gains depends on the covariance between common and distributional shocks and on differences in economic structures, such as different degrees of factor mobility and in wage and price flexibility. Indeed, the distribution of the welfare gains from coordination can become so skewed that a country would find it advantageous to leave the system unless properly compensated by other members. This suggests that the survival of the EMS, and even more so of a monetary union, requires fiscal and regional policies at the EC level to ensure that the benefits of coordination are distributed among all participants. We return to this topic in Chapter 8, where we argue that from a public choice perspective, an income-based tax system is preferable to an expenditure policy as a method of distributing gains among the members.

Chapter 7 presents evidence corroborating the cooperative interpretation of the EMS. The main achievements of the EMS have been the reduction of the exchange-rate and inflation uncertainty. The EMS has traded lower internal for higher external exchange-rate uncertainty: Lower variance of EMS exchange rates goes along with higher variance of exchange rates, both nominal and real, between EMS and non-EMS currencies. To the extent that exchange-rate uncertainty depresses international trade, this trade-off makes the welfare gains of the EMS ambiguous depending on the relative importance of the variances and the relative importance of trade among EMS countries as opposed to trade between EMS and non-EMS countries. Evidence of changes in the stochastic distribution of unexpected inflation suggests that policy coordination in the EMS has achieved a greater degree of symmetry of inflation shocks in the region and has alleviated the impact of shocks originating outside the EMS.

The EMS has provided two safety valves to protect itself against the tensions resulting from wide and lasting inflation differentials: capital and exchange controls and realignments, which manifest the principles of symmetry and flexibility in the design and operation of the system. Capital and exchange controls shelter domestic from international money and capital markets and result in positive differentials between offshore and onshore interest rates. Since 1983, they have been gradually dismantled as required by the Internal Markets Program. Realignments give member countries the freedom to choose long-run monetary trends independently. But realignments cannot be perfectly anticipated; if they were, the EMS would be exposed to speculative attacks. Thus, re-alignments are a source of exchange-rate uncertainty that must be considered in the evaluation of the EMS. The evidence presented in Chapter 7 suggests that realignment uncertainty was significant in the 1980s. Yet the markets learned to form expectations about the size and the timing of the realignments correctly. Chapter 8 deals with economic and monetary union, EMU. European policymakers, with the exception of the British government, appear to be committed to the formation of a monetary union in the EC. From a public choice perspective, monetary union can be seen as a form of collusion among central banks that limits the degree of international competition of monetary policies and thereby reduces the average quality of monetary policy (long-run price stability). But there are also reasons why a monetary union could improve the quality of monetary policy in Europe. Much depends on the appropriate institutional reforms. The future European central bank must be credible in its commitment to a low-inflation policy. To this end, it is imperative that it be completely independent of the national governments and the European Council. The club nature of the future monetary authority suggests that voting rules in the central bank council must be designed to ensure a low-inflation outcome. Similarly, rules for distributing seignorage revenue among the member countries have to be devised to reinforce the incentives for low-inflation policies.

The proper functioning of a monetary union requires that tax laws be harmonized to avoid distortions of relative prices and that income be distributed among EC members to buffer against shocks that affect regions differently. Beyond that, however, greater coordination or centralization of government spending in the monetary union is not only unnecessary but counterproductive. It promotes political entre-preneurship and weakens the position of the European central bank relative to the fiscal authorities. The same principle applies to the call for fiscal restraints advocated by the Delors committee. The strategy of making the European central bank independent and letting the market penalize fiscal profligacy promises to be a better alternative than spending or budget deficit limits that can be easily manipulated by politicians.

Chapter 9 deals with the transition phase to EMU. If EMU is the ultimate goal, how fast should one attempt to reach it? Gradually, so as to give the twelve EC countries time to adjust, or rapidly, so as to lock in the disinflation gains achieved so far? A short transition period would be preferable, because it would raise the cost of policy reversal and thereby raise the credibility of the commitment to EMU. But too rapid a transition entails the premature loss of the flexibility in the adjustment to transitory, asymmetric shocks that is offered through flexible exchange rates and even the EMS. We discuss the various proposals for a strategy to EMU, including the Delors proposal and the "Hard-ECU" strategy of the British government. Strategies based on the introduction of parallel currencies have the advantage of offering a flexible, market-determined, transition path, but there is little reason to believe that the parallel currency can achieve the final goal of monetary union. Strategies based on tightening the EMS constraint, on the other hand, lead to the desired outcome but at the cost of disruptive transition processes, the instability of which jeopardizes the successful outcome and the credibility of the final goal. We conclude by offering our own proposal, which is based on softening of the EMS constraint, strengthening policy coordination in the EC, and depoliticizing exchange-rate adjustments.

Notes

1. The debate of the late 1960s referred to these two strategies as "economist" and "monetarist," respectively.

2

A Description of the European Monetary System

2.1 The Long Road to Monetary Union

The Treaty of Rome, which created the European Economic Community, is very specific about the elimination of trade barriers. In contrast, it contains only vague provisions related to common macroeconomic and, specifically, monetary policies. Altogether there are six articles in the treaty with some bearing on monetary policy. Article 104 defines external equilibrium, full employment, price stability, and external stability of the currencies as the common, general objectives of economic policy in the Community.[1] Article 103 declares that "Member States shall regard their stabilization policies as a matter of common concern" and requires that members share information about such policies. Article 107 equally proclaims exchange-rate policies as a matter of common concern. If exchange rates turn out to be inconsistent with the objectives stated in Article 104, the European Commission, the Community's administration, may authorize member states to take appropriate actions. Article 107 also sanctions the use of exchange and capital controls. Article 105 calls upon the members to coordinate their economic and monetary policies and to facilitate cooperation among the national authorities. This article also foresees the formation of a Monetary Committee in the EC with a simple advisory status: "to facilitate attainment of the objectives set out in Article 104" Article 108 calls for mutual assistance in balance-of-payments problems, but Article 109 in essence says that in an emergency, member states can take any measure without consideration of its effect on others.

A Brief History of Monetary Policy Coordination in the EC

Despite the brevity of the Treaty's provisions, the close coordination of monetary policies has a long tradition in the Community. As early as 1959 the European Parliament proposed the formation of an institution patterned after the U.S. Federal Reserve System (Tsoukalis 1977, 53). A host of important Community politicians—including Jean Monnet, Robert Marjolin, and Pierre Vigny—endorsed some form of exchange-rate union. During the first fifteen years of the EC, exchange-rate stability and a basic framework for policy coordination were actually furnished externally to the EC by the Bretton Woods system. The European Monetary Agreement of 1958 strengthened the provisions of the Bretton Woods system by limiting the bilateral margins of fluctuation among the EC currencies to 3 percent.

The 1960s brought two developments with important consequences for the EC's goal of monetary policy coordination. The rapid progress with the customs union and other forms of economic cooperation, including the "Common Agricultural Policy" (CAP), raised the desirability of stable exchange rates among the EC members. In fact, exchange-rate stability for the EC was regarded as so important that by the mid-1960s it became fashionable in Community circles to assert that Europe already enjoyed a de facto monetary union, because a return to flexible exchange rates was perceived as too harmful (Tsoukalis 1977). With the benefit of hindsight, Tsoukalis called this attitude "agricultural illusion." At the same time, however, the stability of the U.S. dollar, the center currency of the Bretton Woods system, gradually eroded and with it the external basis of European exchange-rate stability.

The Bretton Woods system had been under strain throughout the 1960s. Robert Triffin (1960) foresaw the critical weakness in the gold-dollar standard: the sustained growth of dollar liabilities relative to gold stocks was bound to create a confidence crisis about the ability of the center country to convert its liabilities into gold at the official price of $35 per ounce. By 1968, gold convertibility had virtually ceased; President Nixon formally ended it on August 15, 1971.

As noted in the report by the Commission on the Role of Gold, (1982, 86), "The Bretton Woods system might have been able to survive an end of gold convertibility. It could not survive the inflationary policies of the center country that characterized the decade from the mid-1960s on." Under the strains of the Vietnam War and Lyndon Johnson's Great Society programs, the United States embarked on a path of a higher and more variable inflation rate. In 1969 the French franc was devalued and Germany allowed the mark to appreciate. Subsequently, other countries decided to disconnect their currencies from the dollar. In 1973 the United States announced a 10 percent devaluation of the dollar.

As the crumbling of the old monetary order placed enormous political strain on the Community, new voices called for monetary union as a way to keep the EC together and to enhance the process of economic and political integration.[2] In an effort to repair the damage in French-German relations, the German chancellor Willy Brandt offered a proposal for the creation of a European Monetary Union at the Summit of the European Council, composed of EC heads of governments, in The Hague in December 1969. His proposal was strongly endorsed by the French government, with the result that for the first time, monetary union was declared a long-term goal of the EC. The summit gave impetus to the celebrated *Werner Report* (Council of the EC 1970), which recommended the implementation of a European monetary union in three stages. The first stage, from 1971 to 1974, would create the machinery for coordinated policy making. The second stage would make exchange-rate changes depend on explicit member agreements. A Community central bank, shaped after the U.S. Federal Reserve System, would centralize monetary policy in the final stage. The *Werner Report* led directly to the first European exchange-rate arrangement, the "Snake," in 1972; the creation of the European Monetary Cooperation Fund (EMCF) in 1973; and a spate of directives aimed at institutionalizing policy coordination (Christie and Fratianni, 1978). Subsequently, the *Marjolin Report* (Commission of the EC 1975) discussed the relationship between trade and goods market integration and monetary integration in the EC. It argued that monetary union should be postponed until after the achievement of a high degree of economic integration in the Community. Reducing barriers to trade and factor mobility would create a unified internal market as a sound basis for subsequent monetary unification. The *MacDougall Report* (Commission of the EC 1977) discussed the possibility of monetary integration from the perspective of fiscal federalism. The report stressed the role of a unified fiscal system in a monetary union and concluded that a monetary union would not be viable without a sufficiently large Community budget for fiscal policy.

The international economic and financial turmoil of the early and mid-1970s quickly brought the process of monetary unification to a halt. Recurrent realignments and the exit of several EC members soon made it clear that the Snake was not capable of coordinating Europe's monetary policies. With their very different approaches to stabilizing the economies, the EC countries experienced correspondingly different inflation rates and volatile exchange rates. A fresh impulse for closer monetary coordination had to come again from the political side. In a famous speech in Florence in 1977, European Commission president Roy Jenkins criticized the concept of a gradual *"politique des petits pas"* to build the monetary union on the basis of economic union (Jenkins 1978). Jenkins advocated a big leap forward instead. Monetary union would become the driving political force to obtain economic integration.

In 1978, German chancellor Helmut Schmidt and French president Valéry Giscard d'Estaing embarked on a political tour de force for a new monetary arrangement, at the end of which the EC formed the EMS in December 1978 (Ludlow 1982). The EMS charter set its goals to be "a greater measure of monetary stability," "growth with stability," and "convergence of economic development." But it is clear that the main objective was monetary stability. More than a decade later, it is fair to say that the EMS has surprised many merely for having survived this long. In fact, most conventional macroeconomists expected the EMS to fail for trying to forge high-inflation France and Italy into an exchange-rate arrangement with low-inflation Germany (Fratianni and von Hagen 1990a).

After a period of stagnation in the early 1980s, the process of monetary union regained momentum with the Community's efforts to complete its internal market program, the "Single European Market," or "Europe 1992" program. At its Madrid summit in June 1989, the Council adopted the *Delors Report* (1989) as the official blueprint for monetary unification. Written by central bank representatives from all EC member states, the report represents the first formal acknowledgment of the goal of monetary union by all central banks in the EC. Like the *Werner Report*, the *Delors Report* proposes to build monetary union in three stages and outlines institutional arrangements for each step.[3] It dwells again on the relationship between economic and monetary integration. In a compromise between the positions of the Marjolin and MacDougall reports and the political position of Jenkins (1978), it develops the concept of parallelism: monetary and economic integration are two aspects of the same process and must be pursued simultaneously. The report also deals with the role of fiscal policy in a monetary union, calling repeatedly for fiscal policy coordination and the imposition of binding restraints on members' budgetary policies.

The Madrid summit paved the way for a monetary amendment to the Treaty of Rome. At its Rome summit in December 1990, the European Council inaugurated an intergovernmental conference to prepare the amendment. A first draft of the constitution of the future European Central Bank (ECB) was presented to this summit by the Council of Central Bank Governors. By setting up a second intergovernmental conference dedicated to political union, the same summit made it clear once more how closely monetary and political integration are intertwined in Europe.

Economic Integration and Monetary Integration

Despite declarations in the *Delors Report* and elsewhere, there is no compelling reason why economic integration must be accompanied by monetary integration, understood in the broad sense of either a common money or several monies linked to one another by permanently fixed exchange rates. Monetary integration can, of course, be a valuable complement to economic integration; still, markets for goods, services, labor, and capital can be perfectly integrated, while different national monies are exchanged at flexible rates. What is the basis, then, for the popular claim (made most notably in Community circles) that the Single European Market needs monetary unification for its full development?

One ground is tradition. European policymakers have long wished stable exchange rates. The openness of their economies and their dependence on trade have reinforced the historical view—shaped to a large extent by the disruptive effects of fluctuating exchange rates on interwar trade—that stable exchange rates are a precondition for the orderly functioning of a customs union (Giavazzi and Giovannini 1989, 2-5).

The second reason has to do with the internal dynamics of the process of integration and the incentives of those who oversee and implement Community policy and derive political prestige from its enhancement. To describe these dynamics, Tsoukalis (1977) and van Ypersele and Koeune (1985) postulate the "cumulative logic of integration," according to which the process of integration, once it has started in one area of economic policy, will spread to other areas.

For example, the creation of a customs union such as the EC implies that member countries can no longer rely on commercial policy as an independent policy tool; commercial policy is shifted to the group level. It is a well-known fact that if goods prices move more slowly than asset prices, a devaluation of a currency is equivalent to a tariff on imported goods and a subsidy on exported goods (Dornbusch 1980, 67). The elimination of commercial policy as an independent policy tool creates the temptation to manipulate exchange rates to gain competitive advantages over other members of the customs union. Furthermore, nominal exchange-rate changes result in temporary real exchange-rate changes and "misalignments" (Williamson 1983; De Grauwe 1988; Bini-Smaghi 1990), that is, in incongruencies between real exchange rates and the underlying competitive relationships. Uncontrolled exchange-rate fluctuations, in a nutshell, can undermine the drive for free regional trade.[4] Fixing exchange rates, therefore, reduces conflict and enhances the stability of the customs union.

In addition, the elimination of barriers to trade and to capital and labor mobility raises the degree of economic interdependence, with the result that the effectiveness of national economic policies to achieve national objectives declines. This decline inevitably leads to calls for coordination of economic and monetary policies as a means of restoring the effectiveness of the policy tools over the larger, integrated area. Finally, economic integration generates solidarity among countries, reflected in provisions for mutual assistance and the coordination of policies to share the burden of adjustment to external shocks.

Van Ypersele and Koeune (1985) and Giavazzi and Giovannini (1989) regard CAP as an additional reason for fixing exchange rates in the EC. CAP is an agreement to fix agricultural supply prices in the EC in terms of the common numeraire ECU.[5] Farmers receive the national-currency equivalent of the regulated ECU prices. Changes in a currency's exchange rate against other member currencies and, hence, the ECU alter the international relations of agricultural goods prices and production incentives. One may therefore argue that such changes warp competitive conditions because they are not always related to productivity changes. But this argument is clearly equivocal: Fixed exchange rates in the presence of persistent inflation differentials are as distortive as exchange-rate changes in a world of equal inflation rates.

Nevertheless, the international financial crises of 1969 revealed how much the working of CAP was built on exchange-rate stability in practice. When the French franc was devalued, the French government combined the parity change with the introduction of so-called monetary compensatory amounts (MCAs) aimed at insulating the domestic farmers from the price effects of the devaluation. The German government followed suit when the DM was revalued subsequently. At the time, MCAs were widely regarded as incompatible with CAP rules, and their use was seen to precipitate the collapse of the EC (Tsoukalis 1977). The political significance of the exchange crisis can be attributed largely to these consequences.[6] CAP contributes to the desire for monetary union because permanently fixed exchange rates would make MCAs redundant and strengthen the functioning of CAP. But the importance of CAP in this regard should not be overstated. Ultimately, this particular motivation for fixed exchange rates rests only on the wish to rectify some of the flaws of a policy long recognized to be ill-conceived.

Monetary Integration and Political Integration

Our brief historical review has demonstrated that there is another basis for the quest for European monetary union, one that has little to do with economic reasoning. This is the general political movement for greater integration and unity in Western Europe. The use of a common currency has an obvious symbolic value for the political cohesion of regions and peoples; history shows that national political unification goes hand in hand with monetary unification (Ludlow 1982; Holtfrerich 1989; Sannucci 1989). As noted already by Triffin (1960), European politicians have long recognized this symbolic value and promoted monetary unification as a way to advance the political unification of Europe.[7]

The German chancellors, from Konrad Adenauer to Helmut Kohl, have pursued political unification as a way to integrate West Germany tightly into the Western alliance. The EMS itself stands in this tradition of political considerations. Chancellor Helmut Schmidt and President Giscard d'Estaing prepared for its creation on their own initiative without even notifying the bureaucracy in Brussels. They both clearly saw it as part of a larger political strategy, not just a tool for monetary coordination. Samuel Brittan (1979) speculated that Schmidt wanted to embark on the project because of the "weakness of the American dollar coupled with his well-known personal doubts about the political leadership and abilities of President Carter." The political nature of the decision is also illustrated by the fact that the Bundesbank was purposely kept in the dark because of its notorious opposition to any form of cooperative scheme of monetary policy (Ludlow 1989, 22). Of course, the predominance of political factors in the decisions leading to the EMS does not imply that economic reasons were absent. Both Schmidt and Giscard d'Estaing were preoccupied with the threat of global economic instability caused by erratic U.S. economic policies and volatile oil and raw materials prices.

Helmut Schmidt's memoirs (1990a, 1990b) provide us with valuable insights about the motivation underlying the formation of the EMS.[8] Recalling how Giscard d'Estaing had to defend himself in France against the accusation of having succumbed to German national interests, Schmidt wrote (1990b):

> Giscard developed this argument into a dimension of the "Grand Strategy": He characterized Britain as a power which could not rank with France both in economic and military terms, and called upon the French spirit not to be satisfied with being a secondary economic power, but to strive for parity with Germany. Should France miss this goal, Europe would be dominated by Germany.

After agreeing with Giscard that without France, the Bundesbank would have dominated monetary and credit policies in the EC, Schmidt stated flatly: "I had always regarded the EMS not only as a mere instrument to harmonize the economic policies of the EC member countries, but also as part of a broader strategy for the political self-determination in Europe." And later on: "France under Giscard was prepared for the loss of sovereignty which would come at the end of this road; the Bundesbank and many of the German professors of economics, who think of themselves as experts, were not prepared for it (and still are not today)."

The new rounds of negotiations over monetary union in 1990 and 1991 again revealed the strong political aspect of monetary unification. Indeed, the European Council (1990, 10) emphasized in its October 1990 summit in Rome the role of monetary union as an instrument to forge a politically unified Europe:

> Intergovernmental Conferences on Political Union and Economic and Monetary Union will open in Rome on 15 December 1990. . . . The European Council confirms that the work of the two Conferences will proceed in parallel and should be concluded rapidly and at the same time. The results will be submitted for ratification simultaneously with the objective of ratification before the end of 1992.

And again, the willingness to trade monetary autonomy, including a possible increase of price instability, for political integration seems particularly clear on the part of the German government, which appears more than ever determined to link political union to economic and monetary union. Germany and France would even like to include a common European defense clause in the treaty on political union (*Economist* 1991a, 50).

At the same time, the goal of a European monetary union is not yet fully shared within the Community. The British government under Margaret Thatcher expressed its opposition to monetary union loudly and made no secret of the fact that its opposition resulted largely from the antipathy to greater political integration in Europe and the fear of losing power to an all-embracing central bureaucracy in Brussels.[9] The government of John Major, although more sympathetic to the European "cause," has yet to endorse any move toward European political integration.

Opposition to European monetary integration is not limited to the British. As we have already remarked, the Bundesbank never quite accepted the EMS. Its position cannot be dismissed simply as a case of institutional self-preservation. There is a long political tradition in Germany going back to Ludwig Erhard, Adenauer's economics minister, who with German industrialists favored European free trade but not a commitment to political unification in Europe. It is instructive to quote again from Chancellor Schmidt (1990b):

The opposition which was brought up in Germany against the EMS in 1978 was, just as in France, really a nationalist opposition, but it developed in opposite ways in the two countries. Giscard was criticized because he allegedly delivered the economic welfare of his country to the price-stability oriented regime of the DM; I was criticized because I allegedly delivered the German economy to the inflation-oriented majority rule of the French, Italian and Belgian monetary policy.

On the role of the Bundesbank and its opposition to the EMS, we read: "The obstinate obstruction of the Bundesbank against the further development of the EMS has neither Keynesian nor monetarist foundations. Instead, it is motivated by the DM-focused missionary zeal for price stability."

The old Erhard-Bundesbank position clearly differentiates between economic integration and monetary integration. The British position of the late 1980s fits well into this tradition of recognizing the large promises of economic integration but disregarding the advantages of monetary integration as small and resenting its political dimension.

To summarize, the arguments behind the claim that monetary union must be a precondition for a full economic integration are based more in the nature of political economy than in proper economic reasoning. It is important to emphasize this point to appreciate fully the quest for monetary union in Europe, a quest that rests on the desire for political unification of the EC—with monetary unification as the vehicle for achieving that—rather than the intention to complete economic integration. Similarly, the opposition to monetary union is grounded much less on economic arguments than on a general hostility toward European political union. Recognizing the importance of political considerations obviously does not imply that economic forces have no bearing on European monetary union, much less that economists should not participate in this debate. Our point is that to understand the process toward a European monetary union, one must accept that political considerations dominate economic ones. Ultimately, the decision for or against it will depend on the outcome of the debate, now under way, over the desirability of greater political integration in Europe.

2.2 The EMS: Institutions and Policymaking

The EMS consists of four main institutional elements: (1) a basket currency, the ECU, (2) the Exchange-Rate Mechanism (ERM), (3) credit provisions among the participating central banks, and (4) the pooling of reserve assets among the members.[10] Of these four elements, the ERM has emerged as the most visible and important element of the EMS.

The ECU

The ECU is a basket currency defined by fixed quantities of currencies (see the appendix to this chapter for details). The ECU is the common numeraire of the ERM and is used as a means of payments among participating monetary authorities. As such, it is used for transactions related to central bank interventions in the EMS and the credit facilities of the system. An initial supply of ECU for intervention purposes was created by the EMCF against the deposit of 20 percent of the participating central banks' gold and dollar reserves taking the form of three-month revolving swap operations.

With a fixed quantity of each currency in the basket, the relative weight of a currency in the ECU (as defined in the appendix) decreases as a consequence of a depreciation against the remaining currencies; the relative weight of an appreciating currency rises. This implies that the relative weights change significantly if individual currencies are persistently weak or strong relative to the remaining ones, as has been the case in the history of the EMS. In view of this tendency, the basket quantities of the ECU were adjusted in 1984 and 1989 to prevent the ECU from being dominated by the strong currencies in the system. Table 2.1 shows that the quantities of the two appreciating currencies in the basket, the DM and the Dutch guilder, were reduced, whereas the Italian lira, the French franc, and the Greek drachma—three depreciating currencies— acquired additional units in the basket. This is in line with paragraph 2.3 of the European Council resolution establishing the EMS, which states (Commission of the EC 1979, 95): "The weights of currencies in the ECU will be re-examined and if necessary revised within six months of the entry into force of the system and thereafter every five years or, on request, if the weight of any currency has changed by 25 percent." In September 1989 the Spanish peseta and the Portuguese escudo were admitted to the ECU basket. Room was made for these two currencies primarily by lowering the weights of the deutsche mark and the pound sterling.[11]

The Exchange-Rate Mechanism

The cornerstone of the EMS is the agreement to limit bilateral exchange-rate fluctuations within margins of ±2.25 percent around

TABLE 2.1 The European Currency Unit

Countries	Currency Quantities			Relative Weights*		
	March 3, 1979	Sept. 7, 1984	Sept. 21, 1989	March 3, 1979	Sept. 9, 1984	Sept. 21, 1989
Belgium/ Luxembourg	3.80	3.85	3.431	9.63	8.57	8.09
Denmark	0.217	0.219	0.1976	3.06	2.69	2.53
France	1.15	1.31	1.332	19.83	19.06	19.3
Germany	0.828	0.719	0.6242	32.98	32.07	30.33
Italy	109	140	151.8	9.49	9.98	10.24
Netherlands	0.286	0.256	0.2198	10.51	10.13	9.49
Ireland	0.00759	0.00871	0.008552	1.15	1.2	1.12
Spain	—	—	6.85	—	—	5.16
Portugal	—	—	1.393	—	—	0.89
United Kingdom	0.0885	0.0878	0.08784	13.34	14.98	11.89
Greece	—	1.15	1.44	—	1.31	0.96

*Based on central parities.

Source: San Paolo, *Ecu Newsletter*, various issues.

predetermined central parities.[12] Italy managed to obtain the wider margins of ±6 percent for the lira in 1978; only on January 5, 1990, did the lira enter the narrow band.[13] Spain joined the ERM on June 19, 1989, and the United Kingdom began participating October 8, 1990. Both the Spanish peseta and the British pound enjoy the wider band of ±6 percent. The Greek drachma and the Portuguese escudo remain outside the ERM.

From its beginning, the ERM was not supposed to be a rigid system of fixed exchange rates. There was a common understanding that the central parities would be adjustable to changing economic conditions and the

A Description of the European Monetary System

relative performance of the participating economies. Early proponents of the EMS stressed the point that the frequency of realignments should not be regarded as a criterion of success or failure of the system (Commission of the EC 1979, 78; van Ypersele 1979, 9). Since 1979, there have been twelve realignments (Table 2.2).

The *indicator of divergence*, a technical novelty of the ERM, was designed to quantify the divergence of a currency's development from

TABLE 2.2 Exchange-Rate Realignments Within the EMS (percent)

	DM	HFL	FF	BFR	LIT	DKR	IRL
Sept. 24, 1979	2.0	—	—	—	—	–2.9	—
Nov. 30, 1979	—	—	—	—	—	–4.8	—
Mar. 23, 1981	—	—	—	—	–6.0	—	—
Oct. 5, 1981	5.5	5.5	–3.0	—	–3.0	—	—
Feb. 22, 1982	—	—	—	–8.5	—	–3.0	—
Jun. 14, 1982	4.25	4.25	–5.75	—	–2.75	—	—
Mar. 21, 1983	5.5	3.5	–2.5	1.5	–2.5	2.5	–3.5
Jul. 22, 1985	2.0	2.0	2.0	2.0	–6.0	2.0	2.0
Apr. 7, 1986	3.0	3.0	–3.0	1.0	—	1.0	—
Aug. 4, 1986	—	—	—	—	—	—	–8.0
Jan. 12, 1987	3.0	3.0	—	2.0	—	—	—
Jan. 5, 1990	—	—	—	—	–3.7	—	—

Note: The numbers are percentage changes of a given currency's bilateral central rate against those currencies whose bilateral parities were not realigned. A positive number denotes an appreciation, and a negative number denotes a depreciation. On March 21, 1983, and on July 22, 1985, all parities were realigned.

DM = Deutsche Mark, HFL = Dutch guilder, FF = French franc, BFR = Belgian/ Luxembourg franc, LIT = Italian lira, DKR = Danish kroner, IRL = Irish punt.

Source: Commission of the European Communities.

the average of all other currencies in the system. It is activated when the ECU value of a member currency crosses either the upper or the lower *threshold of divergence*; these two points define an inner band around each currency's ECU parity (see the appendix). Article 3.5 of the Council Resolution establishing the EMS states (Commission of the EC 1979, 95): "When a currency crosses its `threshold of divergence', this results in a presumption that the authorities concerned will correct the situation by adequate measures, namely: (a) diversified intervention; (b) measures of domestic monetary policy; (c) changes in central rates; (d) other measures of economic policy." Note that this presumption applies equally to relatively weak and strong currencies. This reflects the objective of *symmetry* of the EMS, the intention to achieve an equal sharing of the burden of adjustment to balance-of-payments disequilibria between deficit and surplus countries (van Ypersele 1979, 6). The Council Resolution stresses that actions cannot be taken unilaterally but must be in "concertation between central banks" (Article 3.5), another reflection of the concept of symmetry.

Interventions and Financing Facilities

Central banks participating in the ERM are obliged to intervene in the foreign exchange markets if necessary to maintain exchange rates within their bands. If a currency approaches the upper or lower margin of its ERM band, compulsory "interventions at the margin" set in. A weak-currency central bank must sell foreign exchange in the exchange market to prevent its currency from depreciating further; conversely, a strong-currency central bank must sell its own currency for foreign currency. To facilitate intervention, the central banks can resort to the Very Short Term Facility (VSTF) of the EMCF. Weak-currency central banks can borrow, without limits, members' hard currencies under this arrangement. Members are obliged to grant such credits upon request. Credits are due 45 days after the end of the month when the intervention occurred. Repayment of up to 100 percent of the debtor's VSTF quota can be delayed for an additional 30 days. The Nyborg Agreement of 1987 extended this possibility to 200 percent of the debtor's quota and two months. Beyond that, the lender's consent to the prolongation of the terms is required.

VSTF credit is denominated and partly repayable in ECU. A creditor central bank may refuse repayment in ECU only when it exceeds 50 percent of the claim being settled (Commission of the EC 1979, 104). This implies a real wealth transfer from central banks with an appreciating currency to central banks with a depreciating currency and a sharing by weak- and hard-currency central banks of the risk of a parity realignment

(Papadia 1976). The interest paid or received on net positions in the EMCF was initially computed as the weighted average of the discount rates in the member countries. Because discount rates are normally well below market rates, this implied an additional subsidy in the use of ECU, making potential creditors reluctant to run positive net positions in the EMCF. In light of these features, it is not surprising that member countries' net positions in the EMCF were for a long time contained within 10 percent of the initial stock of ECU (Micossi 1985).

The EMCF credit provisions were changed in 1985 for the purpose of promoting the use of the ECU. Positive net ECU positions in the EMCF can now be used to obtain dollars or Community currencies for a period of three months with the possibility of renewal, and ECU can be used to repay more than 50 percent of VSTF loans. The computation of the interest rate on EMCF net positions is now based on money-market interest rates rather than discount rates. Both changes have made the ECU more attractive as a reserve asset of high liquidity (Micossi 1985, 340).

In practice, weak-currency central banks obtain hard currency for compulsory interventions by drawing on the VSTF, and the EMCF receives the funds simultaneously from the hard-currency central bank involved. A liability is created on the weak-currency central bank's balance sheet, and a claim is created on the hard-currency central bank's balance sheet as a result. Hence, the monetary base of the former declines; the monetary base of the latter rises. If the hard-currency central bank intervenes at the margin, it will sell its own currency for weak currency. According to EMCF rules, the reserves thus acquired are automatically transferred to the EMCF, where they are credited to the hard-currency central bank's account and debited to the weak-currency central bank's account. Again, the result is a new liability on the weak-currency central bank's balance sheet and a new claim on the hard-currency central bank's balance sheet, so that the monetary base of the former falls and the base of the latter increases. Thus, the rules of the EMS assure that the immediate effects of interventions on the monetary bases of the countries involved are perfectly symmetric. The immediate liquidity effects will thus be the same, irrespective of whether the actual intervention is executed by the weak- or the hard-currency central bank.

The fact that the immediate liquidity effects are symmetric does not mean, however, that the final liquidity effects will be symmetric as well. Central banks can "sterilize" foreign exchange interventions—that is, they can neutralize their impact on the monetary base through offsetting changes in the domestic components of the monetary base, such as credit to domestic commercial banks or open market operations. The EMS does not stipulate any rules for sterilization. Therefore, the final allocation of the liquidity effects remains indeterminate in the EMS because it depends on the ability and desire of the central banks to sterilize interventions in the foreign exchange market. Some authors have argued that this indeterminacy gives rise to an asymmetry in the system: hard-currency central banks will find it easier to sterilize intervention than will weak-currency central banks, because the former accumulate foreign exchange reserves but the latter lose reserves in the process.[14] This suggests that weak-currency central banks have to yield to the pressure from the ERM and change their policies earlier than the hard-currency partners. The strength of this argument is reduced, however, by the weak-currency central banks' opportunities to borrow reserves from the hard-currency central banks. Furthermore, hard-currency central banks like the Bundesbank will find it difficult to squeeze the domestic component of the monetary base because in many European countries, the domestic component consists mainly of loans to commercial banks. A lasting reduction of the domestic component of the monetary base, therefore, is likely to meet strong opposition by the banking industry.[15]

In addition to interventions at the margins of the exchange-rate bands, central banks may choose to intervene while exchange rates fluctuate within the margins. Such "intramarginal" interventions are not compulsory. They can be used to curb undesired exchange-rate developments early, before they require compulsory intervention. Under the original rules of the EMS, intramarginal interventions in member currencies required the consent of the central bank issuing the intervention currency. Fearing that such interventions might thwart the conduct of its monetary policy, the Bundesbank had insisted on this requirement to prevent other EMS central banks from accumulating large DM balances. As a result, the bulk of intramarginal interventions were executed in U.S. dollars and therefore did not have symmetric liquidity effects in the weak- and strong-currency countries. Since the early 1980s, the Bundesbank has loosened its strict opposition and, on occasion, has actually encouraged other central banks to build up DM reserves. The previously mentioned Nyborg Agreement made intramarginal interventions of up to 200 percent of a member's quota in the VSTF eligible for EMCF financing and stipulated the general presumption that the central bank issuing the intervention currency accepts intramarginal interventions financed with VSTF resources. As a result, a sizable number of intramarginal interventions also now have symmetric immediate liquidity effects, further strengthening the principle of symmetrical burden sharing.

There remains, however, some ambiguity in the interpretation of the Nyborg Agreement. The then French finance minister, Edward Balladur, interpreted it as giving a country a presumption of automatic access to VSTF credit, whereas Karl Otto Pöhl, then president of the Bundesbank, read the decision as giving the Bundesbank the discretion to decide each case on its merits (*Economist* 1987). This difference of views reflects the natural desire of traditionally weak-currency countries to obtain access to credit facilities for intramarginal interventions and the concern of hard-currency countries to minimize the risk that credit facilities do not become an engine of excessive monetary creation.

2.3 The Economic Record of the EMS

Exchange-Rate Stability

Since 1979, there have been twelve realignments in the EMS. Of these, the last one on January 5, 1990, can be considered a mere "technical" readjustment easing the lira's entry into the narrow band.[16] Of the remaining eleven realignments, seven occurred during the first four years and four in the subsequent four years (Table 2.2). In the roughly eight years from March 1979 to January 1987, when the eleventh realignment occurred, the lira experienced the largest parity depreciation vis-à-vis the DM (45 percent); the Dutch guilder had the smallest depreciation against the DM (4 percent). The smallest bilateral parity change (2.6 percent) occurred between the Irish punt and the French franc. The evidence from the central parities shows that the EMS did not prevent sizable nominal exchange-rate changes over time. This is consistent with the view that the monetary authorities did not regard the system as a truly fixed exchange-rate arrangement but rather as one aiming at lower variability of nominal exchange rates.

Did these parity changes compensate fully for inflation differentials within the EMS countries? In Table 2.3 we show cumulative bilateral inflation differentials, measured in terms of consumption deflators, over the period from 1979 to 1990 for seven EMS countries—Belgium, Denmark, France, Germany, Ireland, Italy, and the Netherlands—and nine non-EMS countries—Australia, Austria, Canada, Finland, Greece, Japan, Switzerland, the United Kingdom, and the United States.[17] The largest inflation differential among EMS countries occurred between Italy and the Netherlands (99 percent), the smallest between Germany and the Netherlands (1 percent). These two countries had virtually identical inflation experiences and are natural candidates for a monetary union. The largest inflation differential among non-EMS countries occurred between Greece and Japan (196 percent), the smallest between Austria and Switzerland and between the United Kingdom and Finland (4 percent). Finally, the largest differential between non-EMS and EMS countries occurred between Greece and the Netherlands (190 percent),

TABLE 2.3 Cumulative Bilateral Inflation Differential Measured by the Consumption Deflator Over the 1979–1990 Period (in percent)

	B	DK	F	D	EIRE	I	NL	AUS	AUT	CAN	FIN	GRE	J	CH	UK	USA
B		23.8	30.6	-20.8	43.3	77.4	-22.1	42.9	-8.8	17.7	28.4	167.7	-28.0	-12.7	32.2	10.2
DK			6.8	-44.6	19.5	53.6	-45.9	19.0	-32.6	-6.1	4.6	143.9	-51.8	-36.5	8.3	-13.6
F				-51.4	12.7	46.8	-52.7	12.3	-39.4	-12.9	-2.1	137.1	-58.6	-43.3	1.6	-20.4
D					64.1	98.2	-1.3	63.7	11.1	38.5	49.3	188.5	-7.2	8.1	53.0	31.0
EIRE						34.1	-65.4	-0.4	-52.1	-25.6	-14.8	24.4	-71.3	-56.0	-11.1	-33.1
I							-99.5	-34.6	-86.2	-59.8	-49.0	90.3	-105.4	-90.1	-45.3	-67.2
NL								64.9	13.3	39.7	50.5	189.8	-5.9	9.4	54.2	32.3
AUS									-51.7	-25.2	-14.4	124.8	-70.9	-55.6	-10.7	-32.6
AUT										26.5	37.3	176.5	-19.2	-3.9	41.0	19.0
CAN											10.8	150.0	-45.7	-30.4	14.5	-7.4
FIN												139.2	-56.5	-41.2	3.7	-18.2
GRE													-195.7	-180.4	-135.5	-157.5
J														15.3	60.2	38.2
CH															44.9	22.9
UK																-21.9
USA																

Note: A positive (negative) number indicates that the inflation rate of the country shown in the column heading is cumulatively higher (lower) than that of the country shown in the row heading.

B = Belgium, DK = Denmark, F = France, D = Germany, Eire = Ireland, I = Italy, NL = Netherlands, AUS = Australia, AUT = Austria, CAN = Canada, FIN = Finland, GRE = Greece, J = Japan, CH = Switzerland, UK = United Kingdom, USA = United States.

Source: OECD, *Economic Outlook* data diskettes N. 41 and N. 47.

the smallest between the United Kingdom and France (2 percent). This suggests that the United Kingdom could have joined the ERM well before October 1990 with as good a chance as France to stay in the system. Greek inflation, on the other hand, stands out so sharply with respect to all EMS countries as to suggest that participation in the ERM would have led either to frequent realignments, a drastic alteration in Greek monetary policy, or both.

Bilateral exchange-rate depreciations during this period were positively associated with inflation differentials. This positive association, however, was far from complete, implying significant real exchange-rate changes (Table 2.4). For example, France, Italy, and Ireland, three EMS countries with above-average inflation, experienced sizable real appreciations of their currencies in the EMS. Real appreciation of the French franc against the DM was approximately 11 percent, of the Italian lira 42 percent, and of the Irish punt 23 percent. This pattern is not unique to the EMS countries. The pound sterling experienced hefty real appreciations against the Belgian franc, the Danish kroner, the French franc, the DM, and the Dutch guilder, but a real depreciation against the lira. The Greek pattern is similar to the United Kingdom's. In sum, positive inflation differences tend to be associated with a real appreciation of the currency that is subject to the higher inflation. For the EMS, this association is more than purely statistical. In fact, at realignments high-inflation countries readjusted their parities in such a way as to obtain a real appreciation, a deliberate policy decision that relies on the exchange rate to disinflate the economy.

We will explore the evidence on exchange-rate variability in detail in Chapter 7. Here we simply note some findings. Ample evidence exists that nominal and real exchange-rate variability has declined within the EMS but not outside the EMS. The evidence concerning the interaction between EMS and non-EMS countries is more subtle. Ungerer et al. (1986, tables 28 and 29) find no evidence that the effective exchange rates of EMS countries behaved differently in the EMS period than before. Table 2.5 illustrates a similar finding. The table reports the F-ratio of the sample variances of EMS and pre-EMS (1973-1978) annual percentage changes of effective exchange rates for the seven EMS countries and nine non-EMS countries. The results indicate a significant *increase* in variability for two of the EMS countries—Belgium and the Netherlands—but constant variability for the remaining EMS and non-EMS countries, except Austria. Given the reduced variability of intra-EMS exchange rates, and that effective exchange rates are weighted averages of exchange rates vis-à-vis EMS and non-EMS countries, this observation accords with the hypothesis that the reduced exchange-rate variability within the EMS countries came partly at the expense of a higher variability between EMS and non-EMS

TABLE 2.4 Cumulative Percentage Change in Bilateral Real Exchange Rates Over the 1979–1990 Period

	B	DK	F	D	EIRE	I	NL	AUS	AUT	CAN	FIN	GRE	J	CH	UK	USA
B		-14.0	-17.7	-6.8	-30.1	-48.8	-1.0	-10.4	-17.0	-21.2	-41.6	-27.3	-15.1	-18.0	-30.9	-20.0
DK			-3.7	7.2	-16.1	-34.8	12.9	3.6	-3.1	-7.2	-27.7	-13.4	-1.1	-4.0	-16.9	-2.0
F				10.9	-12.4	-31.1	16.6	7.3	0.6	-3.5	-24.0	-9.7	2.6	-0.3	-13.2	1.7
D					-23.3	-42.0	5.7	-3.6	-10.3	-14.4	-34.9	-20.6	-8.3	-11.2	-24.1	-9.2
EIRE						-18.8	29.0	19.7	13.0	8.9	-11.6	2.7	15.0	12.1	-0.8	14.1
I							47.8	38.4	31.8	27.6	7.2	21.5	33.7	30.8	17.9	32.8
NL								-9.4	-16.0	-20.2	-40.6	-26.3	-14.0	-16.9	-29.9	-15.0
AUS									-6.6	-10.8	-31.2	-16.9	-4.7	-7.6	-20.5	-5.6
AUT										-4.1	-24.6	-10.3	2.0	-0.9	-13.8	1.1
CAN											-20.5	-6.1	6.1	3.2	-9.7	5.2
FIN												14.3	26.6	23.7	10.8	25.7
GRE													12.2	9.4	-3.6	11.3
J														-2.9	-15.8	-0.9
CH															-12.9	1.9
UK																14.9
USA																

Note: A positive (negative) number indicates a real depreciation (appreciation) of the country's currency shown in the column heading with respect to the country's currency shown in the row heading. The real exchange-rate changes were obtained by subtracting the cumulative inflation differences of Table 2.3 from the nominal exchange-rate changes.

B = Belgium, DK = Denmark, F = France, D = Germany, EIRE = Ireland, I = Italy, NL = Netherlands, AUS = Australia, AUT = Austria, CAN = Canada, FIN = Finland, GRE = Greece, J = Japan, CH = Switzerland, UK = United Kingdom, USA = United States.

Source: OECD, *Economic Outlook* data diskettes N. 41 and N. 48

TABLE 2.5   F-Ratio of the Variability of the Annual Growth of the Effective
Exchange Rate 1979–1990 vs. 1973–1978

EMS		Non-EMS	
Belgium	6.64*	Australia	1.12
Denmark	2.70	Austria	48.00**
France	0.41	Canada	0.38
Germany	1.65	Finland	0.64
Ireland	3.65	Greece	0.62
Italy	0.55	Japan	1.04
Netherlands	16.23*	Switzerland	0.27
		United Kingdom	0.87
		United States	2.73

Note: * Significant at the 5 percent level; ** significant at the 1 percent level. The
value of the F (11,5) statistic at the 1 percent level is 10.02; at the 5 percent level it is
4.71.

countries. The result Ungerer and his colleagues derived (1986, table
22)—that the coefficient of variation of bilateral exchange rates with
respect to non-EMS currencies rose from 39.6 (1974-1978) to 42.8 (1979-
1985) for the non-EMS countries but from 36.3 to 46.7 in the period 1979-
1985 for the EMS countries—lends additional support to this hypothesis.

Inflation Rates and Money Growth

Proponents of the EMS have pointed to the reduction in inflation
rates in the EMS countries as a sign of the system's success. Statements of
this kind need to be scrutinized carefully. Meaningful statistical inference
cannot be made by simply comparing two periods because they will most
likely differ by the size and nature of the shocks to the economies in
addition to the exchange-rate regime under consideration. Without the
heroic assumption that the shocks were the same in the 1970s and 1980s,
the decline in inflation rates over time, therefore, cannot be attributed
simply to the exchange-rate regime. To mitigate somewhat this problem,
one may compare the performance of the EMS economies with that of a
group of non-EMS economies sufficiently similar to the EMS economies,
except for the exchange-rate regime. For this purpose, our group of nine
non-EMS countries is quite suitable.

In Figure 2.1 we have graphed the inflation rates for the seven EMS
countries and the nine non-EMS countries for the period 1973-1990.[18] It is

FIGURE 2.1 EMS and Non-EMS Inflation Rates

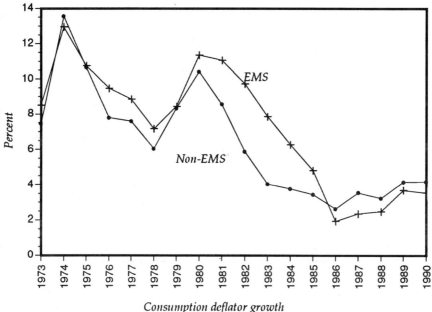

Consumption deflator growth

Source: OECD

clear that both the EMS and the non-EMS inflation rates behaved very similarly. Both rose after the second oil price shock at the end of the 1970s, both declined sharply from 1980 to 1986, and both increased moderately after 1986. This exercise does not deny the disinflation achieved by the EMS countries; it simply underscores that the EMS record is not different from that of the non-EMS countries. A possible interpretation of Figure 2.1 is that exogenous shocks or policy factors, affecting both groups similarly, were more important than EMS membership in explaining European disinflation.

A similar argument can be made with respect to monetary base growth. In Figure 2.2 we have plotted the difference between the monetary base growth rates of the EMS and the non-EMS countries.[19] This difference was 0.5 percent on average between 1973 and 1978 and 1.2 percent between 1979 and 1990. Neither difference was significantly different from zero at conventional confidence levels. In sum, inflation and money growth do not suggest that the performance of the EMS countries was much different from that of countries outside the EMS.

FIGURE 2.2 EMS Minus Non-EMS Money Base Growth

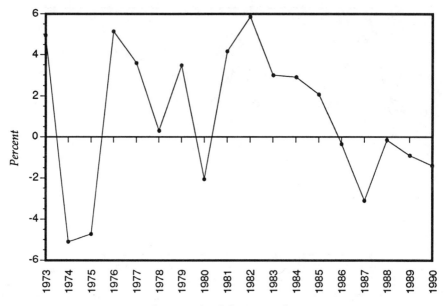

Consumption deflator growth

Source: OECD

Interest Rates

Financial market integration implies that in the absence of expected real exchange-rate changes, real rates of interest cannot differ among countries for assets of equal risk. Rogoff (1985b) shows that short-term real interest rate differentials between Germany and France and between Germany and Italy increased during the EMS period. Furthermore, the conditional variances of these interest rates rose as well. Giavazzi and Pagano (1985) show that the spread between offshore and onshore interest rates widened and became more variable when the likelihood of a parity realignment increased, an indication that binding capital and exchange controls were driving a wedge between German, French, and Italian interest rates. The overall conclusion is that the reduced exchange-rate variability came, to a large extent, from the impediments to capital mobility rather than from coordinated monetary policy.[20]

This evidence, however, relates only to the early EMS until 1984. Since then, an important financial liberalization process has occurred in France and Italy in connection with the Single Market program. Controls have been dismantled, which has forced real interest rates in these countries to rise relative to rates abroad. In Table 2.6 we have computed real interest rates using current inflation as a proxy for expected inflation. Real interest rates sharply increased throughout the world in the 1980s, but the differentials across countries have petered out and almost disappeared among EMS countries. For example, the German real rate

TABLE 2.6 Real Interest Rates

	1973–1978		1979–1990	
	Average	*Standard Deviation*	*Average*	*Standard Deviation*
Belgium	–0.55	3.11	5.82	1.34
Denmark	2.92	1.74	5.26	1.53
France	–1.04	1.85	3.56	2.61
Germany	1.89	2.21	3.97	1.13
Ireland	–4.32	3.98	4.01	3.91
Italy	–4.46	2.37	3.87	3.72
Netherlands	–2.70	2.26	4.23	1.02
EMS	–0.76	0.67	3.97	1.74
Australia	–2.93	3.94	5.87	3.13
Austria	–0.42	2.21	3.19	1.52
Canada	0.26	1.61	5.57	1.92
Finland	–2.90	3.62	5.30	3.60
Greece	–3.27	4.75	2.80	3.81
Japan	–3.52	3.00	4.17	0.82
Switzerland	–1.99	2.31	0.95	1.84
United Kingdom	–2.65	7.53	5.02	3.00
United States	–1.03	1.39	3.30	1.70
Non-EMS	–1.70	1.94	3.81	1.33

Note: Calculated as current short-term interest rates minus current growth rate of consumption deflator.

Source: OECD, data diskettes.

was, on average, 635 basis points (100 basis points = 1 percent) higher than the Italian rate in the pre-EMS period but only 10 basis points higher in the EMS period. Once again, the record of the EMS is not statistically different from that of the non-EMS group.

Economic Growth and Unemployment

How did the real sectors of the EMS economies perform in relation to non-EMS countries? Unemployment rates increased sharply in the EMS period in all EMS countries as well as in the three European non-EMS countries in our group. In contrast, Canada, Japan, and the United States experienced much more modest increases. These patterns are reflected in Figure 2.3 where we have plotted the difference between the EMS unemployment rate and the non-EMS unemployment rate. The figure shows the sharp upward trend of this difference beginning in 1982 and reaching a peak of almost 400 basis points in 1989. The average difference is statistically highly significant.

The relative underperformance of the EMS countries, however, does not carry over to output growth. Average growth rates of real gross

FIGURE 2.3 EMS Minus Non-EMS Unemployment Rates

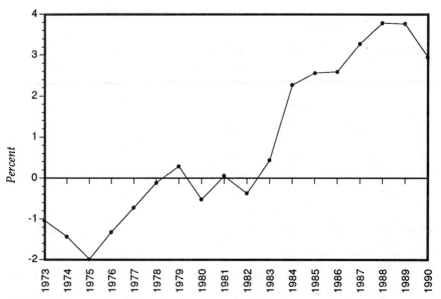

Source: OECD

FIGURE 2.4 EMS Minus Non-EMS Real GDP Growth

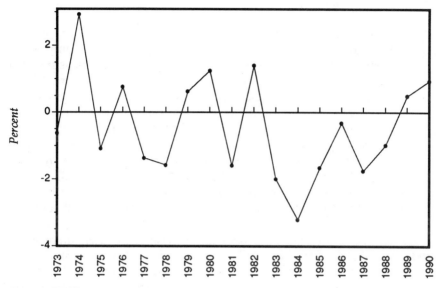

Source: OECD

domestic product (GDP) were higher in the non-EMS countries than in the EMS between 1982 and 1990 but not statistically different (see Figure 2.4). Only Switzerland, the United Kingdom and the United States experienced a significantly higher output growth rate than the EMS average.

The nature and size of the real slowdown in Europe are controversial. Few economists, however, believe that the EMS was responsible for the higher unemployment rates.[21] Indeed, it is hard to blame the EMS for lasting reductions in output and employment growth—after all, the system is a voluntary agreement.   Member countries were free to leave the EMS and would have done so had they perceived its real cost as excessive. A literature on Eurosclerosis and hysteresis emerged during the 1980s (e.g., Commission of the EC 1984; Lawrence and Schultze 1987) that focuses on supply-side constraints instead of the constraints imposed by the EMS and proposes supply-side remedies to reduce the wedge between the private and the social cost of labor and to stimulate the expansion of productive capacity rather than changes in the exchange-rate regime (e.g., Dreze et al. 1987).

Fiscal Policies in the EMS

The discussion so far has highlighted the monetary policy aspects of the EMS. But the exchange-rate regime may have had important consequences for fiscal policies too. For a quantitative measure of a country's overall fiscal stance, we use its ratio of net government debt to GDP. Net government debt is calculated by subtracting government assets from total debt. The time profile of net debt reflects the relative size of budget deficits; an increase in the ratio signifies a fiscal expansion. All countries participating in the ERM experienced a rise in their net debt ratios during the period 1979-1990. This ratio rose much faster than the equivalent ratio for the nine non-EMS countries (see Figure 2.5). In fact, the two debt ratios were virtually identical in 1977, whereas by 1990 the EMS ratio was almost twice as large as the non-EMS ratio. Furthermore, the debt ratio of the non-EMS countries peaked around 1986 and has declined ever since; the EMS debt is still rising. In brief, there is no indication that the EMS has acted as a brake on fiscal expansion.

It is also informative to check the relative fiscal expansion inside the EMS group for the entire EMS period and for the shorter period from 1984 to 1990, when there were fewer parity realignments. To assess the relative performance of these countries, we calculate the difference between each country's net debt ratio and the weighted average ratio of the EMS. If we define a positive (negative) difference expansive (contractive) and a difference close to zero neutral, the result can be summarized as follows:

	1979–1990	*1984–1990*
Belgium	Expansive	Expansive
Denmark	Expansive	Neutral
France	Contractive	Contractive
Germany	Neutral	Contractive
Ireland	Expansive	Expansive
Italy	Neutral	Expansive
Netherlands	Neutral	Expansive

Thus, for example, Italy's fiscal policy did not differ from the EMS average over the entire period, but was more expansive from 1984 to 1990. The French debt ratio, in contrast, fell in relation to the EMS average over the entire EMS period. These simple comparisons show that fiscal policies in the EMS diverged, and did so most noticeably during the second half of the 1980s. Thus, the exchange-rate system does not appear to have promoted the convergence of fiscal policies. In sum, the ERM has neither exerted discipline on nor promoted convergence of fiscal policies.

FIGURE 2.5 Net Debt-to-GDP Ratio, EMS Versus Non-EMS

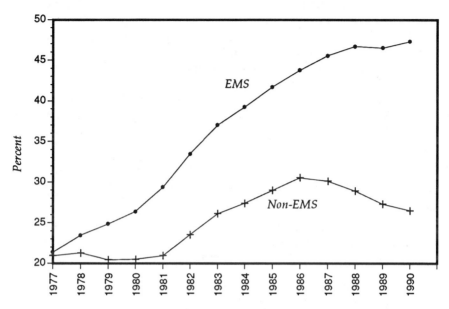

Source: OECD

2.4 Conclusions

We have reviewed in this chapter the history leading to the creation of the EMS, its basic institutional structure, and its basic economic performance since 1979. Our synopsis illustrates that the quest for monetary unification in Europe, of which the EMS is a critical element, is most of all the result of a drive to unify Europe politically. This is not to say that economic considerations did not or do not play a role; in fact, the EMS was created to coordinate and strengthen the effectiveness of monetary policies in the region. Yet decisive impulses to enhance monetary integration have always originated in the political area.

The institutional design of the EMS is marked by flexibility and symmetry. The principle of symmetry is reflected in the provisions for equal burden sharing in the external adjustment, such as the indicator of divergence, the use of the ECU as the common numeraire, and the various credit facilities. The principle of flexibility is reflected most of all in the provision of realignments but also in the tolerance for capital and exchange controls in the earlier phases of the EMS.

Contrary to popular expectations at the time of its foundation, the EMS has not collapsed. The inflation bias, feared by many economists when the system was instituted, has not materialized. On the other hand, the reduction of inflation rates, greatly praised by the proponents of the EMS, has proved no better than the reduction achieved by other countries. On the real side of the economy, the EMS record falls short of non-EMS countries, especially concerning unemployment. Yet it would be difficult to blame the EMS for such a performance. The most noticeable achievement, therefore, is lower exchange-rate variability.

The prima facie evidence leaves unanswered the question of whether the EMS has been a success. In the following chapters we present two alternative interpretations of the EMS to answer that question more effectively.

Notes

1. The latter objective can be inferred from the treaty's goal of maintaining confidence in member currencies.

2. See Tsoukalis (1977) for a detailed review of the political and economic debate.

3. For a detailed view of the *Delors Report* and its strategy to achieve EMU, see Fratianni and von Hagen (1990c) and Chapter 9 (this volume).

4. Article 107 of the Treaty of Rome explicitly recognizes this problem and authorizes retaliation against EC-member countries that use exchange-rate changes for reasons of commercial policy.

5. Before 1978, the ECU prices were set in terms of the European unit of account.

6. Member countries with depreciating currencies should pay MCAs by taxing agricultural exports whose supply has increased as a result of the devaluation; countries with appreciating currencies should receive MCAs by subsidizing agricultural exports whose supply has declined because of the appreciation (Giavazzi and Giovannini 1989, 15). In other words, the purpose of MCAs is to undo the adverse incentive effects of the exchange-rate change. In practice, things do not quite work this way. Giavazzi and Giovannini (1989) point out that in countries regularly receiving MCAs—Germany and the Netherlands— agricultural prices are higher than in countries paying MCAs. The asymmetry in the MCAs simply reflects the unwillingness of farmers to accept cuts in domestic currency prices.

7. See also von Hagen (1992) and Tyrie (1990).

8. The following translations from the German original are our own.

9. See, for example, the speeches of the governor of the Bank of England, reprinted in the Bank of England *Quarterly Bulletin* (1990a, 1990b).

10. See Commission of the European Communities (EC) (1979, 1982) for detailed descriptions.

11. The creation of ECU has spurred significant financial innovations, an aspect we are not treating in this book. Banks have issued ECU deposits, and an active market for ECU-denominated securities has developed; see the works by

Allen (1989), Lomax (1989), Jozzo (1989), Commission of the EC (1990), and Fratianni (1992).

12. More precisely, the upper part of the band is 2.275 percent above the central parity, whereas the lower part of the band is 2.225 percent below the central parity.

13. For an account of the hectic negotiations that won Italy the wider margins, see Baffi (1989).

14. This argument goes back to Triffin (1960). Wyplosz (1988) and Bofinger (1988) see it as the source of asymmetry in the EMS.

15. For an empirical account of the Bundesbank's sterilization practice, see von Hagen (1989b). There it is shown that generally during the 1980s, the Bundesbank did not completely sterilize EMS interventions.

16. In fact, the new central rate was set at approximately the then-prevailing market value of the lira. The lower intervention level of the narrow band remained identical to the intervention level of the previous broad band. (Bank for International Settlements 1990, 196).

17. In the following tables and figures, we will be constructing EMS and non-EMS aggregate series for a variety of macroeconomic variables. Country series will be added according to 1982 GDP weights expressed in 1982 U.S. dollars, as computed by the OECD. The weights for the EMS series are as follows: Belgium = 0.0455, Denmark = 0.0297, France = 0.2884, Germany = 0.3442, Ireland = 0.0099, Italy = 0.2107, and the Netherlands = 0.0722. The weights for the non-EMS series are as follows: Australia = 0.0308, Austria = 0.0123, Canada = 0.0561, Finland = 0.0094, Greece = 0.0071, Japan = 0.2003, Switzerland = 0.0179, United Kingdom = 0.0898, and United States = 0.5763.

18. Inflation is measured in terms of the consumption deflators. The data are annual and from the diskettes of the OECD, *Economic Outlook* N. 41 (June 1987) and N. 47 (July 1990). The aggregation over countries was made by multiplying the country's growth rate by the country's weight based on GNP share calculated in 1982 prices and exchange rates. The OECD weights were normalized so that the weights for each group add to unity. The normalized weights for the EMS countries are Belgium = 0.0462, Denmark = 0.0294, France = 0.294, Germany = 0.3571, Ireland = 0.0084, Italy = 0.1891, the Netherlands = 0.0756; for the non-EMS countries they are: Austria = 0.0134, Canada = 0.058, Japan = 0.208, Switzerland = 0.0179, United Kingdom = 0.094, and United States = 0.609.

19. The data are from the IMF, *International Financial Statistics*.

20. Goodhart (1986) argued against the United Kingdom's entry into the EMS on the strength of this evidence, because the crucial role of London as a major financial center requires freedom of capital movement. Walters (1986) rejected the EMS on these grounds as well as on considerations of political economy.

21. See, however, Katseli (1987) for a different opinion.

Appendix 2A

The ECU, Central Parities,
and the Indicator of Divergence

Equation (2.1) defines the value of the ECU in terms of a currency i, ECU_i, based on the quantities of the individual currencies q_j and the exchange rates between currency i and the remaining currencies, s_{ij}, defined as units of currency i per unit of currency j:

$$(2.1) \qquad\qquad ECU_i = \sum_{j=1}^{n} q_j s_{ij}.$$

The relative weight of currency j in the *value* of the ECU, w_j, is the ratio

$$(2.2) \qquad\qquad w_j = s_{ij} q_j / ECU_i.$$

Central parities in the ERM are stated in two equivalent ways: either as a parity grid of all member currencies, or by relating each currency to its ECU central parity, from which bilateral central parities can be derived. Table 2.1A shows the parity grid with its intervention points as of January 7, 1990. Each member currency has an ECU central rate, which is obtained by applying formula (2.1) with the corresponding bilateral central rates of Table 2.1A instead of s_{ij}.

TABLE 2.1A EMS Bilateral Central Rates and Intervention Points, January 7, 1990

		Bruxelles *in BFR*	*Amsterdam* *in HFL*	*Copenhagen* *in DKR*	*Frankfurt* *in DM*	*Milan* *in LIT*	*Paris* *in FF*	*Dublin* *in IRL*	*Madrid* *in PST*
1ECU		42.1679	2.30358	7.79845	2.04446	1529.7	6.85684	0.763159	132.889
	min		5.5872	18.9145	4.95868	3,710.17	16.6307	1.85098	334.62
BFR	100	100.00	5.4629	18.4938	4.84838	3,627.64	16.2608	1.80981	315.14
	max		5.3413	18.0823	4.74050	3,546.93	15.8990	1.76954	296.80
	min	1,872.18		346.238	90.771	67,916.06	304.432	33.8830	6,125.4
HFL	100	1,830.54	100.00	338.536	88.751	66,405.33	297.660	33.1293	5,768.8
	max	1,789.81		331.004	86.777	64,927.82	291.037	32.3921	5,433.1
	min	553.023	30.2110		26.813	20,061.69	89.9260	10.0087	1,809.4
DKR	100	540.722	29.5389	100.00	26.216	19,615.44	87.9257	9.7860	1,704.0
	max	528.690	28.8817		25.633	19,178.99	85.9693	9.5683	1,604.9
	min	2,109.5	115.238	390.121		76,523.91	343.016	38.1774	6,901.7
DM	100	2,062.5	112.674	381.443	100.00	74,821.71	335.386	37.3281	6,500.0
	max	2,016.7	110.167	372.956		73,156.93	327.924	36.4976	6,121.7
	min	28.1933	1.5402	5.2140	1.3669		4.5844	0.5102	92.2422
LIT	1000	27.5661	1.5059	5.0980	1.3365	1000.00	4.4825	0.4989	86.8726
	max	26.9528	1.4724	4.9846	1.3068		4.3827	0.4878	81.8166
	min	628.966	34.360	116.320	30.495	22,816.64		11.3831	2,057.8
FF	100	614.976	33.595	113.732	29.816	22,309.11	100.00	11.1299	1,938.1
	max	601.292	32.848	111.202	29.153	21,812.73		10.8823	1,825.3
	min	56.5114	3.0872	10.4511	2.7399	2,050.03	9.18922		184.893
IRL	1	55.2544	3.0185	10.2186	2.6789	2,004.43	8.98481	1.00	174.130
	max	54.0250	2.9513	9.9913	2.6193	1,959.83	8.78490		163.996
	min	33.693	1.841	6.231	1.634	1,222.26	5.479	0.60978	
PST	100	21.732	1.733	5.868	1.538	1,151.11	5.160	0.57428	100
	max	29.885	1.633	5.527	1.449	1,084.12	4.860	0.54086	

Note: The indicator of divergence is based on the thresholds of divergence, for each currency i, the upper threshold is set at $0.75\,IP_{uj}\,(1 - w_i)$, and the lower threshold at $(-0.75)\,IP_{l,i}\,(1 - w_i)$, where $IP_{u,i}$ and $IP_{l,i}$ are the (theoretical) upper and lower intervention points with regard to the ECU, i.e., 2.25 percent (6 percent for countries in the wide band) above or below the currency's central rate against the ECU. Since intervention points and ECU weights are different for individual currencies, the margins between the thresholds of divergence are different for each currency, too. For example, on January 7, 1990, Germany had the tightest threshold margin with ±1.172 percent and the peseta had the widest threshold margin with ±4.26 percent.

Source: San Paolo, *ECU Newsletter*, Janaury 1990.

3

Cooperation or Discipline:
The Political Economy of the EMS

An exchange-rate union like the EMS commits the participating monetary authorities to a specific form of policy coordination. It requires that every member relinquish a part of its monetary policy independence. This implication of the agreement is commonly known as the *N-degrees of freedom paradigm*: An exchange-rate union among N countries predetermines N–1 central parities and leaves only one degree of freedom to choose the union's common monetary policy. In the short run, this remaining degree of freedom is used to determine the union's response to fluctuations in aggregate demand, aggregate supply, world interest rates, world market prices, and the like, factors that affect all members jointly. In the long run, the role of the last degree of freedom is to set the union's inflation trend and its rate of depreciation against other nonmember currencies.

The N-degrees of freedom paradigm implies that there can be at most one monetary authority in the union that determines its policy independently of the other members. Thus, it is important in the design of an exchange-rate union to determine which member is assigned the authority over the remaining degree of freedom and, consequently, how the burden of adjustment to external shocks is distributed. To a large extent, this is a result of how the institutions of the union are framed: the rules for foreign exchange market interventions and their sterilization, which stipulate whose monetary base is affected by the efforts to maintain the central parities; the tolerance for barriers to international capital flows, which shield monetary conditions in one country from the rest of the system and allow the country to retain some monetary independence even within the union; and the rules for changing central parities.

Two extreme solutions delimit the range of possibilities. On the one hand, the Nth degree of freedom can be resolved by assigning policy independence to a single member of the union. This is the hegemonic solution: one country, most likely the largest member, unilaterally determines the union's common monetary policy. Britain's role in the classical gold-standard period and the role of the United States in the Bretton Woods system have been interpreted in this way (Eichengreen 1989; Kindleberger 1973). Kindleberger indeed argues that all stable international monetary arrangements require a hegemon that provides stability as a public good to the system, a proposition that has been called the *hegemonic stability theorem* (Keohane 1984; Eichengreen 1989). On the other hand, the Nth degree of freedom can be shared equally among the participants. This is the cooperative solution, in which the joint monetary policy is the outcome of a cooperative decisionmaking process of all members.

Much of the debate about the design and the performance of exchange-rate unions centers around the question of how the Nth degree of freedom is distributed and used in practice. The EMS is no exception. Since it came into being, two views have been offered in the literature. The *cooperative interpretation* regards the EMS as an arrangement to facilitate monetary policy coordination among its members with the purpose of improving their responses to exogenous economic shocks from the outside, such as the oil price hikes of the mid and late 1970s or the large swings in U.S. monetary policy in the early 1980s. The *disciplinary interpretation*, in contrast, argues that high-inflation countries, like France or Italy, have used the EMS to achieve a lower inflation trend under the strict leadership of the Bundesbank. The two views may not seem incompatible at first, because the former focuses on short-run stabilization policies around a given trend, while the latter addresses the choice of the long-run inflation trend itself. However, they are based on very different views of how the Nth degree of freedom in the EMS is allocated. The cooperative interpretation sees a collective determination of monetary policy in the EMS. The disciplinary view, in contrast, corresponds to the hegemonic paradigm; here, the Bundesbank acts as the hegemon of the system.

In the remainder of this chapter, we discuss these two interpretations in broad terms. In the last section of the chapter, we present a model of monetary policy making in the EMS that is used for a more thorough analysis of the two views in the following chapters.

3.1 The Cooperative Interpretation of the EMS

The cooperative interpretation of the EMS rests on the observation that even under flexible exchange rates, monetary policy in one country creates spillover effects on other countries. Flexible exchange rates do not insulate countries from the impact of economic fluctuations and policies in other countries.[1] Therefore, in contrast to what many economists and policymakers had hoped after the breakdown of the Bretton Woods system, flexible exchange rates do not eliminate the international interdependency of monetary policies. In economies as open as those of Europe, such interdependency becomes particularly acute and critical for policymaking.

Standard microeconomic theory suggests that independent decisionmaking by national monetary authorities leads to inefficient policy outcomes if there are significant spillover effects of monetary policies across countries. Independent policymakers do not take into account the effects of their actions on the foreign economies and therefore do not recognize their impact on the foreign authorities. Coordination of national policies, in contrast, can internalize such spillovers and achieve more efficient policy results. Exchange-rate arrangements create one particular form of such coordination. Recent game-theoretic literature has analyzed the conditions under which they yield optimal (or at least feasible and satisfactory) forms of coordination (e.g., Canzoneri and Gray 1985; Mélitz 1985; Laskar 1986; Canzoneri and Henderson 1988 and 1991; Fratianni and von Hagen 1990c).

The cooperative view regards the EMS as a strategic coalition of monetary authorities whose purpose is to coordinate their monetary policies and improve their stabilization efforts. Consider the following quote by Helmut Schmidt (1990a), the former German chancellor and one of the creators of the EMS:

> Giscard and Barre [then the French prime minister] were convinced that they absolutely needed the EMS to realize their own economic policies; I was similarly convinced of that. We knew that the European economies were unable to shield themselves individually against the turbulence of the World. Therefore, we wanted the unification and the joint success.
>
> When Giscard and I envisaged the common monetary system for the EC, France was outside the so-called Snake. France had left it hoping to free itself from the strict discipline imposed by the exchange rates, and yet maintain a proximate balance-of-payments equilibrium by imposing capital controls and other market interventions.
>
> As it turned out, however, this had only very unsatisfactory success— similar to the cases of England and Italy which had left the Snake earlier. Furthermore, the conduct of monetary and exchange rate policies in the U.S. and the dependency of the European countries' monetary policies on the dollar, on dollar interest rates, and dollar speculation, had been particularly harmful.

Schmidt and Giscard's hope was that policy coordination in the EMS would strengthen the members' ability to cope with adverse economic shocks. The declarations of the European Council in Bremen of July 1978 and in Brussels of December 1978 equally reflect this view (Commission of the EC 1979, 67 and 93):

> The European Council has discussed the attached scheme for the creation of a closer monetary cooperation (European Monetary System) leading to a zone of monetary stability in Europe. . . . The European Council regards such a zone as a highly desirable objective. . . . Participating countries will coordinate their exchange rate policies vis-à-vis third countries.

> The purpose of the European Monetary System is to establish a greater measure of monetary stability in the Community. It should be seen as a fundamental component of a more comprehensive strategy aimed at lasting growth with stability, a progressive return to full employment, the harmonization of living standards and the lessening of regional disparities in the Community.

The EMS was intended as an instrument to strengthen the coordination of monetary policies among the European economies to overcome the unsatisfactory performance of the uncoordinated regime of flexible exchange rates. Using fixed exchange rates as clear and readily observable criteria of coordination, and specifying a set of rules for cooperation and adjustment of policies, members would create an institutional framework to facilitate policy coordination (van Ypersele 1979; Padoa-Schioppa 1985b).

The use of fixed exchange rates as a vehicle for policy coordination to enhance the absorption of exogenous economic shocks creates a conflict between the desire to adopt a joint monetary policy in the short run and the desire of the participants to choose their domestic inflation rates independently of others in the long run, unless there is a general agreement on the group's joint inflation rate. But in the late 1970s, the European governments were far from reaching such an agreement. To resolve this inherent conflict, the design of the EMS was based on two principles, *flexibility* and *symmetry*. Flexibility meant that the central parities in the EMS should not be regarded as rigidly fixed. They could be changed in realignments with the consent of all EMS members. Early proponents of the system stressed the point that the frequency of realignments should not be taken as a criterion of success of the EMS (Commission of the EC 1979, 78; van Ypersele 1979, 9). Flexibility also meant accepting that individual members might impose capital and exchange controls to preserve some effectiveness and independence of their domestic monetary policies. Finally, flexibility was reflected in the absence of any formal rules of intervention and sterilization of foreign exchange market operations.

The principle of symmetry says that no EMS member country should carry a disproportionate cost of adjustment to balance-of-payments disequilibria (van Ypersele 1979, 6). To quote again from the 1978 Bremen Resolution of the European Council (Commission of the EC 1979, 93): "A system of closer monetary cooperation will only be successful if participating countries pursue policies conducive to greater stability at home and abroad; this applies to the deficit and surplus countries alike." There is a clear presumption that both hard- and soft-currency members of the EMS would take appropriate measures to adjust their policies to the EMS average. Various institutional elements of the EMS, such as the indicator of divergence and the credit facilities (see Chapter 2) result from this principle.

Flexibility and symmetry together imply that the long-run inflation trend of the EMS was left undetermined. Many of the early critics of the EMS focused on this indeterminacy and expressed their concern that EMS membership would set incentives for the low-inflation countries to adopt a more inflationary policy stance without exerting enough pressure on the high-inflation countries to pursue a more disciplinary course. Vaubel (1980) argued that the EMS would effectively take power away from the staunchest antiinflationist institution in the region, the Bundesbank. In the EMS, the Bundesbank would have to adopt policies consistent with the exchange-rate constraint. The central parities with other European currencies, realignments, and financial support to other central banks would become important parameters of German monetary policy. Because the authority to set these parameters would be with the Ministry of Finance, the EMS would give the latter more clout in German monetary policy and weaken the Bundesbank's independence from government. In this way, the EMS would likely endanger price stability, particularly in Germany. Furthermore, the EMS would lower the degree of currency competition in the region and reduce the demonstration effect that successful antiinflation policies have for less disciplined countries. The provision that both weak- and strong-currency countries would have to intervene to maintain their parities would favor convergence at the average rather than at the low end of the inflation range.[2] Finally, the fact that credits in the EMS are denominated in ECU implies that a country can lower its real credit burden by inflating its own currency, which would create inflationary incentives for weak-currency countries.

Caesar and Dickertmann (1979, 300 et seq.) and Cohen (1981, 20) argued that the extended credit facilities would encourage member countries to postpone actions aimed at correcting balance-of-payments deficits. Lomax (1983) pointed out that Belgium, Ireland, and Denmark gained additional creditworthiness in the international credit markets by joining forces with the Bundesbank, which would likely use its dollar and gold reserves to help these countries in the case of a liquidity crisis. The credit facilities in the EMS would therefore undermine the weak-currency countries' incentive to change their policies in favor of greater price stability.

Vaubel (1980) and Schröder (1979, 244) raised the additional objection that the EMS would tend to destabilize exchange rates in the region. The need to reach formal agreements to realign central parities would lead politicians in the member countries to time and shape realignments to their own political benefit. As bureaucratic decisions, realignments would tend to lag behind optimal timing (Lomax 1983, 42; Korteweg 1980, 42). Expectations of necessary realignments would then trigger speculative attacks on weak currencies and force member central banks to intervene heavily. In the end, EMS exchange-rate movements would be discontinuous and disruptive rather than continuous and smooth as under flexible rates.

3.2 The Disciplinary View of the EMS

During the 1980s, the pendulum of the discussion swung increasingly from the cooperative view held by the founders of the EMS toward the new disciplinary interpretation. The disciplinary view sees EMS membership as a method to achieve greater monetary discipline in countries with traditionally high inflation rates, like France, Italy, or Ireland. It rests on the positive analysis of central bank credibility of Barro and Gordon (1983), which holds that the institutional design of monetary authorities and the degree to which they can credibly commit to low-inflation policies are important determinants of a country's inflation trend. With its large degree of political independence, Germany's Bundesbank is the institution with the most credible commitment to price stability in the EMS. Other central banks, in contrast, find themselves exposed to more political pressure and are locked in unfavorable, high-inflation equilibria. These central banks have used the EMS to delegate part of their monetary autonomy to the Bundesbank and enjoy the effects of its greater credibility in return.

The disciplinary view generates the empirically testable implication that the Bundesbank unilaterally sets monetary policy in the EMS. We call this implication the *German-Dominance Hypothesis*, or GDH for short. Descriptions of the EMS in terms of GDH are numerous. For example, Katseli (1987, 28) claims that "within Europe, domestic central banks have chosen to lose some of the 'economic effectiveness' of domestic monetary policy and accept the leadership of the Bundesbank. . . ." Fischer (1987, 41) regards the EMS "as an arrangement by France and Italy to accept

German leadership, imposing constraints on their domestic monetary and fiscal policies." Giavazzi and Giovannini (1987, 237) assert that "Germany is the center country and runs monetary policy for the whole system." Goodhart (1989, 5) describes the Bundesbank as having played a "central, hegemonic role within the EMS, and a significant political influence on the impetus for EMU." Similarly, Russo and Tullio (1988, 332) conclude that "After 1983 an implicit agreement on inflation emerged, namely to converge towards the German inflation rate and to let Germany determine the 'anchor' inflation rate of the system." Gros and Thygesen (1988, 62) state flatly that "the EMS has thus become a hierarchic and asymmetric system." Finally, the *Delors Report* (1989, para. 5) asserts that the deutsche mark is an "anchor" for monetary policies in the EMS.

The same view is also expressed by the press. The *Economist* (1987) speaks of "no parity of power in the EMS" and argues that "[i]f sterling does join, the biggest change will be the transfer of responsibility for Britain's monetary policy from the Bank of England to Germany's Bundesbank which, as the central bank keenest on sound money, sets the pace for others to follow." Reginald Dale (1987), writing in the *International Herald Tribune*, asks "whether Germany will continue to dominate European economic policy-making through its leadership of the European Community's eight-nation currency block."

GDH can be interpreted in various ways. The "relative size" version of the argument simply states the obvious: that the EMS combines countries of different economic size. The relatively large German financial markets naturally give German interest rate movements and, hence, German monetary policy a greater impact on other countries, compared to the impact other, smaller countries' monetary policies have in the system. More interesting and relevant is the "strategic" version of GDH, according to which the EMS is a strictly hierarchical system that allows the Bundesbank alone to pursue its domestic policy goals independently of other EMS central banks. The attempt to benefit from the credibility of the Bundesbank's commitment to price stability has left the remaining central banks with no freedom at all to pursue independent goals. Instead, the ERM constraint forces them to adopt the Bundesbank's policy stance, even if it goes against their interests. We use the term "German dominance" exclusively in this strategic sense because, as we demonstrate in Chapter 5, this version provides a basis for an empirical test of the disciplinary view of the EMS.

A critical assumption of the disciplinary interpretation is that the monetary authorities in the high-inflation countries can credibly commit to an exchange-rate target compatible with low inflation, although they cannot commit themselves to a low-inflation monetary target. Therefore, to make this interpretation work, there must be something special about an exchange-rate target as compared to a domestic monetary target, commitment to which can be credible only if backing out of it is less attractive to the policymaker than keeping it. Thus, some feature of an exchange-rate target makes it costly to renege. The EMS arrangement itself does not clarify the nature of this extra cost because it does not spell out penalties should members break their commitments. Mélitz (1988), among others, argues that exchange-rate targets have a greater political weight than monetary targets because voters regard exchange-rate changes in the EMS as political events rather than market outcomes and punish policymakers for the perceived loss of international reputation following a devaluation. In essence, the politician associates the failure to maintain a commitment to a low-inflation exchange-rate target with a loss of electoral support.

Sachs and Wyplosz (1986) make a similar point in their account of the end of the French "Mitterrand experiment" with its expansive demand policies under the EMS constraint. In fact, the "Mitterrand experiment" from 1981 to 1983 is often mentioned as a classical example of the discipline theory (e.g., Sachs and Wyplosz 1986; Giavazzi and Giovannini 1989). In 1981, the newly elected government of President François Mitterrand embarked on a strongly expansionary program, increasing transfer payments to households, public-enterprise investment, public employment, and the minimum wage rate and shortening the workweek. The government budget deficit rose from zero in 1980 to 3.1 percent of GDP in 1982; public debt jumped from 9.1 percent of GDP in 1980 to 15 percent in 1983. The fiscal program was combined with accommodative monetary policy. The money supply (M1) rose by 15.9 percent in 1981 and 10.9 percent in 1982. Inflation declined slightly from 12.2 percent to 11.8 percent in 1981 and rose again to 12.6 percent in 1982, compared to 4.2 percent and 4.5 percent in West Germany. But the results of this stimulative package were disappointing for the government. Real GDP growth fell from 1 percent in 1980 to 0.5 percent in 1981 and rose a mere 1.8 percent in 1982. The unemployment rate increased from 6.5 percent in 1980 to 8.1 percent in 1982. Sachs and Wyplosz attribute the lack of success largely to the recessionary world environment: Germany, for example, suffered reductions in real GDP in 1981 and 1982, and the French performance was still relatively better than the performance of many other OECD countries.

By 1982, however, the French government was faced with a mounting external imbalance. Despite devaluations of the franc's central parity in the EMS in October 1981, February 1982, and June 1982 by a total of 10 percent against the ECU and 14 percent against the DM, the current account deficit rose to 2.2 percent of GDP in 1982. At the same time, interventions to support the franc depleted the international reserves of the Banque de France. During the second half of 1982, and more decidedly after the March 1983 realignment, the French government finally performed a full turnaround to a policy of austerity geared toward external balance and price stability.

Sachs and Wyplosz (1986) contend that EMS membership played a critical role in this decision. The political threat of having to abandon the EMS otherwise forced the government to adopt the new, unpopular policies. Yet a closer look shows the example is quite ambiguous. Sachs and Wyplosz explain that the Mitterrand experiment resulted in unsustainable external imbalances that demanded correction in one way or another. The French government had realized that a more restrictive policy was unavoidable and pondered the alternative options for reversing the trends of high inflation and devaluation of the franc (Eggerstädt and Sinn 1987). Thus, the relevant policy question was not whether to take corrective action but rather whether to do so inside or outside the EMS. The OECD (1988) review of the case argues that based on the French experience in the 1970s, the authorities expected adjustment under a flexible exchange rate to be even more harmful than adjustment within the EMS. Furthermore, the EMS offered recourse to financial assistance: The French stabilization program was supported by an ECU 4 billion loan through the medium-term facility in May 1983 (Ungerer et al. 1986, 6). Thus, remaining in the EMS could be regarded as the lesser evil in the unavoidable policy adjustment. Such a view, however, contradicts the very essence of the credibility hypothesis. If EMS membership promises to reduce the economic cost of reversing inflationary demand policies, it must increase the incentive to use such policies to serve short-run political interests in the first place. EMS membership would then lower rather than raise the credibility of the monetary authorities' commitment to price stability.[3]

Sachs and Wyplosz argue that the importance of the EMS in the French turnaround rested largely on the perception—widely diffused in French government circles—that leaving the EMS would have meant leaving other spheres of European cooperation and integration as well. This contention can be cast in more general terms: Breaking the EMS commitment would have entailed the loss of other economic benefits from EMS and EC membership, such as the positive effects of exchange-rate stability on trade, the reduced information and transaction cost resulting from fixed exchange rates, and the benefits of the customs union. However, the implication of such an argument for central bank credibility is again ambiguous, because such benefits naturally accrue to all participants. This implies that all participants face a welfare loss if one of them withdraws from the EMS. In particular, the French move out of the EMS would have imposed a cost on low-inflation Germany as well. But this would have given the French central bank some leverage over German monetary policy. Had the Bundesbank been forced to face a significant economic cost arising from a breakdown of the EMS, it might have preferred accommodating a French monetary expansion and preserving the fixed exchange rate to going back to a flexible exchange rate and maintaining its independent policy. The EMS would have damaged the credibility of the Bundesbank's low-inflation policy; the result would have been higher European equilibrium inflation.

The history of the Italian disinflation is equally ambiguous with respect to the credibility hypothesis. In the 1970s, the Italian Treasury could automatically expand the monetary base through an overdraft facility with the Banca d'Italia and through reliance on the central bank as the residual buyer of government debt at Treasury auctions. The absence of a secondary market for government debt prevented the Banca d'Italia from neutralizing these automatic sources of base-money creation. In 1976, the Treasury began offering securities to the public, a step that gave the central bank some monetary independence by allowing it use of open market operations. Its independence was strengthened when the government in 1981 completely released the Banca d'Italia from being the residual buyer of government debt at Treasury auctions. The reasons for this so-called divorce had little to do with the EMS; its purpose was rather to enforce greater fiscal discipline on the government (Tabellini 1988, 97).

In 1984, the Italian opposition, together with militant labor unions, called for a national referendum against the government's attempts to limit wage indexation. In their empirical studies of inflation expectations in Italy, Gressani et al. (1988) and Giavazzi and Spaventa (1989) found that the effect of the government's firm stand in this affair, which led to eventual defeat of the referendum, was much larger and more significant than the effect of Italy's EMS membership. One may conclude that the government had to prove its willingness to bear the cost of unpopular domestic policies first, before wage and price setters became convinced that the commitment to the new monetary regime was lasting. Giavazzi and Spaventa speculate that EMS membership gave Italian politicians the justification for unpopular policies. But the use of the EMS as a scapegoat conflicts with the credibility hypothesis. By reducing the threat of having to face up to the political consequences of reversing expansionary monetary policies, policymakers would have undermined the credibility of their commitment to price stability.

Dornbusch (1989) has reviewed the Irish experience in the 1980s. He argues that the main element in the disinflation process was the restoration of balance to the government budget. In early 1982, the long-term interest rate differential between Ireland and Germany began to fall, an indication of increasing credibility of the Irish stabilization program.

Dornbusch suggests that the Irish decision not to seek a devaluation in the 1982 realignments contributed somewhat to this credibility gain. More important, however, was the fact that after 1982 the stabilization program was carried by a broad domestic political consensus, which became most obvious when the new Irish government, in March 1982, submitted essentially the same tight budget for which the previous government had fallen. Again, this example is a clear demonstration that policymakers' willingness to bear the political cost of unpopular policies seems to have been much more important than EMS membership.

Another critical weakness of the disciplinary view is that it does not explain German membership in the EMS. The point is important because as Snidal (1985) points out, hegemonic-stability theorems have the peculiar characteristic that the hegemon incurs a welfare loss from supplying stability to the system. The disciplinary view therefore embeds a conflict between the high-inflation countries and low-inflation Germany. To resolve this conflict, some authors have argued that Germany seeks trade advantages in the EMS resulting from a tendency to undervalue the DM between realignments (Mélitz 1988; Giavazzi and Pagano 1988). But such mercantilistic suggestions are not convincing. An exchange-rate arrangement with permanent trade imbalances would be unsustainable because of the drain on the weak-currency countries' foreign currency reserves. As markets realize this nonsustainability, speculative attacks on the central parities would follow and precipitate the breakdown of the system.[4] For the EMS to be sustainable, there cannot be systematic overvaluation or undervaluation of a member currency.

Another explanation for German membership offered in the literature is that the Bundesbank seeks greater financial integration in the EMS. Giavazzi and Pagano (1985) note that Germany has historically borne the brunt of speculative capital flows originating from the U.S. dollar market. Under fixed exchange rates, increased substitutability between DM- and other EMS currency-denominated assets produces a more equitable distribution of speculative capital flows.[5] The problem here is that until the second half of the 1980s, the EMS relied heavily on artificial barriers to capital and financial flows in the weak-currency countries to preserve its stability. At least at the inception of the system, it was therefore not clear whether these barriers to financial integration in Europe would serve German interest.

3.3 A Model of Monetary Policy Making in the EMS

This section develops the analytical tools we use throughout the remainder of this book. It sets up a macroeconomic model of three economies linked together by trade in goods and financial assets. The purpose of the model is to analyze monetary policy and policy coordination in the EMS. Here, we introduce the model's general framework and describe its basic characteristics. Later on, we use more restricted versions suitable for the particular problem in question.

Our device belongs to the class of game-theoretic models of international monetary policy presented by Canzoneri and Henderson (1988) and Fratianni and von Hagen (1990a). To avoid misunderstanding, we stress at the outset that the model is not meant to achieve a detailed and realistic description of the economies involved but rather to highlight certain aspects and problems of strategic interaction among central banks. The model deliberately simplifies many aspects of the economies to concentrate on the policy issues.

Table 3.1 displays the model. All variables except interest rates are defined in logarithms. Time subscripts are suppressed to simplify notation where possible. All parameters are positive. There are three countries, called Germany, Italy, and the United States, indexed by i = 1, 2, 3, respectively. Each country produces a homogeneous output good y_i, each an imperfect substitute for outputs produced by other countries. Production takes place according to the Cobb-Douglas production functions (3.1) using domestic labor (n_i) as the only variable input. The two exogenous stochastic shocks ξ_j, j = 1, 2, are serially and mutually uncorrelated random variables, whose expected value is zero. Labor demand is given by equations (3.2), where w is the nominal wage rate and P denotes an output price. It is based on the assumption of profit maximizing given the production functions (3.1).

Labor is immobile across countries. An important ingredient of our model is the assumption that labor markets are governed by some nominal wage rigidity. Labor supply is described by a wage-setting function (3.3). Wages are tied to the predetermined output price expectations P^e and, with intertemporal substitution, to unexpected changes in the current interest rate.[6] Labor supply is assumed perfectly elastic at this wage. Expectations are based on information available at the end of the previous period.

Aggregate demand for domestic output, equation (3.4), consists of a domestic and an export component. The domestic component depends positively on domestic real income and negatively on the real interest rate $r = R - (P_{+1}^e - P)$. The export component depends positively on foreign real income and the relative price of foreign and domestic output. In equation (3.4), β_{ij} is the share of country i's output in country j's consumption, and ρ_i is country i's marginal propensity to consume out of real income. The relative prices are expressed by three real exchange

TABLE 3.1 A Model of Policymaking in the EMS

(3.1) Production Functions
$$y_1 = y_1^n + (1 - \alpha_1)n_1 + a_{11}\xi_1 + a_{12}\xi_2 \, ;$$
$$y_2 = y_2^n + (1 - \alpha_2)n_2 + a_{21}\xi_1 + a_{22}\xi_2 \, ;$$
$$y_3 = y_3^n + (1 - \alpha_3)n_3 + a_{31}\xi_1 + a_{32}\xi_2 \, .$$

(3.2) Demand for Labor
$$w_1 - p_1 = -\alpha_1 n_1 + a_{11}\xi_1 + a_{12}\xi_2 \, ;$$
$$w_2 - p_2 = -\alpha_2 n_2 + a_{21}\xi_1 + a_{22}\xi_2 \, ;$$
$$w_3 - p_3 = -\alpha_3 n_3 + a_{31}\xi_1 + a_{32}\xi_2 \, .$$

(3.3) Supply of Labor
$$w_1 = P_1^e + \lambda_1(R_1 - R_1^e) \, ;$$
$$w_2 = P_2^e + \lambda_2(R_2 - R_2^e) \, ;$$
$$w_3 = P_3^e + \lambda_3(R_3 - R_2^e) \, .$$

(3.4) Demand for Output
$$y_1^d = \phi_{11}q_{12} + \phi_{13}q_{13} - \gamma_1 r_1 + \sum_{j=1}^{3} \beta_{1j}\rho_j y_j + c_{11}\eta_1 + c_{12}\eta_2 \, ;$$

$$y_2^d = -\phi_{21}q_{12} + \phi_{23}q_{23} - \gamma_2 r_2 + \sum_{j=1}^{3} \beta_{2j}\rho_j y_j + c_{21}\eta_1 + c_{22}\eta_2 \, ;$$

$$y_3^d = -\phi_{31}q_{13} - \phi_{32}q_{23} - \gamma_3 r_3 + \sum_{j=1}^{3} \beta_{3j}\rho_j y_j + c_{31}\eta_1 + c_{32}\eta_2 \, .$$

(3.5) Money-market Equilibrium
$$m_1 - P_1 = y_1 - y_1^e - \theta_1(R_1 - R_1^e) \, ;$$
$$m_2 - P_2 = y_2 - y_2^e - \theta_2(R_2 - R_2^e) \, ;$$
$$m_3 - P_3 = y_3 - y_3^e - \theta_3(R_3 - R_3^e) \, .$$

(3.6) Triangular Arbitrage
$$s_{23} = s_{13} - s_{12} \, .$$

(3.7) Open Interest Parity
$$R_1 = R_2 + s^e_{12, t+1} - s_{12} = R_3 + s^e_{13, t+1} - s_{13} \, .$$

(3.8) Consumer Price Levels
$$Q_i = \sum_{j=1}^{3} \beta_{ij}(s_{ij} + P_j) = P_i + \sum_{j=1}^{3} \beta_{ij} q_{ij},$$
where $s_{ii} = 1$.

(3.9) Preferences of the Monetary Authorities
$$2U_i = -\sigma_i (n_i - N_i)^2 - (Q_i)^2 .$$

rates: between Germany and Italy, q_{12}; between Germany and the United States, q_{13}; and between Italy and the United States, q_{23}. For example, $q_{12} = s_{12} + P_2 - P_1$, where s_{12} is the nominal spot DM-lira exchange rate, quoted as DM per lira. The exogenous shocks η_j, $j = 1, 2$, are serially and mutually uncorrelated demand shocks with expectation zero.

Domestic money of each country is held only by domestic residents. Money-market equilibrium is given by equations (3.5). The demand for real balances depends positively on real income and negatively on the domestic interest rate. For analytical simplification, we normalize the demand for real balances by the expected level of real output, y^e, and the expected interest rates, R^e. We take the money supply as the monetary policy instrument in all three countries. In addition to money, there are nominal, interest-bearing bonds denominated in the three currencies. Residents of each country may hold foreign currency-denominated bonds in addition to their own bonds. The model is closed by two arbitrage conditions and a price-level definition. Equation (3.6) is the triangular arbitrage in the foreign currency markets. Equation (3.7) is the open interest parity that equals the expected yield on all three bonds in a given currency. Equation (3.8) expresses the national price level, the consumer price index (CPI), as the weighted average of prices of domestic goods and imported goods expressed in local currency.

Policymakers in all three countries pursue two policy goals. On the one hand, they aim at minimizing fluctuations of employment around a target level of employment. On the other hand, they attempt to minimize fluctuations of the consumer price level. These policy goals are expressed in the preference functions (3.9), where $\sigma > 0$ is the relative weight placed on employment fluctuations, and $N_i \geq 0$ is the level of employment above natural employment the central banks wish to realize. Such an employment target can be justified by the existence of distortionary taxes, which drive a wedge between the individually optimal (the natural) and the socially optimal level of employment; alternatively, the target may simply reflect pressures exerted on the central bank to boost employment for reasons of political opportunism.[7] By normalizing the price level of the previous period to zero in logarithms, we can interpret the current CPIs as the increments of the current over the previous price levels. The preference functions then express a distaste for inflation (as well as deflation) together with a preference for above-normal employment. Throughout the remainder of the book, we adhere to the unfortunate but common (to economists) abuse of language in calling an increase in a policymaker's preference or utility level as a "welfare improvement." Although we are aware of the problems in equating the preference functions (3.9) with national or public welfare, we follow the language convention to avoid the cumbersome wording that would otherwise be convention to avoid the cumbersome wording that would otherwise be needed.

The linear stochastic structure of our model implies that it is separable in the determination of trend values for all endogenous variables and the determination of fluctuations around these trends. Monetary policy, therefore, has two separate aspects: The long-run growth rate of the money supply determines the long-run rate of inflation, exchange-rate depreciation, and nominal rate of interest. Short-run deviations of money growth from its trend cause deviations of interest rates, exchange rates, inflation, output, and employment from their long-run values. As a consequence, the model opens two areas for policy coordination: coordination of the choice of inflation trends and coordination of short-run stabilization policies geared at counteracting the stochastic shocks that affect the three economies. These two options correspond to the discipline and the cooperation views of the system. We discuss these two paradigms in the following chapters.

Notes

1. The conditions under which flexible exchange rates provide partial or full insulation from foreign shocks have been studied extensively in the post-Bretton Woods literature. They depend critically on the nature of the shocks, the information available to economic agents, and the degree of wage indexation. See, for example, Frenkel and Aizeman (1985), von Hagen (1990), von Hagen and Neumann (1990), and Wihlborg and Willett (1991).

2. We return to these themes in Chapter 8 when we compare the collusive and competitive theories of central banking.

3. von Hagen (1992). See also Wihlborg and Willett (1991) for a similar argument.

4. See Wyplosz (1986) for an analysis of speculative attacks.

5. Additionally, Giavazzi and Giovannini (1987) argue that intervention practices in the EMS free the Bundesbank from the need to adjust to EMS portfolio shocks, a point, however, that holds strictly only for nonobligatory, intramarginal interventions.

6. Because expectations based on information available at the beginning of a period and nominal interest and exchange rates are the only observable variables in the system, an unexpected rise in the real interest rate is equivalent to an unexpected rise in the nominal interest rate.

7. For a discussion of such output or employment targets, see Barro and Gordon (1983), Rogoff (1985a), Fratianni et al. (1991).

4

The EMS
and Central Bank Credibility

In Section 3.2 of the previous chapter we have outlined the general thrust of the disciplinary interpretation of the EMS, which states that the system enhances central bank credibility in the high-inflation countries of the EC. In this chapter, we expand analytically on this view.

4.1 Theoretical Considerations

The disciplinary interpretation of the EMS has been put forth persuasively by Giavazzi and Pagano (1988) and Giavazzi and Giovannini (1987, 1988, 1989). These authors build on Barro and Gordon's (1983) seminal article on central bank credibility. According to Barro and Gordon, governments cannot credibly precommit themselves to a low-inflation monetary policy rule, because, in practice, they cannot be punished if they deviate from such a commitment. Barro and Gordon show that if nominal wages are rigid and markets understand policymakers' incentives, the nonenforceability of policy commitments biases monetary policy outcomes toward inflation. The equilibrium inflation rate is positive, yet there are no output or employment gains because the announcement of a zero-inflation policy rule is not credible. Both society and policymakers would benefit from an enforceable precommitment.

Thompson (1981) and Rogoff (1985a) propose to cope with this institutional deficiency by delegating the authority over monetary policy to an agent whose preferences about inflation and other policy goals are markedly different from the government's preferences. They argue that the appointment of a "conservative" central banker, who would put more emphasis on fighting inflation than would politicians or policymakers, will lead the public to reduce inflation expectations and, thus, will produce a lower equilibrium rate of inflation.[1] The disciplinary view of the EMS fits into this general theme. In particular, it is argued that members having traditionally high inflation rates and monetary authorities with little credibility use the ERM to delegate their monetary policy authority to the Bundesbank. The Bundesbank, relying on its high degree of political independence and credibility, assumes the role of the conservative central banker in the EMS. Interpreting the EMS in this fashion, one can answer the puzzle raised by conventional economics—namely, why countries with very different inflation rates would want to join an exchange-rate arrangement like the ERM.

To assess the validity of the discipline hypothesis, we use a simplified version of the model presented in Section 3.3 (see Table 4.1). The model is reduced to two countries, Germany and a high-inflation country (say, Italy) and to abstracts from bond markets; money is the only financial asset. The economies are perfectly symmetric, and with the focus on inflation trends rather than stochastic fluctuations, all exogenous shocks are set equal to zero. The reduced-form solutions for employment and the consumer price level of this version are

(4.8) $$n_1 = m_1 - m_1^e; n_2 = m_2 - m_2^e;$$

(4.9) $$Q_1 = m_1 - (1 - \alpha)(m_1 - m_1^e) + \varepsilon(m_1 - m_1^e - (m_2 - m_2^e)),$$
$$Q_2 = m_2 - (1 - \alpha)(m_2 - m_2^e) + \varepsilon(m_2 - m_2^e - (m_1 - m_1^e)),$$

where $\varepsilon = \phi\beta^2(1 - \alpha)$. Percentage deviations of aggregate employment from natural employment are proportional to the unexpected growth in the domestic money supply. A monetary expansion leads to an equal relative increase in the price level if the expansion is fully anticipated. In contrast, the inflation effect of a monetary surprise is reduced by its output effect, $(1 - \alpha)(m_i - m_i^e)$, and is increased by the devaluation of the domestic currency it causes, $\varepsilon(m_i - m_i^e)$. Note that a domestic monetary surprise causes a devaluation only if it differs from the foreign monetary surprise.

The disciplinary view of the EMS focuses on the temptation policymakers face to use monetary surprises to bring employment closer to the target level, N_i. Suppose the Banca d'Italia announces a zero-inflation policy, or, $m_2 = 0$. If the Italian private sector regards the announcement as credible, the expected money supply is $m_2^e = 0$, and $w_2 = P_2^e = 0$. Honoring its announcement, the central bank attains the utility level $2U_2 = -\sigma N_2^2$. But because the monetary authority acts after wage contracts have been set in accordance with expectations, it will maximize its preferences given the private sector's expectations and wage contracts.[2] In the current scenario, the marginal utility of a monetary

TABLE 4.1 A Simplified Model

(4.1) Production Functions
$$y_1 = y_{1n} + (1 - \alpha)n_1;$$
$$y_2 = y_{2n} + (1 - \alpha)n_2.$$

(4.2) Labor Demand Functions
$$w_1 - P_1 = -\alpha n_1;$$
$$w_2 - P_2 = -\alpha n_2.$$

(4.3) Wage Setting
$$w_1 = P_1^e;$$
$$w_2 = P_2^e.$$

(4.4) Demand for Output
$$y_1 = \phi^{-1}q + \beta y_2 + (1 - \beta)y_1;$$
$$y_2 = -\phi^{-1}q + \beta y_1 + (1 - \beta)y_2.$$

(4.5) Money-Market Equilibrium
$$m_1 - P_1 = y_1 - y_{1n};$$
$$m_2 - P_2 = y_2 - y_{2n}.$$

(4.6) Definition of real exchange rate
$$q = s_{12} + P_2 - P_1.$$

(4.7) Definition of the consumer price level
$$Q_1 = P_1 + \beta q;$$
$$Q_2 = P_2 - \beta q.$$

---

surprise is positive, when $m_2 = m_2^e$, namely $(dU_2/dm_2) = \sigma N_2 > 0$, which reflects the possibility of a utility gain resulting from the employment effect of a monetary surprise. It follows that it is optimal for the Banca d'Italia to renege on its announcement and instead choose the money supply $m_2 = \sigma N_2/[\sigma + (\alpha + \varepsilon)^2] > 0$, which yields the utility level $2U_2 = -\sigma N_2^2(\varepsilon + \alpha)^2/(\sigma + (\varepsilon + \alpha)^2) > -\sigma N_2^2$.

The private sector is aware of the authorities' preferences and the temptation to trade employment for price stability. Being rational, the private sector must incorporate in its expectations the behavior of the policymakers and realize that it is optimal to renege on an announcement unless the marginal utility of a monetary surprise is zero. Because the marginal utility of a monetary surprise decreases with an increase in expected inflation, the equilibrium inflation rate must be large enough to eliminate the temptation to renege. In sum, the announcement of a zero-inflation policy is not credible because it contradicts rationality.

With a flexible DM/lira exchange rate, the two monetary authorities choose their money supplies independently. The resulting "subgame perfect" Nash equilibrium is[3]

(4.10) $m_{1N} = Q_{1N} = \sigma N_1/(\varepsilon + \alpha); m_{2N} = Q_{2N} = \sigma N_2/(\varepsilon + \alpha).$

A basic assumption of the disciplinary view is that the Italian employment target exceeds the German target, $N_2 > N_1 > 0$.[4] This makes Italy's equilibrium inflation rate higher than Germany's. The utility levels associated with this equilibrium are[5]

(4.11) $2U_{1N} = -\sigma N_1^2[1 + \sigma/(\varepsilon + \alpha)^2]; 2U_{2N} = -\sigma N_2^2[1 + \sigma/(\varepsilon + \alpha)^2] < 2U_{1N}.$

In equilibrium, inflation is fully anticipated and hence yields no employment benefits. Yet the authorities' desire to raise employment above the natural employment levels results in positive equilibrium inflation. This outcome is inefficient in the sense that the authorities would be better off if they could credibly commit to noninflationary policies.

The disciplinary view of the EMS asserts that Italy can improve on this outcome by pegging the lira to the DM at a predetermined rate.[6] Giavazzi and Giovannini (1987) and Giavazzi and Pagano (1988) present the argument in the most persuasive way, assuming that German monetary policy remains unaffected by the creation of the EMS. In the present model, pegging the DM/lira exchange rate requires that Italy adopt the same monetary policy as Germany, or $m_2 = m_1$. In this sense, Germany dominates monetary policy making in the EMS, and Italian monetary policy has been delegated to the Bundesbank. The resulting utility, under these circumstances, is

(4.12) $2U_{2P} = -\sigma[N_2^2 + \sigma N_1^2/(\varepsilon+\alpha)^2] > 2U_{2N}.$

Pegging the exchange rate in the EMS seems to promise a clear-cut welfare gain to the Italian authorities. Giavazzi and Giovannini call it the "advantage of tying one's hands" (see also Giavazzi and Pagano 1988). By delegating Italian policy to the Bundesbank, the Banca d'Italia borrows credibility from the Bundesbank and achieves a reduction in its inflation bias.

Canzoneri and Henderson (1988) point out that the principle embedded in the "advantage of tying one's hands" seems to contradict a basic microeconomic proposition—decisionmakers cannot gain by reducing their options (the choice set). This proposition would suggest that an exchange-rate peg can yield, at best, the same utility as flexible exchange rates for the Italian authorities, because with flexible rates they have a broader range of alternative actions from which to choose. The solution to this contradiction lies in the implicit yet all-important assumption on which the disciplinary argument rests: that the Banca d'Italia can credibly commit itself to a low-inflation exchange-rate target. That is, the EMS implicitly enlarges the central bank's choice set by the new option called credible precommitment, which by assumption does not exist under the flexible exchange-rate regime.

So far, the result that Italy unambiguously benefits from a fixed exchange rate rests on the premise that German monetary policy does not change with the creation of the EMS. However, this is a flawed premise. The fact that Italy adopts the exchange-rate target and follows German monetary policy changes the policy constraints faced by the Bundesbank. By accepting the Bundesbank as the leader of the system and by pegging the exchange rate, the Banca d'Italia automatically mimics monetary surprises initiated by the Bundesbank. This implication of the exchange-rate peg changes the Bundesbank's behavior, because it reduces the effect of a Bundesbank monetary surprise on the German inflation rate. This can be seen in equation (4.9), where the term $\varepsilon(m_1 - m_1^e - (m_2 - m_2^e))$ vanishes under the fixed exchange rate. Intuitively, a part of the domestic price level effect of a German monetary expansion is now exported to Italy. The EMS thus reduces the surprise inflation necessary to achieve a given increase in German employment, leaving the Bundesbank with a greater incentive for monetary surprises.[7] Recognizing this change, the private sector adjusts its expectations m_1^e. The subgame perfect equilibrium for the EMS becomes

(4.13) $\qquad m_{1E} = Q_{1E} = m_{2E} = Q_{2E} = \sigma N_1/\alpha > \sigma N_1/(\varepsilon + \alpha).$

German inflation in the EMS unambiguously exceeds German inflation under flexible rates. By allowing the Banca d'Italia to borrow credibility, the Bundesbank loses some credibility itself. In turn, this loss affects the utility levels of both authorities:

(4.14) $\quad 2U_{1E} = -\sigma N_1^2(1 + \sigma/\alpha^2) < 2U_{1N} ; 2U_{2E} = -\sigma[N_2^2 + \sigma N_1^2/\alpha^2].$

Equation (4.14) shows that Italy's incentive to join the EMS becomes ambiguous once the endogenous basis of Germany's policy is recognized. The Banca d'Italia's utility gain is

(4.15) $\qquad 2(U_{2E} - U_{2N}) = \sigma^2[N_2^2/(\varepsilon + \alpha)^2 - N_1^2/\alpha^2].$

Italy benefits from the EMS only if $(\varepsilon + \alpha)/\alpha < N_2/N_1$. This condition links the structural characteristics of the economies to the central bank's preferences. For a sufficiently small value of ε the condition will hold by assumption. But ε is small when β, the income elasticity of import demand, is small and when $1/\phi$, the real exchange-rate elasticity of import demand, is large. Both conditions can be interpreted to mean that the more the two countries are economically integrated, the less likely the EMS yields a benefit to Italy. The disciplinary view thus runs counter to the common notion that monetary policy coordination in the EMS is a part of the European integration process. Furthermore, the long-run objective of a complete internal market—"Europe 1992"—contradicts Italy's interest in achieving a low-inflation equilibrium in the EMS.

Even if the condition just described is satisfied, however, it is not clear that joining the EMS is a credible strategy for the Banca d'Italia. The crucial issue is what makes markets believe in the bank's commitment to a low-inflation exchange-rate target. Formally, EMS membership with the adoption of the German money rule is not a subgame perfect strategy. To see this, consider the marginal utility of a monetary surprise to the Italian central bank once expectations, hence wages, have been set according to the EMS:

$$(4.16) \qquad dU_{2E}/dm_2 \bigg|_{m_2 = m_2^e = m_1 = m_1^e} = \sigma[N_2 - (\alpha + \varepsilon)N_1/\alpha].$$

The marginal utility is positive if $N_2/N_1 > 1 + \varepsilon/\alpha$, which is exactly the condition assuring that Italy gains from the EMS. Given EMS expectations, the Banca d'Italia has an immediate incentive to abandon the exchange-rate target. In practice, the central bank can do so by leaving the EMS formally, or by pressing for a realignment or using capital and exchange controls to reduce the EMS constraint while remaining in the system. Seeing through this incentive structure, the public will not consider the Italian EMS commitment a credible one and will not form expectations according to equation (4.13). It follows that Italy can expect no welfare gain from the EMS.

To overturn this negative conclusion, one must assume that once the EMS has been put into place, there is a cost associated with reneging on the exchange-rate target. Formally, let the Italian preference function be $2U_2' = 2U_2 - 2\zeta P_2$, where the index variable ζ is zero if Italy honors the exchange-rate commitment and one otherwise, and P_2 is the utility loss incurred by the Italian authorities as a result of reneging. The new marginal utility of a monetary surprise then is $dU_2'/dm_2 = dU_2/dm_2 - P_2$. To make the EMS credible, the extra cost P_2 must obey

$$(4.17) \qquad P_2 \geq \sigma[N_2 - (\alpha + \varepsilon)N_1/\alpha],$$

that is, it must balance the temporary employment gain. The larger the weight of the employment target and the larger the difference in the pre-EMS inflation biases, the larger the extra cost of leaving the EMS must be to make Italy's EMS membership feasible. Because this extra cost is not an intrinsic part of the exchange-rate arrangement itself, it is erroneous to call the EMS a "disciplinary device" (Giavazzi and Pagano 1988). The discipline must come from some other source.

The superiority of EMS membership as a monetary strategy for Italy thus hinges entirely on the assumption that the EMS fills the institutional void behind the inflation bias by creating threats to the policymaker for breaking a commitment. The empirical strength of the argument then depends critically on the possibility of identifying the nature and force of these new threats in practice. Unfortunately, no satisfactory answer has been given so far in the literature. We pointed out in Section 3.2 that the evidence of a political threat—the risk of losing electoral support—as a basis of EMS discipline is quite inconclusive. Similarly, the historical accounts of the French, Italian, and Irish disinflations offer only vague and ambiguous evidence about the nature and the importance of a specific cost of reneging on the EMS exchange-rate target.

One may argue that such reneging is politically unattractive because it requires the consultation and consent of the other EMS members (De Grauwe 1992). But it is not obvious that peer pressure exists among EMS policymakers. Realizing that they all face similar constraints, politicians are equally likely to exert solidarity with a government asking for a realignment. After all, realignments are decided upon by treasury ministers, who may well be inclined to grant them easily and to help their fellow politicians save face rather than blame them for profligacy. In this way, mutual consultation and official statements of consent can lower the cost of surprise inflation.

Hughes-Hallett and Minford (1990) pursue another route to identify the source of greater monetary discipline in the EMS. Although these authors do not claim that such discipline raises the credibility of low-inflation policies in the EMS, their argument must be mentioned in our context. Using simulations of hypothetical reflations in EMS countries other than Germany, they argue that EMS membership has raised the cost and reduced the benefit of reflation. In their model, an independent monetary surprise causes a revaluation of the domestic currency and a rise in the real interest rate, so that the output and employment effects become "perverse." This suggests that the EMS would raise the credibility of low-inflation policies by deterring central banks from independent reflation. Hughes-Hallett and Minford's results, however, depend crucially on an unrealistic way of modeling realignments. In their model, realignments are permitted only at fixed and long intervals, a specification that is consistent neither with EMS principles nor with the experience until 1987. Furthermore, their argument implies that governments are exposed to the temptation of surprise deflation, which would equally undermine their credibility. In conclusion, there is no convincing evidence that the necessary condition allowing the EMS to give greater credibility to the high-inflation central banks is fulfilled in practice.

Germany's change in utility from EMS membership is

(4.18) $2(U_{1E} - U_{1N}) = \sigma^2 N_1^2 [1/(\varepsilon + \alpha)^2 - 1/\alpha^2] < 0,$

a welfare loss resulting from the higher German equilibrium inflation rate under the fixed exchange rate. This welfare loss is larger the more the two economies are integrated, that is, the larger is the parameter ε. Credibility cannot be transferred freely among central banks. Consequently, the disciplinary view cannot explain German membership in the EMS.

The increase in the German inflation rate results from the fact that in the EMS, the extra inflation necessary to raise employment in Germany by a given rate is lower than with a flexible exchange rate. In other words, the inflation cost of a rise in employment is lower, or the German Phillips curve is flatter, in the EMS. One may respond that the fixing of the exchange rate can have the opposite effect, because in reality a domestic inflation increases domestic production costs as well as output prices (De Grauwe 1992). With a fixed exchange rate, domestic producers would lose competitiveness and employment would fall. As a result, the German Phillips curve would be steeper in the EMS and German inflation would fall rather than increase.

A slight modification of our model helps to show that this does not solve the problem. The idea that domestic inflation increases production costs can be incorporated straightforwardly by changing our wage-setting equation to allow for partial indexation:

(4.19) $w_i = P_i^e + \chi Q_i, i = 1, 2,$

where χ is the indexation parameter, $0 \leq \chi \leq 1$. With this assumption, the inflation effects of a monetary surprise in Germany under flexible and fixed exchange rates are:

(4.20) $dQ_1/dm_1 \Big|_{flex} = [(1 - \chi(1 - \alpha - \varepsilon))(\alpha + \varepsilon) - \chi\varepsilon^2]/[(1 - \chi(1 - \alpha - \varepsilon))^2 - \chi^2 \varepsilon^2]$

(4.21) $dQ_1/dm_1 \Big|_{fix} = [(1 - \chi(1 - \alpha))\alpha]/[(1 - \chi(1 - \alpha))^2].$

Note that with full indexation, both effects are unity, but with less than complete indexation, the effect under a flexible rate exceeds the effect under a fixed rate. The employment effect of a monetary surprise is $dn_1/dm_1 = 1 - \chi dQ_1/dm_1$, which is zero under full indexation. It follows that even if domestic cost rises as a result of inflation, the inflation cost of an increase in German employment is lower with a fixed exchange rate.

Another way to tackle the problem of German membership in the EMS is based on the potential conflict between the Bundesbank and the German government. According to German law, exchange-rate arrangements are decided by the Ministry of Finance and not by the Bundesbank; this was certainly true for the EMS. One may therefore argue that EMS membership was forced on the Bundesbank against its will.[8] But if credibility is relevant to explain the EMS, this only redirects the question: Why would the German government want a higher rate of inflation? Credibility considerations suggest that, in contrast, the government should keep the Bundesbank independent to minimize the inflation bias of German monetary policy.[9]

An alternative approach to solving the problem of German membership comes from the realization that the EMS is not, in reality, an agreement between two isolated countries. To see what happens in a more general framework, we can analyze the German inflation bias arising in the three-country version of our model. With a few simplifying assumptions, it can be shown that the German inflation bias under a flexible exchange rate can be smaller or larger than if the DM/lira rate is fixed.[10] The reason is that when the DM/lira rate is fixed, the DM/dollar and the lira/dollar rates must move together, and a German monetary surprise may require a larger depreciation of the mark against the dollar than otherwise. The German inflation bias could be smaller in the EMS if the share of U.S. imports in German consumption is significantly larger than the share of EMS imports, or if the price elasticity of output demand is smaller with regard to changes in the relative price of U.S. goods than in the relative price of goods produced in other EMS countries. Although the second condition seems plausible in view of the greater proximity of the markets, the first condition is unlikely to hold.

Alternatively, one might argue that Germany seeks some other benefit in the arrangement and is willing to incur a higher inflation rate in return. The disciplinary view then requires that to induce German membership in the EMS, the other members must somehow compensate the German authorities for their loss of credibility. In technical terms, the EMS requires "side payments" of some form to the German authorities. In Section 3.2 we explored some alternatives to motivate German membership in the EMS along these lines. As in the case of the alleged extra costs that keep high-inflation countries in the EMS, the side

payments received by Germany must come from outside the model, and
their nature and significance have not been clarified satisfactorily, at least
not so far. But side payments are likely to lower the high-inflation
countries' incentive to join the system. If this is true, a necessary condition
for the disciplinary view to explain the EMS is that Italy's welfare gain
from reduced inflation in the EMS exceeds the German loss, so that the
aggregate utility change of both countries is positive. The following
condition states when Italy's utility gain exceeds Germany's utility loss,
making side payments feasible:

$$(4.22) \quad 2(U_{2E} - U_{2N}) + 2(U_{1E} - U_{1N}) = -\sigma^2 N_1^2 [2/\alpha^2 - (1 + (N_2/N_1)^2)/ (\alpha + \varepsilon)^2] > 0.$$

The aggregate change in utility is positive if $(1 + \varepsilon/\alpha)^2 < 0.5[1 + (N_2/N_1)^2]$.
This condition is more restrictive than the condition that Italy alone gains
from EMS membership if $\beta_2 \phi \geq 3.5 \alpha/(1 - \alpha)$. Again, it means that the
degree of integration of the Italian and German economies must not be
too high.

In conclusion, the disciplinary view of the EMS leaves important
questions unanswered, such as how to explain German membership in
the system and what is the exact source of greater credibility of the
exchange-rate target. Still, it provides a suggestive explanation for the
EMS that has some plausibility given that disinflation has taken place in
traditionally high-inflation countries. Despite its shortcomings, therefore,
the disciplinary view should not be discarded a priori.

4.2 Evidence from Inflation Rates

Proponents of the disciplinary view of the EMS have focused primarily
on the reduction and convergence of EMS inflation rates during the
1980s. This evidence is presented in Table 4.2, where this time we have
measured inflation in terms of consumer price indexes instead of
consumption price deflators (Figure 2.1).[11] The average inflation rate in
the EMS peaked in 1980 at 11.6 percent and declined steadily thereafter
to 2.2 percent in 1987. At the same time, the standard deviation of
inflation rates among the members fell from 6.2 percent to 1.9 percent.
Inflation has risen since 1987, but its standard deviation has not. By itself,
this evidence seems to show that EMS inflation rates were pulled toward
the German rate. Supporters of the disciplinary view infer from this that
the Bundesbank dominates the system.

But as we noted in Chapter 2, this inference is less convincing when
we consider our group of nine non-EMS countries, whose inflation

TABLE 4.2 CPI Inflation Rates, EMS and Non-EMS Countries (Percent)

EMS	1977	1978	1979	1980	1981	1982	1983	1984	1985	1986	1987	1988	1989	1990
Belgium	7.1	4.5	4.5	6.6	7.6	8.7	7.7	6.3	4.9	1.3	1.5	1.2	3.1	3.4
Denmark	11.1	10.1	9.6	12.3	11.7	10.1	6.9	6.3	4.7	3.6	4.0	4.5	4.8	4.8
France	9.4	9.1	10.7	13.8	13.4	11.8	9.6	7.4	5.8	2.5	3.3	2.7	3.5	3.4
Germany	3.7	2.7	4.1	5.4	6.3	5.3	3.3	2.4	2.2	-0.2	0.2	1.3	2.8	2.7
Ireland	13.6	7.6	13.2	18.2	20.4	17.1	10.5	8.6	5.4	3.8	3.1	2.2	4.1	3.4
Italy	17.0	12.1	14.8	21.2	17.8	16.5	14.7	10.8	9.2	5.9	4.7	5.0	6.2	6.5
Netherlands	6.5	4.2	4.2	6.5	6.7	5.9	2.8	3.3	2.2	0.1	0.0	0.7	1.1	2.5
Average	8.8	5.9	8.5	11.6	11.2	10.0	7.9	6.0	4.9	2.6	2.2	2.5	3.7	3.8
St.D.	4.9	5.3	4.4	6.2	4.6	4.4	4.4	3.2	2.7	1.7	1.9	1.5	1.5	1.5
Non-EMS														
Australia	12.3	7.9	9.1	10.1	9.7	11.1	10.1	4.5	6.7	8.7	8.6	7.6	7.6	7.3
Austria	5.5	3.6	3.7	6.4	6.8	5.4	3.3	5.7	3.2	1.7	1.4	1.9	2.6	3.3
Canada	8.0	9.0	9.1	10.2	12.4	10.8	5.8	4.3	4.0	4.1	4.4	4.0	5.0	4.8
Finland	12.7	7.8	7.5	11.6	12.0	9.3	8.4	7.1	5.9	2.9	4.1	5.1	6.6	6.1
Greece	12.2	12.5	19.0	24.9	24.5	21.0	20.2	18.4	19.3	23.0	16.4	13.5	13.7	20.4
Japan	8.0	3.8	3.6	8.0	4.9	2.6	1.8	2.3	2.0	0.6	0.0	0.7	2.3	3.1
Switzerland	1.3	1.1	3.6	4.0	6.5	5.7	3.0	2.9	3.4	0.7	1.4	1.9	3.2	5.4
U.K.	15.8	8.3	13.4	18.0	11.9	8.6	4.6	5.0	6.1	3.4	4.2	4.8	7.8	9.5
U.S.	6.5	7.6	11.3	13.5	10.4	6.2	3.2	4.3	3.6	2.0	3.6	4.0	4.8	5.4
Average	9.0	5.7	6.9	10.3	8.3	6.2	3.7	3.9	3.4	2.3	3.2	3.5	4.7	5.4
St. D.	5.4	8.6	4.7	5.0	3.5	3.8	3.6	2.2	3.3	2.3	2.1	1.9	1.7	2.8

Notes: Averages and standard deviations (St.D.) are weighted with the following 1982 real GNP-based weights (percents). EMS: Belgium 4.55, Denmark 2.97, France 28.84, Germany 34.42, Ireland 0.99, Italy 21.07, Netherlands 7.22. Non-EMS: Australia 3.08, Austria 5.61, Canada 1.23, Finland 0.94, Greece 0.71, Japan 20.03, Switzerland 1.79, U.K. 8.98, U.S. 57.63.

Source: International Monetary Fund, *International Financial Statistics*, various issues.

performance is similar to that of the EMS (see also Ungerer et al. 1986; Fratianni 1988). Average inflation in this group also peaked in 1980 and declined from then on to about 3 percent in 1987. The pattern is similar to that in the EMS, which had a noticeable convergence of inflation rates at the low end. The non-EMS standard deviation of inflation rates declined from 5.1 percent to 2.1 percent. Thus, disinflation and convergence are by no means special characteristics of the EMS.

There are at least two alternative interpretations of these data. One is that all industrial countries, whether in the EMS or not, have responded to the same external shocks and constraints during the 1980s, shocks that facilitated disinflation, such as the tightening of U.S. monetary policy in the early years of the decade and the decline in oil prices. The other is that policymakers inside and outside the EMS generally became dissatisfied with the stagflationary consequences of the active demand management policies they had pursued during the 1970s. In their disenchantment, they were willing to adopt less activist policies oriented toward greater price stability during the 1980s.[12] Both hypotheses have the same implication for the inflation performance inside and outside the EMS: They predict that inflation rates decline and converge at the lower level. The data presented in Table 4.2 are therefore observationally equivalent to the disciplinary view of the EMS. However, they provide no basis for giving credit to the EMS in achieving disinflation and convergence. Consequently, it is impossible to infer the empirical strength of the disciplinary view on the basis of inflation rates.

The well-known "Lucas critique" suggests that changes in policy regimes that induce changes in the private sector's expectation formation cause parameter instabilities in reduced-form econometric models (Lucas 1976). Giavazzi and Giovannini (1988) and Kremers (1990) follow this suggestion and use regression analysis to explore the impact of the EMS on inflation expectations. Giavazzi and Giovannini present vector autoregressions of real output, wages, and inflation in the EMS countries. Although they do not find structural breaks in the model parameters resulting from the EMS, simulations of inflation and output growth in the 1980s based on parameter estimations using data up to 1979 tend to overpredict inflation in France, Italy, and Denmark, underpredict inflation in Germany and real growth in Denmark, and overpredict real growth in Germany. This analysis would support the hypothesis of a systematic reduction in inflation expectations in France, Italy, and Denmark and a systematic rise in Germany, consistent with the credibility hypothesis. Unfortunately, their results do not meet standard statistical properties and are therefore inconclusive.

Kremers (1990) estimates a rational-expectations model of inflation expectations in Ireland. He finds a significant break in the model structure between 1979 and 1982. The impact of U.K. inflation on Irish inflation expectations vanishes and is replaced by average EMS inflation. At the same time, the effect of lagged real exchange rates, a measure of competitiveness, rises.[13] Kremers interprets these findings as indications of credibility gains.

Another approach to evaluating the empirical strength of the disciplinary view is to compare the economic cost of disinflation in the EMS with that in nonmember countries. This is based on the proposition that a central bank with greater credibility should find it more difficult to convince the private sector of its willingness to reduce inflation; consequently, its disinflation would cause less unemployment. Giavazzi and Spaventa (1989) and Dornbusch (1989) compare sacrifice ratios inside and outside the EMS. The "sacrifice ratio" is the ratio of cumulated unemployment above a base-year level to the total reduction in inflation. The authors do not find that sacrifice ratios in the EMS are lower than outside the EMS. The evidence on unemployment rates and growth rates of real output presented in Chapter 2 confirms these findings.

De Grauwe (1990) uses the "misery index"—the sum of unemployment and inflation rates—to measure the cost of disinflation. This index was higher on average in the EMS than in some non-EMS OECD countries, both before and after 1979. More important, the EMS index rose during the 1980s; the index of the other countries fell. Comparing alternative hypothetical preference structures, De Grauwe concludes that an adverse EMS effect on the misery index can be negated only if it is assumed that EMS governments care much more about inflation than about unemployment. By studying plots of the unemployment-inflation combinations in the EMS and the non-EMS OECD countries since the mid-1970s, De Grauwe illustrates that the main difference between the two groups has to do with the much lower speed of disinflation in the EMS. Disinflation outside the EMS follows a shock-therapy pattern, causing relatively deep but short recessions. In contrast, disinflation in the EMS was more gradual, stretching the economic cost over a much longer time interval. A lower total cost as claimed by the credibility hypothesis would accrue only if EMS governments had significantly higher time preferences than others.

In summary, the empirical evidence from inflation and unemployment rates and real growth is at best inconclusive with regard to the disciplinary view of the EMS. Despite the popularity of the argument, the performance of the EMS in terms of policy outcomes gives little reason to accept this view. In the next chapter, we turn to a test of the disciplinary interpretation based on a model of central bank interaction rather than policy outcomes.

Notes

1. Implicit in this argument is the assumption that once appointed, the central banker cannot be removed easily from office at the discretion of the government. Otherwise, the banker would have no more credibility of pursuing a low-inflation course than would the government itself (Lohmann 1992; Mélitz 1988).

2. The present discussion assumes that $m_1 = m_1^e$.

3. An important characteristic of the present policy game between the central banks and the private sector is that central banks act after wage setters. In this game, a subgame perfect equilibrium is such that the central bank has no incentive to deviate from the equilibrium strategy after wages have been set. More generally, reoptimization at the time of action does not lead to choosing an alternative policy; consequently, actual policies match expected policies.

4. An alternative way to express this difference between the Italian and the German central banks is to assume that the preference weight for the employment target is larger in Italy, $\sigma_2 > \sigma_1$. It is straightforward to show that the model yields qualitatively the same results under this assumption (and $N_2 = N_1$); however, the formal solutions are more complicated.

5. Note that $2U_{2N} < \sigma N_2^2$, the utility attained if the central bank could credibly commit to a zero-inflation policy. In this sense, the lack of a credible precommitment possibility creates an inefficiency.

6. Pegging the exchange rate at a predetermined rate must be distinguished from using the exchange rate as a policy instrument that is chosen optimally during the period. In the latter case, Italy's monetary policy would still be independent of Germany's. See Canzoneri and Henderson (1988) for a discussion.

7. See Canzoneri and Henderson (1988) and Fratianni and von Hagen (1990a). The employment-inflation relation in this model is $(dn_i/dQ_i) = [(dn_i/dm_i)/dQ_i/dm_i)]$, which for Germany is $1/(\alpha + \varepsilon)$ under a flexible exchange rate, and $1/\alpha$ under a fixed rate.

8. See the discussion in Chapter 2 on this issue.

9. One might argue that the German government joined the EMS to overcome an alleged deflation bias imposed by Bundesbank policy. Katseli (1987), for example, appeals to a class-based hypothesis to justify that workers desire a higher rate of inflation, whereas central bankers and the people they represent desire a lower rate of inflation. The dominance of the central bank group translates into an overall deflation bias. The hypothesis that such a deflation bias exists, however, is contested by Willett (1988) and is found lacking empirical foundation and plausibility by Neumann and von Hagen (1992).

10. Again we neglect bond markets in the assumptions, which are $\beta_{12} = \beta_{21}$, $\beta_{32} = \beta_{31}$, $\beta_{11} = \beta_{22}$, $\alpha_1 = \alpha_2 = \alpha_3$, $\phi_{11} = \phi_{21}$, $\phi_{13} = \phi_{23} = \phi_{31} = \phi_{32}$, $\rho_j = 1$, $j = 1, 2, 3$. Germany's inflation bias with flexible exchange rates is $\sigma N_1/(\alpha_1 + \varepsilon_1 + \varepsilon_2)$; the bias with a fixed DM/lira rate is $\sigma N_1/(\alpha_1 + 2\varepsilon_2)$, where $\varepsilon_1 = (1 - \alpha_1)\beta_{12}^2/2\phi_{12}$, and $\varepsilon_2 = (1 - \alpha_1)\beta_{13}^2/2\phi_{13}$.

11. Table 2.3 gives more detailed information about the evolution of inflation in the two groups of countries. The difference between CPI and consumption deflator measures of inflation is minor.

12. Chouraqui and Price (1984) review the changes in policies in several

OECD countries in the early 1980s and attribute them to changes in public and political preferences and attitudes toward the economy.

13. The pre-EMS role of U.K. inflation results from the Irish peg of the pound sterling since 1926.

5

German Dominance in the EMS: The Empirical Evidence

In Chapter 3, we pointed out a distinctive feature of the disciplinary interpretation, namely the claim that the EMS has become a strongly asymmetric system, in which Germany dominates monetary policy making. This "German-dominance hypothesis" (GDH) claims that the Bundesbank unilaterally determines the course of monetary policy for the entire EMS. The other countries have tied their monetary policies to the Bundesbank's policy in the attempt to benefit from its credibility as a low-inflation central bank, and they follow German monetary policy passively. GDH imposes tight restrictions on how EMS countries interact at the level of monetary policy making. It limits all interaction within the EMS to stimuli from and reaction to Bundesbank policy. In addition, it excludes the unconstrained reaction of other EMS members to policies and events originating outside the system. Thus, GDH has important implications both for the internal structure of EMS monetary policies and for the system's relationship with non-member countries.

This "strategic" version of German dominance in the EMS is of particular relevance because it makes the disciplinary interpretation different from other views of the EMS and other explanations of the European disinflation of the 1980s. With its focus on the structure of central bank behavior in the EMS rather than on policy outcomes, it suggests that one can devise more powerful empirical tests of the disciplinary view by looking at variables closely related to central bank actions and interaction rather than considering the inflation performance of the EMS (which as previously noted is compatible with a number of explanations that give the EMS no credit at all). In this chapter, we present such tests.

5.1 Testable Implications of German Dominance

Our tests are based on the premise that the structure of the monetary policy game in the EMS can be inferred from a system of equations characterizing the dynamics and interaction of central bank policy variables. One interpretation of such a system is in terms of a system of central bank reaction functions. Let ΔY be a 7x1 vector of policy variables summarizing all central bank actions in the EMS. Let X be a 7xm matrix of domestic target variables of the monetary authorities, such as domestic output growth, unemployment, or inflation, and let ΔW be a 7x1 vector of variables representing monetary policy actions in the rest of the world that might also influence the monetary authorities in the EMS. We set up the following system of dynamic linear equations:

$$(5.1) \qquad A(L)\Delta Y_t = b + B(L)\Delta X_t + C(L)\Delta W_t + e_t,$$

where $A(L) = [a_{ij}(L)]$, $B(L) = [b_{ij}(L)]$, and $C(L) = [c_i(L)]$ are 7x7, 7x7m, and 7x1 polynomial matrices in the lag operator L, respectively, and b is a fixed intercept vector. The vector of residuals e_t has the properties $E(e_{it}) = 0$ and $E(e_{it}^2) = \sigma_{ii}$, where $i = 1, ...,7$, indicates the ith member of the EMS. We make use of the following identifying restrictions[1]:

$(5.2) \qquad$ a) the leading coefficient of $a_{ii}(L)$, $a_{ii,1} = 1$, $i = 1,...,7$;
$\qquad$ b) $\qquad E(e_t\, e'_t) = \mathrm{diag}(\sigma_{ii})$, $i = 1,...,7$;
$\qquad$ c) $\qquad E(e_t\, e'_{t^*}) = 0$ for $t \neq t^*$;
$\qquad$ d) $\qquad b_{ij}(L) = 0$, $i = 1,...,7$; $j \neq k$; $j, k = 0 ,..., m - 1$.

Condition (5.2a) is a natural normalization of the system. Conditions (5.2b) and (5.2c) force all interaction in the EMS policy variables to show up in the coefficients of the polynomial matrix A(L). Condition (5.2d) stipulates that the authorities in country j do not respond to the domestic targets of the authorities in country i. This assures the identification of the system when German dominance does not hold empirically. Finally, we take Germany as country $i = 1$, France as $i = 2$, Italy as $i = 3$, and Belgium, the Netherlands, Ireland, and Denmark as $i = 4$ through 7, respectively.

German dominance consists of four joint hypotheses that can now be formulated as restrictions on the system (5.1). First, GDH implies that the other EMS countries do not react independently to monetary policy actions occurring outside the EMS. The world at large can influence the other EMS countries only through its impact on German monetary policy. This is stated as

H1: World Insularity $c_i = 0$, $i = 2,...,7$.

Rejection of H1 by an EMS member implies that its monetary policy is influenced directly by central bank policies outside the EMS, even if the German influence on this country is controlled for. That is, the country responds independently to the rest of the world over and beyond what is implied by adherence to the German rule; such independent response would represent a violation of GDH.

Second, German dominance implies that each EMS country reacts only to Germany and not to other members' policies:

H2: EMS Insularity $a_{ij} = 0$, $i \neq j$, $i, j = 2,...,7$.

Rejecting H2 signifies that EMS countries interact independently with one another although Germany's impact on their policy is controlled for. Again, this is inconsistent with a common, strict adherence of all other members to the path set by the Bundesbank.

Third, GDH implies that monetary policy in a member country depends on German policy, and we must reject

H3: Independence from Germany $a_{i1} = 0$, $i = 2,...,7$.

Finally, to make German dominance meaningful, Germany itself must not be influenced by the monetary policy actions of other members:

H4: German Policy Independence $a_{1i} = 0$, $i = 2,...,7$.

Rejecting H4 implies that Bundesbank policy responds to policies in other parts of the EMS. Although the Bundesbank could still be an important player in the EMS in this case, this would deny its ability to decide unilaterally the course of its own monetary policy, much less to impose its own preferred course on the other members.

In this formulation, GDH excludes any short-run deviation of other members' policies from the path set by the Bundesbank. We call this the *strong* form of GDH. A less restrictive—and therefore more realistic and plausible—view of German dominance is to allow short-run deviations from the Bundesbank rule but no long-run deviations. To formulate this *weak* form of German dominance, we define the operators g(.) such that $g(a_{ij})$ and $g(c_i)$ are the sums of all coefficients of a lag polynomial $a_{ij}(L)$ or $c_i(L)$. The weak form of GDH can be expressed as follows:

H1W: Weak World Insularity $g(c_i) = 0$, $i = 2,..., 7$;
H2W: Weak EMS Insularity $g(a_{ij}) = 0$, $i \neq j$, $i, j = 2,..., 7$;

H3W: Weak Independence from Germany $g(a_{i1}) = 0, i = 2,..., 7;$
H4W: Weak German Independence $g(a_{1i}) = 0, i = 2,..., 7.$

With the identifying restrictions (5.2a) through (5.2d) imposed on the system, the strong versions of our four subhypotheses H1 through H4 can be interpreted in terms of Granger causality. Note that in the context of testing GDH, Granger causality includes instantaneous causality because we have to allow for interaction among the policies within a time period.[2] GDH implies the following causality structure: Policy variables outside the EMS do not Granger-cause EMS policy variables other than Germany's, once the effect of German policy on the EMS is controlled for; policy variables in a member country other than Germany do not Granger-cause policy variables in any other EMS country given Germany's policy; German policy variables do Granger-cause policy variables in other EMS countries; and finally, policy variables in other EMS countries do not Granger-cause the German policy variables. In particular, GDH excludes Granger feedback between EMS policy variables. Altogether, then, GDH implies the joint validity of 6 causality relations (H3) and 42 noncausality relations.

We present two versions of our test for GDH using different empirical policy variables as endogenous variables directed at different aspects of the EMS. The first version takes a long-run perspective and aims at characterizing the EMS in terms of the interaction of monetary trends behind its inflation performance. Here, the growth rate of the monetary base is an appropriate policy variable because the monetary base summarizes the money supply effects of all central bank actions. The second version of the test aims at characterizing the EMS monetary policy game in the way policymakers perceive it in their daily decisions. In practice, central banks in the EMS commonly express and assess the short-run impact of their monetary policy actions in terms of the resulting changes in domestic money-market interest rates.[3] Over a monthly time horizon, money-market interest rates are therefore very closely related to central bank policies. This suggests the use of changes in money-market interest rates to approximate monetary policy actions and interactions in the short run.

5.2 The Long-Run View of GDH:
Evidence from Monetary Base Growth

In our first application, we choose monetary base growth rates as the endogenous policy variables. In addition to its own lags and monetary base growth rates in other EMS countries, the growth rate in an EMS country may depend on the linear time trend and quarterly seasonal dummies, a measure of the domestic government budget deficit, and a weighted average of the monetary base growth rates in the United States, Japan, Canada, and the United Kingdom. Trend, seasonal dummies, and own lags capture the basic dynamics of monetary base growth in the country. They can be thought of as representing underlying determinants of base growth, such as trend growth of real income, velocity, and target inflation rates.[4] The deficit variable allows for interaction of monetary policy with domestic fiscal policy. We divide the government deficit by the lagged monetary base to make the dimension of the variables commensurate. The final variable captures monetary policy action in the rest of the world.

We estimate the resulting system using quarterly data from the *International Financial Statistics* published by the International Monetary Fund. The monetary base is "reserve money" (line 14 in *IFS*); the deficit variable is "government deficit" (line 80). The weights applied in aggregating the world policy variable are real GNP weights on the basis of 1982.[5] A dummy variable in the Danish equation is added to capture institutional changes in Danish monetary policy during the sample period.[6] The net sample period for estimation goes from the second quarter of 1979 to the second quarter of 1988.

To reduce the parameter space and make the system operational for estimation, we need some further restrictions on the coefficients of system (5.1) to save degrees of freedom. We assume that monetary base growth in an EMS country other than Germany affects policies in another EMS country only through its effect on the average growth rate in the EMS without Germany. Let α_i be the share of EMS country i in the total 1982 real GNP of the EMS. We impose the following restrictions:

$$(5.3) \qquad \alpha_j a_{ij} = \alpha_k a_{ik}, \; i \neq j, \; k; \; i = 1,...,7; \; j, \; k = 2,...,7.$$

This condition restricts the off-diagonal polynomials of matrix A(L) other than the first column such that each member may react to German growth rate and to the weighted average growth rate in the rest of the EMS. Note that restricting the system in this way biases the test toward accepting GDH; therefore, if GDH is rejected in the restricted system, it would be rejected even more strongly in an unrestricted system.

Our empirical strategy is to estimate a broad specification of the model—first by allowing for up to five lags of all variables—and to eliminate variables that contribute little to the explanatory power of the model. The selection process has to satisfy the twin criteria that the reduction process neither lowers the information value of the model, as measured by the Akaike BIC statistic, nor generates residual serial correlation. The shrunken version of the model is then estimated with 3SLS and used for testing GDH. Table 5.1 shows some general characteristics of the final structure.

Table 5.2 reports the results of testing the restrictions of H1 through H4. Each subhypothesis is tested in two ways. First, the restrictions are imposed on one equation at a time leaving all others unrestricted; then the restrictions are imposed on all equations at one time. The results of the first series of tests are shown under the individual country labels in the Tables 5.1 and 5.2; the results of the comprehensive tests are given under the EMS column. In each case, however, the test statistics are calculated using the system's estimator.

We consider the strong version of German dominance first (Table 5.2). "World insularity" is strongly rejected for all countries except Belgium. "EMS insularity" is rejected for all countries but Denmark and France, and "independence from Germany" is strongly rejected except for Belgium and Denmark. Finally, "German independence" is rejected as well, although the F-value is only barely significant at the 5 percent level. Overall, this suggests that the EMS is a strongly interactive system; the results do not lend support to the German-dominance hypothesis.

TABLE 5.1 Model Characteristics, Dependent Variable: Quarterly Monetary Base Growth Rates

	F	$D.o.f.1$	$RMSE(\%)$	$Q(6)$	$D.o.f.2$	ΔBIC
Belgium	57.2**	13,23	0.8	7.0	6	−51.8
Denmark	13.9**	12,24	6.8	3.0	6	−44.0
France	4.1**	9,27	4.6	3.0	6	−3.2
Germany	4.6**	7,29	2.9	4.6	5	−16.5
Ireland	3.8**	13,23	2.6	6.7	5	−16.9
Italy	15.3**	12,24	1.8	7.4	5	−6.5
Netherlands	10.7**	12,24	1.2	5.0	6	−28.5
EMS	5.5**	78,174	1.0	—	—	—
DM Area	8.2**	6,30	2.5	3.5	5	—

Note: F is the F-statistic for overall model significance for the reduced model specification of each equation, with d.o.f.1 degrees of freedom. RMSE(%) is the percentage root mean square error for the reduced specification. Q(6) is the Box-Ljung statistic for residual autocorrelation, calculated by lag six, with d.o.f.2 degrees of freedom. ΔBIC is the difference between the Akaike information statistic for the reduced and the broad specification. A negative sign indicates a reduction of entropy by the elimination of regressors. * and ** denote significance at the 5 and 1 percent levels.

TABLE 5.2 Hypothesis Tests for German Dominance, Based on Quarterly Monetary Base Growth Rates

			Strong Dominance				
Belgium	*Denmark*	*France*	*Germany*	*Ireland*	*Italy*	*Netherlands*	*EMS*
H1: World Insularity							
0.9	12.4**	12.1**	4.1*	6.4**	6.8**	6.5**	8.7**
2	2	1	2	3	2	3	13
H2: EMS Insularity							
3.1*	0.3	0.2	—	2.8	9.3**	3.0*	3.9**
2	2	2	—	2	3	2	13
H3: Independence from German Policy							
0.9	0.7	3.4**	—	4.9**	9.7**	2.6*	4.7**
5	5	5	—	5	5	5	30
H4: German Policy Independence							
—	—	—	2.9*	—	—	—	—
—	—	—	2	—	—	—	—

			Weak Dominance				
Belgium	*Denmark*	*France*	*Germany*	*Ireland*	*Italy*	*Netherlands*	*EMS*
H1: World Insularity							
0.2	2.6	12.1**	0.7	9.7**	4.9*	12.9**	7.1**
1	1	1	1	1	1	1	6
H2: EMS Insularity							
6.2*	0.6	0.3	—	2.1	20.7**	5.9*	5.9**
1	1	1	—	1	1	1	6
H3: Independence from German Policy							
0.0	1.0	0.0	—	4.0*	19.5**	1.1	5.0**
1	1	1	—	1	1	1	6
H4: German Policy Independence							
—	—	—	3.5	—	—	—	—
—	—	—	1	—	—	—	—

Note: Upper-row entries are F-statistics for each test. Lower-row entries are the pertaining numerator degrees of freedom. Denominator degrees of freedom are 174 in all cases. * and ** denote significance at the 5 and 1 percent levels.

Turning to the weak version of GDH, we find that the French, Irish, Dutch, and Italian reactions to monetary base growth outside the EMS remain significant in the long run. Belgium, Italy, and the Netherlands violate the weak "EMS-insularity" restriction. Only the Italian monetary base growth gives a convincing rejection of the weak form of "independence from Germany"; the rejection for Ireland is at the 5 percent margin. Note that the strong rejection of H3W for the EMS as a whole results entirely from the rejection in the Italian case: Testing H3W jointly for the other five countries results in an F-statistic of 1.8, which is below the 10 percent significance level. Thus, Italy seems to be the only country in the EMS that has established an effective long-run link of its monetary policy to the course of the Bundesbank. In all other member countries, Germany's policy has no lasting influence on the conduct of monetary policy. In turn, Germany's base growth rate does not show a significant long-run dependence on the growth rates in the other EMS countries.

These results suggest that France and Denmark are the two countries least influenced in the long run by monetary policies in the EMS. Both conform to weak EMS insularity and weak independence from Germany. On this basis, one would expect that money growth in these two countries deviated more from the rest of the EMS than money growth in any other member country. This conclusion is consistent with the observation that during the sample period, France and Denmark used realignments to adjust their central rates more frequently than the other member countries (see Table 2.2).

The picture emerging from this evidence is clearly at odds with GDH. Monetary policies in all member countries interact; they respond to the policy impulses coming from outside the EMS not only through their reaction to Germany but also independently of it. Germany, to be sure, is an important player in the EMS policy game, but the hypothesis of a dominating Bundesbank is empirically unwarranted. Italy, the one country in the EMS that shows a strong long-run link of its monetary policy to the Bundesbank's course, responds to other EMS countries and to monetary policies outside the system as well, which refutes the dominance hypothesis also for this country.

Still, the tests for weak dominance reveal that the German position in the EMS is special. All EMS members except Denmark show significant and lasting reactions to German monetary policy, to other EMS members, or to the rest of the world, but German responses to the rest of the EMS and the rest of the world vanish after several quarters. One may conclude that in the long run, the Bundesbank pursues its own policy independently, showing no lasting response to the monetary policies of other EMS members. But German independence in the EMS is not equivalent to GDH. It is a much weaker claim because it carries no implication that other EMS countries are compelled to follow the course of German monetary policy.

According to a popular argument, the central banks in the smaller countries neighboring Germany generally move very closely in accordance with German monetary policy and thereby create a kind of "DM area." In the present context, this suggests that the EMS may be dominated by a DM area, if not by the Bundesbank. To explore this issue, we aggregate the monetary base growth rates of Germany, Belgium, Denmark, and the Netherlands to a weighted average and replace the German growth rate by this average in our tests. Thus this question: Are France, Italy, and Ireland dominated by the DM area? Table 5.3 presents the results of tests pertaining to this hypothesis. Here, "world insularity"

TABLE 5.3 Hypothesis Tests for Dominance of the DM Area, Based on Quarterly Monetary Base Growth Rate

	Strong Dominance					Weak Dominance			
DM Area	France	Ireland	Italy	EMS	DM Area	France	Ireland	Italy	EMS
H1: World insularity									
—	3.1	6.0**	2.8	4.5**	—	3.1	9.9**	0.9	5.4**
—	1	3	2	6	—	1	1	1	3
H2: EMS insularity									
—	1.1	2.6	9.9**	4.5**	—	2.0	1.4	20.0**	4.5**
—	2	2	3	7	—	1	1	1	3
H3: Independence from DM-area policy									
—	3.3**	3.9**	8.2**	6.6**	—	0.0	3.6	5.3*	2.9*
—	5	5	5	15	—	1	1	1	3
H4: DM-area policy independence									
4.3*	—	—	—	—	2.4	—	—	—	—
2	—	—	—	—	1	—	—	—	—

H2*: Independence of rest of EMS

Belgium	Denmark	Netherlands	Belgium	Denmark	Netherlands
2.1	1.1	1.3	3.6	2.2	2.6
2	2	2	1	1	1

Note: First-row entries are F-values; second-row entries are numerator degrees of freedom. Denominator degrees of freedom are 175. * and ** denote significance at the 5 and 1 percent levels.

is not rejected for France and Italy. "EMS insularity," which now means the absence of independent interaction among France, Italy, and Ireland, is strongly rejected only for Italy. For all three countries, "independence from the DM area" is rejected in the strong version but only for Italy in the weak version. The suggested DM area responds significantly to the rest of the system, but these reactions cancel out in the long run. None of the smaller countries reacts significantly to policies in France, Italy, or Ireland.

Overall, these results again refute the hypothesis of dominance. But the table helps to clarify the structure of the EMS. The results suggest that Germany and its smaller neighbors indeed form a core group in the EMS. Its characteristic is that its members interact with one another but also with EMS members outside the core group. Furthermore, French and Italian reactions to the rest of the world run entirely in accordance with the core group's reactions, indicating that France and Italy coordinate their policies vis-à-vis outside players with the core group. These results do not imply dominance by the DM area, but they tell us that there is indeed a large degree of conformity of EMS policies with regard to outsiders.

5.3 The Short-Run View of GDH: Evidence from Interest Rates

Our second empirical application takes changes in domestic money-market rates as the endogenous policy variable. Measures of domestic inflation and domestic output growth represent domestic policy goals, and the U.S. interest rate approximates monetary policies outside the system. The data are monthly and the source is again the *International Financial Statistics* of the International Monetary Fund. Interest rates are "money-market rates" (line 60b in the *IFS*). Domestic output is measured as "industrial production" (line 66..c), domestic inflation in terms of "consumer prices" (line 64). With the exception of domestic output, all data are seasonally unadjusted.

To reduce the number of free parameters in this system, we impose the additional restrictions

$$(5.4) \qquad \alpha_j a_{ij} = \alpha_k a_{ik}, \ i \neq k, \ j; \ j, \ k = 4, \ ..., 7; \ i = 1, \ ..., 7.$$

Under condition (5.4), we use in the equations for Germany, France, and Italy a weighted average of the Belgian, Dutch, Danish, and Irish interest rates rather than each interest rate individually.[7] In the equation for each of these four countries, we use the weighted average rate of the remaining three countries together with the German, French, and Italian interest rates. The latter are left unrestricted in all equations.

Preliminary data inspection reveals significant heteroskedasticity of interest rate changes in the EMS if the sample is split after March 1983. Because this date approximately coincides with the end of the "Mitterrand experiment," there is more than a statistical reason for splitting the sample period into two subperiods. To account for the reduction in variances, we use the adjustment factors H reported in Table 5.4. The Belgian and Danish equations are augmented by dummy variables to eliminate a few extreme observations. Finally, we define the 7x1 dummy vector D_t, the elements of which are zero before March 1983 and one thereafter. All lagged regressors in the model and the contemporaneous U.S. interest rate are multiplied by this dummy, and the resulting terms are added to the model. In this way, we can allow and adjust for possible parameter changes at the sample break point.

With the introduction of the shift parameters, the model is now

$$(5.5) \quad A_0 \Delta Y_t = d + d^* ID_t + \sum_{j=1}^{k} (A_j + A_j^* ID_t) \Delta Y_{t-j} + \sum_{j=1}^{m} (B_j + B_j^* ID_t) \Delta X_{t-j}$$

$$+ \sum_{j=0}^{n} (C_j + C_j^* ID_t) \Delta W_{t-j} + e_t,$$

where I is an identity matrix and the elements of d^*, A^*, B^*, and C^* are the differences in pre- and post-March 1983 parameter values. The model thus has two parameterizations: the pre-1983 parameter values, given by the matrices d, A, B, and C; the post-1983 values, given by the sums of d and d^*, A and A^*, B and B^*, and C and C^*.

With these preliminaries, our empirical analysis proceeds as before. Table 5.4 characterizes the 3SLS estimates. All regressions are highly significant. The statistic S is the F-test for joint significance of the interactive dummy terms retained in each equation. Only the French interest rate model does not change significantly over the sample period; the Italian equation contains the largest number of shifts.

Table 5.5 shows that testing the strong version of GDH leads to a clear rejection of the four subhypotheses in almost all cases, for the system as a whole, and for both sample periods. We do not discuss these results in detail but instead focus on the more differentiated and hence more interesting results of testing the weak version of GDH. This evidence, presented in Table 5.6, is somewhat more favorable to GDH. In the first EMS period, H1 (world insularity) is rejected for Denmark and the

TABLE 5.4 Monthly Money-Market Rates, Summary of Estimates

	Broad Specification					*Reduced Specification*					
	H	*R^2*	*SE*	*Number of Para- meters*	*SE*	*R^2*	*F*	*ΔBIC*	*AR(6)*	*S*	
Germany	0.33	0.50	0.15	20	0.17	0.38	2.66**	−23.5	1.30	3.18**	(5)
France	0.33	0.56	0.22	12	0.26	0.40	5.37**	−31.7	5.80	1.90	(1)
Italy	1.00	0.61	0.38	23	0.42	0.51	3.86**	−17.7	6.20	2.98**	(9)
Belgium	0.66	0.68	0.68	21	0.76	0.57	5.41**	−30.7	4.37	3.09**	(5)
Netherlands	0.25	0.57	0.33	19	0.34	0.48	4.33**	−43.3	5.33	6.23**	(5)
Ireland	0.60	0.57	0.84	23	0.91	0.49	3.58**	−28.7	8.60	5.00**	(6)
Denmark	0.48	0.87	0.72	26	0.74	0.84	16.12**	−29.8	3.50	5.62**	(7)

Note: H is the heteroskedasticity adjustment factor for the period 1979-March 1983 and March 1983-April 1988. F is the F-test of model significance for the reduced specification and is from the second-stage estimation. Degrees of freedom are the number of parameters and 108 less the number of parameters. AR(6) is the LaGrange Multiplier test for residual autocorrelation up to lag six. AR(6) has a Chi-square distribution with 6 d.o.f. under the Null. ΔBIC is the difference in Akaike's BIC criteria for the two specifications, based on the second step estimates. S is the F-test for parameter stability; numbers in parentheses are numerator d.o.f.; denominator d.o.f. are 612. SE is the standard error of the regression. **indicates significance at the 1 percent level.

Netherlands; H2 (EMS insularity) is rejected for Denmark, Ireland, and Italy; both hypotheses are rejected at the system level. H3 (independence from Germany) cannot be rejected for Belgium, Denmark, and Italy; for the other countries Germany is a significantly influential player. However, H4 (German independence) must be rejected. In the post-March 1983 period, H3 is clearly rejected for Belgium, France, and the Netherlands; for the same countries, we do not reject H2. H1 is rejected only for Italy, but cannot be rejected at the system level. German interest rates still react significantly to interest rate changes elsewhere in the EMS in this subperiod.

The characterization of the EMS policy game emerging from these results is as follows: overall, monetary policy in the EMS is interactive. Germany is a significant player, but so are the other central banks, particularly the French and the Italian. The strictly hierarchical structure suggested by GDH is not confirmed by the data.

Furthermore, and particularly after March 1983, only one EMS member shows a lasting reaction to policy actions taken outside the system that

TABLE 5.5 Testing Strong German Dominance, Based on Monthly Money-Market Rates

	April 1979–March 1983				April 1983–April 1988			
	H1	H2	H3	H4	H1	H2	H3	H4
Germany	1.87 (3)	—	—	3.92** (8)	1.51 (3)	—	—	4.31** (8)
Belgium	0.99	2.74** (7)	0.91 (3)	—	0.99 (2)	2.58** (8)	4.41** (3)	—
Denmark	5.16** (2)	9.14** (5)	3.24* (3)	—	0.63 (2)	2.24* (6)	1.12 (3)	—
France	7.42** (2)	3.70* (2)	7.92** (4)	—	7.42** (2)	3.70* (2)	7.92** (4)	—
Ireland	3.13* (3)	6.56** (6)	2.61* (3)	—	3.94** (3)	5.94** (7)	4.26** (3)	—
Italy	1.95 (3)	4.81* (3)	2.27 (2)	—	2.44* (4)	4.48** (4)	2.18 (3)	—
Netherlands	2.45* (2)	5.83** (7)	5.04** (3)	—	4.97** (3)	4.78** (8)	5.04** (3)	—
EMS	3.51** (14)	5.55** (30)	4.09* (18)	—	3.24** (14)	3.94** (35)	4.39** (19)	—

H1 refers to world insularity; H2 to EMS insularity; H3 to independence from German policy; H4 to German policy independence.

Note: All tests reported in this table are based on parameter estimates for the total sample, but make no use of the estimated parameter shifts after March 1983. Entries are results of F-tests based on the 3SLS estimates. Numbers in parentheses are numerator degrees of freedom. Denominator degrees of freedom are 612 for all tests. * and ** denote significance at the 5 and 1 percent levels.

might cause divergent interest rate movements. If nothing else mattered, this would be reason enough to regard the EMS as an asymmetric arrangement, in which German leadership prevents other countries from reacting independently to the rest of the world. But the rejections of the "German independence" and "EMS insularity" subhypotheses make it clear that this is not the same as German dominance.

The results of the weak-dominance tests reveal a striking difference between the French and the Italian positions in the EMS. French interest rate responses accord well with all three restrictions posed by the German dominance hypothesis, but the Italian responses do not. This indicates that French interest rates are much more closely bound to German interest rates than are Italian rates. But we recall from the previous section that a

TABLE 5.6 Testing Weak German Dominance, Based on Monthly Money-Market Rates

	April 1979–March 1983				April 1983–April 1988			
	H1	H2	H3	H4	H1	H2	H3	H4
Germany	—	—	—	3.08*	—	—	—	4.31**
Belgium	1.31	1.67	0.11	—	1.31	2.33	5.47*	—
		(3)			(3)			
Denmark	10.24**	2.86*	0.20	—	0.59	2.61*	1.10	—
		(3)				(3)		
France	0.39	0.2	20.41**	—	0.74	0.20	20.40**	—
		(1)				(1)		
Ireland	0.91	5.14**	3.82*	—	1.53	4.89**	0.63	—
		(3)				(3)		
Italy	0.34	7.16**	2.99	—	6.51**	8.61**	0.12	—
		(2)				(2)		
Netherlands	4.81*	1.13	13.47**	—	1.23	1.52	13.47**	—
	(3)	(3)				(3)		
EMS	3.36**	2.98**	6.77**	—	2.06	3.32**	7.00**	—
	(6)	(15)	(6)		(6)	(15)	(6)	

H1 refers to world insularity; H2 to EMS insularity; H3 to independence from German policy; H4 to German policy independence.

Note: H1 refers to world insularity; H2 to EMS insularity; H3 to independence from German policy; H4 to German policy independence. Entries are values of the F-tests based on 3SLS estimates. Numbers in parentheses are numerator degrees of freedom. Denominator degrees of freedom are 612 for all tests. * and ** denote significance at the 5 and 1 percent level, respectively.

significant difference between the French and the Italian positions in the system is that Italy's monetary growth path depends importantly on Germany's in the long run; the French does not. This raises two puzzles. Why does the close link between German and French short-run policy actions, expressed by interest rates, not show up in the monetary base growth rates; and why are Italian short-run interest rate movements more disconnected from Germany's despite the apparently closer long-run association of Italian policy with German policy? The answers lie in the institutional arrangements of the EMS. Although monetary policies are intertwined in the short run, realignments give member countries the ability to choose their own trend monetary growth and inflation rates.

The stark contrast between the French interest rate and the monetary base results, therefore, is resolved by the fact that France has used realignments more often and effectively than other countries to set its own monetary trend. As for Italy, the EMS has granted this country more short-run flexibility than France because of the wider exchange rate band (12 percent versus 4.5 percent). Consequently, Italy's need to align with other EMS countries in the short run is weaker.

To summarize, we have tested GDH in a strong form, requiring strict adherence to the monetary path set by the Bundesbank at all times, and a weak form, which allows for short-run deviations from this path. The empirical results reject German dominance in the EMS in both forms. Overall, the system appears to be more interactive than hierarchical. But the tests indicate that other asymmetries exist in the system. One asymmetry is German long-run monetary policy independence. Another is that the Banque de France, most likely because of the narrower exchange-rate band, is more restricted than the Banca d'Italia by the short-run constraints of the system. Finally, the smaller members of the EMS except Ireland are more closely associated with an EMS core group, consisting of these countries and Germany, than with the rest of the EMS.

5.4 Other Evidence for German Dominance

Cohen and Wyplosz (1989) test the German-dominance hypothesis for a subgroup of EMS countries using vector autoregressions of domestic interest rates and monetary base growth rates. They find that German interest rates and monetary base growth rates significantly affect the same variables in other EMS countries. However, the opposite is also true. Other researchers report a similar outcome for base growth rates (Mastropasqua, et al. 1988). Weber (1990) uses three-month offshore and onshore interest rates, call money rates, and long-term government bond yields, as well as growth rates of narrow and broad money, reserve money, and foreign reserves, from the same countries used in the Cohen and Wyplosz study. Weber tests our hypotheses of EMS insularity, independence from Germany, and German independence in bilateral causality tests. His results point to significant interaction among the EMS members, which is inconsistent with GDH. In broad agreement with our results, Weber concludes that Germany's position in the EMS is a "non-dominated" one, yet not one of dominance. Again, German dominance fails the empirical test. Kirchgässner and Wolters (1991) investigate long-run international interest rate links in the EMS on the basis of cointegration methods. Their results confirm our conclusion that GDH must be rejected.

De Grauwe (1988) presents an alternative approach to testing GDH. His test asks whether expected exchange-rate devaluations of an EMS member country against the DM affect short-term interest rates only in this country, as GDH would suggest, or both in Germany and the depreciating country. He finds that the German interest rate does not respond to expected devaluations of the Belgian franc, the French franc, and the Italian lira. However, interest rates in these three countries do not fully adjust either. It follows that capital controls and dual exchange-rate systems are critical in isolating domestic money markets from international forces. For the Netherlands, where there are no capital controls, De Grauwe finds that interest rate adjustments are shared between Germany and that country, a result consistent with ours. De Grauwe concludes that his findings provide no support for German dominance.

Another group of authors has looked at central bank interventions in the EMS to infer German dominance. These researchers (Bofinger 1988; Camen 1986; Mastropasqua et al. 1988; and Roubini 1988) all estimate the extent to which the Bundesbank can sterilize foreign exchange market interventions. The common result is that sterilization is very high, suggesting that the Bundesbank can pursue its own policy objectives independently of the EMS. However, this conclusion is flawed. The estimations presented by these authors fail to account for important institutional characteristics of Bundesbank monetary policy. The Bundesbank's operating procedure distinguishes between the short-run control of domestic money-market conditions and the control of the growth rate of the monetary base over a longer time horizon. The Bundesbank uses different monetary instruments to pursue its short-run and long-run objectives. Most significantly, the monetary base growth effects of short-run control actions (so-called reversible operations) are generally repealed over one or two quarters.[8] Complete and quasi-automatic sterilization of foreign exchange market interventions commonly occurs at the time of the actual intervention through use of short-run control instruments. Because these operations are reversed, however, during the following one or two quarters, the more relevant question is how interventions affect the growth of the monetary base over a longer time horizon. Von Hagen (1989) shows that German monetary base growth, in general, has been affected by the Bundesbank's foreign exchange market interventions if one considers a time horizon of four to six months. This implies that the EMS has at times effectively constrained Bundesbank policies.

A final argument to justify GDH comes from the observation that in a fixed exchange-rate system, only one country can independently choose the exchange rate vis-à-vis an outside currency. German dominance could therefore consist of the imposition of a dollar policy on the EMS by the Bundesbank (Sarcinelli 1986). The Bundesbank's engagement in the policy coordination efforts among the five major industrialized countries (the G-5) between 1985 and 1988 could then be interpreted as evidence of German dominance.[9] But how independent of EMS considerations was Germany's role in the G-5 coordination process? To answer this question, we resort to Funabashi's (1988) detailed historical account of the coordination efforts from the Plaza to the Louvre agreements, between 1985 and 1987. Funabashi repeatedly stresses three points. First, Germany participated in the process only reluctantly. The Bundesbank in particular was skeptical about the success of coordinated interventions in the dollar market. In fact, the German authorities more than once tried to slow the process and opposed any commitment to specific dollar targets. The United States and Japan complained about German "stubbornness" and Germany's unwillingness to engage in coordinated monetary policy action beyond intervention.

Furthermore, German reluctance to participate was largely motivated by the Bundesbank's concern that such policies would create tensions in the EMS. Swings in the value of the dollar have repeatedly affected the DM more than other EMS currencies and precipitated or increased pressure for a realignment. The Bundesbank's main preoccupation in the Plaza Agreement was to minimize the need for realignments in the EMS and to safeguard the currency relations of the system. On several occasions, the Bundesbank argued explicitly from an EMS position rather than a German point of view.

Finally, other EMS members were consulted by the Bundesbank and even participated actively in the joint dollar-market interventions. German officials deliberated with French and British representatives on the eve of the Plaza meeting about the potential consequences for the EMS. After the agreement, the Bundesbank and the Banque de France immediately notified the other EMS central banks of the accord. To ease tensions in the EMS, the Intervention Redistribution Plan was devised, an internal swap arrangement allowing EMS members to borrow dollars from the Bundesbank and intervene in support of their own currencies. In September 1986, Germany initiated a meeting of the European finance ministers to receive an endorsement of its position. Finally, both France and Italy actively took part in the interventions following the Plaza Agreement. France, itself a member of the G-5, recognized these coordination efforts as a welcome opportunity to push Germany toward more expansionary policies. Indeed, French-German bargaining over dollar targets provided much of the impetus to the Louvre Agreement. In summary, Funabashi's report does not support the view that Germany dominated the EMS through an independent dollar policy.

5.5 Asymmetries in the EMS

An alternative way to assess German dominance in the EMS is to look at the estimated interest rate responses in the EMS countries to interest rate innovations (e_t) in other member countries. For this purpose, we use the parameter estimates obtained for the system to compute the impulse response functions of the individual interest rates. The value of an impulse response function $h_{ij}(k)$ indicates the current change in country j's interest rate due to an autonomous, unit-size, positive change in country i's interest rate k periods ago. The total effect of this "impulse" on the level of country j's interest rate Y_j is then given by the cumulative change over the k periods:

$$(5.6) \qquad\qquad H_{ij}(k) = \sum_{n=0}^{k} h_{ij}(n).$$

Table 5.7 reports the estimated values of $H_{1j}(k)$ and $H_{j1}(k)$, j = 2, ..., 7, for lags k = 0, 1, and 6. The first column specifies the response of other members to a unit increase in the German interest rate; the second column gives the German response to an increase in other members' rates. All responses are positive. In most cases, other members' responses to Germany increase over the six-month horizon. During the first sample period, the French and Italian interest rate reactions reach unity after six months; the reactions of the other countries remain lower. In contrast, German responses to other countries remain constant over time or decline after the first month except in the case of the Netherlands. The German response to Italian interest rate innovations vanishes after six months. The picture changes in the second period. The German impact on France and Italy falls. At the same time, the German reaction to French interest rate innovations declines over time, but the reaction to Belgium, Italy, and the Netherlands increases over time.[10]

The interest rate responses in Table 5.7 suggest two interpretations of the EMS. On the one hand, Germany is a relatively strong player in the system in the sense that other countries react more strongly to its policy than vice versa. However, this result may reflect the sheer relative size of the German financial markets in the EMS and does not necessarily support GDH. On the other hand, France and Italy appear to be relatively weak players in the sense that they adjust more fully than other EMS members to German policies, and their policies have less of an impact on German policy. This relative weakness is particularly noticeable during the first sample period. Table 5.7 thus provides some justification for the

TABLE 5.7 Responses to Unit Interest Rate Innovations

	Lag 0		Lag 1		Lag 6	
	H_{1j}	H_{j1}	H_{1j}	H_{j1}	H_{1j}	H_{j1}
April 1979–March 1983						
France	0.29	0.36	0.56	0.30	1.06	0.38
Italy	0.28	0.39	0.57	0.02	1.11	0.00
Belgium	0.09	0.16	0.16	0.12	0.34	0.20
Netherlands	0.26	0.30	0.28	0.21	0.56	0.41
Ireland	0.31	0.03	0.27	0.03	0.25	0.05
Denmark	0.03	0.09	0.09	0.06	0.27	0.10
EMS	—	—	—	—	—	—
April 1983–April 1988						
France	0.28	0.36	0.58	0.17	0.75	0.08
Italy	0.29	0.39	0.43	0.70	0.23	0.51
Belgium	0.09	0.16	0.75	0.22	0.68	0.21
Netherlands	0.26	0.30	0.22	0.40	0.53	0.55
Ireland	0.30	0.03	0.18	0.04	0.23	0.07
Denmark	0.03	0.09	0.35	0.11	0.36	0.09
EMS	—	—	—	—	—	—

Note: H_{1j} denotes the response in country j to a German innovation. H_{j1} denotes the German response to an innovation in country j.

dissatisfaction French and Italian officials have expressed about Germany counting too much in the EMS.

Using the currency weights w_i of the ECU, we construct an average money-market rate for the EMS, $Y_{EMS} = \Sigma_{i=1,7}w_iY_i$, which is the return on an ECU portfolio invested in the seven money markets.[11] The effect of a unit innovation in country j's interest rate k periods ago on the current, average EMS rate is the weighted sum of its effects on the individual rates, $\Sigma_{i=1,7}w_iH_{ji}(k)$. The total change in the average rate due to unit shocks originating in all EMS countries is then $\Sigma_{j=1,7}\Sigma_{i=1,7}w_iH_{ji}(k)$. Thus, if all other things remain the same, we can estimate the relative contribution of an innovation in an individual rate, Y_j, to a change in the average EMS rate as

(5.7)
$$\sum_{i=1}^{7} w_iH_{ji}(k)/[\sum_{j=1}^{7} \sum_{i=1}^{7} w_iH_{ji}(k)].$$

Expression (5.7) can be interpreted as an approximate measure of country j's relative importance in the short-run EMS policy game. Empirical estimates of this measure for lags k = 0, 1, and 6 are shown on the left side of Table 5.8. Germany's contribution is clearly the largest in both periods. During the first sample period, the French and Italian contributions at lag 6 correspond to their relative weights in the ECU. In contrast, the French contribution is much smaller than the ECU weight for France in the second period; the Italian and the Dutch contributions are larger than their weights. These observations confirm the results of Table 5.7, namely that Germany is a relatively strong player and that France and Italy are relatively weak players in the EMS, France even more so in the second sample period.

If all other things remain the same, changes in an EMS money-market rate i are the results of current or lagged innovations in this and all other rates in the system, $\Sigma_{j=1,7} H_{ji}(k)$. Consequently, the relative importance of the EMS for an individual country can be approximated by

$$(5.8) \qquad \sum_{j \neq i}^{7} H_{ji}(k) / [\sum_{j=1}^{7} H_{ji}(k)] = 1 - H_{ii}(k) / [\sum_{j=1}^{7} H_{ji}(k)] ,$$

which indicates the relative contribution of interest rate innovations in all other EMS countries k lags ago to changes in country i's interest rate. The closer to zero is this measure, the more independent is country i in the EMS; the closer to one is the measure, the less independent is the country.

The right-hand side of Table 5.8 reports the estimates of this measure. For Belgium, Denmark, France, Italy, and the Netherlands, it increases with the length of the lag. In contrast, for Germany it decreases or remains the same. Before 1983, Germany's measure at lag 6 is the smallest of all EMS countries, meaning that the Bundesbank, more so than any other EMS central bank, was able to pursue a relatively independent policy. However, a relatively high degree of independence of German monetary policy is not equivalent to German dominance in the EMS. In contrast, Germany's measure is much more in line with the other countries after 1983. This suggests that the Bundesbank lost much of its relative independence in the EMS after 1983 as realignments became less frequent.

5.6 Conclusions

The empirical evidence presented in this chapter rejects the German-dominance hypothesis. The Bundesbank's position in the EMS is best described as long-run independence but not dominance.

TABLE 5.8 Decomposition of Interest Rate Changes

	Relative Contribution of Domestic Rates to Changes in EMS Rate							Relative Contribution of EMS Rate to Changes in Domestic Rate						
Lag	G	F	I	B	NL	Ire	Dk	G	F	I	B	NL	Ire	Dk
March 1979–March 1983														
0	0.31	0.21	0.18	0.10	0.16	0.02	0.04	0.53	0.32	0.46	0.35	0.35	0.60	0.17
1	0.35	0.25	0.10	0.09	0.15	0.02	0.04	0.40	0.40	0.57	0.45	0.33	0.38	0.58
6	0.41	0.20	0.08	0.09	0.17	0.02	0.04	0.40	0.56	0.64	0.58	0.53	0.58	0.68
April 1983–April 1988														
1	0.28	0.17	0.24	0.10	0.16	0.02	0.04	0.57	0.47	0.49	0.68	0.31	0.58	0.71
6	0.32	0.10	0.20	0.09	0.23	0.03	0.03	0.56	0.61	0.51	0.70	0.47	0.53	0.64

Note: G = Germany, F = France, I = Italy, B = Belgium, NL = Netherlands, Ire = Ireland, and Dk = Denmark.

In Chapter 3 we stressed the importance of the N-degrees of freedom paradigm to understand exchange-rate arrangements. This paradigm would suggest that German long-run independence in the EMS is equivalent to German dominance in the system. Only one country can occupy the Nth degree of freedom and set monetary policy for the entire system. Our results therefore raise this question: Why does the EMS not conform to the paradigm? The answer lies in its institutional structure. The EMS has two "safety valves," that allow individual member countries to escape the pressure the ERM exerts on their monetary policies. One is the possibility for countries to use capital and exchange controls to shield domestic financial markets from international markets. Giavazzi and Giovannini (1987) argue that such controls have been particularly important in France and Italy before realignments. Wyplosz (1988) explains that capital controls have been used by the French authorities exactly to provide room for independent domestic monetary policy in the short run under the EMS arrangement. Realignments themselves are the second safety valve. They permit individual countries to decouple their long-run monetary growth from the rest of the EMS. Although France and Italy removed their capital and exchange controls by 1990 and the realignment option has not been used since 1987, these two "safety valves" continue to be available and remain important characteristics of the EMS. Both assure that German long-run independence is not equivalent to German dominance.

Still, we do find some significant asymmetries in the EMS policy game. Apart from showing Germany's independent position, the data point to the existence in the system of a core group, consisting of Germany and its smaller neighbors. The members of this group interact more closely with one another than with the rest of the system, especially than with the other two large members, France and Italy. Furthermore, the French and Italian positions have been relatively weak, especially in the early phase of the EMS. Indeed, the relative weakness of France in the system is the most striking asymmetry in the EMS. French underrepresentation and the fact that the ERM constrained French interest rates more tightly than Italian rates may well explain why the complaints about German dominance have come most forcefully from the French side. We conclude that many observers have mistaken German long-run independence and French underrepresentation in the EMS for German dominance.

Rejecting the German-Dominance Hypothesis implies discarding the disciplinary interpretation of the EMS. Indirectly, our findings corroborate the alternative explanation that the European disinflation of the 1980s was the outcome of a consensus in the region to reduce inflation and of the resulting willingness of policymakers to bear the political cost of restrictive domestic policies; these forces were far more important than

EMS membership. The Bundesbank, with its strong and successful commitment to price stability, may have strengthened this consensus and facilitated the development of low-inflation monetary strategies, thus serving as a role model for monetary authorities elsewhere in the EMS.[12] But such a coordinating role is much weaker—yet more plausible—than the assertion that the Bundesbank dominated monetary policy in the EMS.

Notes

1. We adopt the following notational convention: for a polynomial a_{ij} (L), $a_{ij} = 0$ means a_{ij} (L) is identically zero; $c_i = 0$ and $b_{ij} = 0$ have the corresponding meaning for the polynomials c_i (L) and b_{ij} (L).

2. Some critics of our tests have contended that the use of instantaneous causality is a weakness that makes our tests inconclusive. This critique is based on the observation that in a bivariate, contemporaneous causal relationship, one cannot identify the source of action or the direction of causality (e.g., Weber 1990). They propose that causality tests of GDH must involve only lags greater than zero. This critique, however, is based on a flawed understanding of causality testing. First, as discussed at length in Cooley and LeRoy (1985), the regression residual in pure vector autoregressive systems is not identifiable in the sense of structural random variables unless the error covariance matrix is diagonal. That is, causality tests involving only lags greater than zero are in no way more informative than our tests; instead, they hide the problem of identifying the source of action. Second, the inclusion of domestic target variables in addition to the policy variables means that our system is not a pure vector autoregression and allows us to identify the individual equations.

3. For a detailed account of the operating procedures of various central banks, see Kneeshaw and van den Bergh (1989); Batten et al. (1990); and the various country chapters in Fratianni and Salvatore (1992).

4. One may argue that it is preferable to enter variables like real income explicitly if they play a role. The use of more explanatory variables, however, which would all enter with additional lags, is prohibitive because of the limited sample size.

5. The actual weights applied are 0.06 for Canada, 0.215 for Japan, 0.097 for the United Kingdom, and 0.626 for the United States.

6. See Danmarks Nationalbank (1985, 1986). The dummy is zero except in the third quarter of 1985 and the second quarter of 1986.

7. The weights are 1982 real GNP weights.

8. Short-run control instruments of the Bundesbank consist mainly of credit operations of maturities of 2 to 28 days with domestic commercial banks. They are used to fine-tune the domestic money market. Long-run control instruments include reserve requirements, credit operations with maturities of 30 to 90 days, and open market operations in government paper. These instruments are used to control the trend growth of the money supply (Neumann and von Hagen, 1992).

9. This interpretation was suggested to us by Allan Meltzer. On the G-5 exchange-rate intervention policies, see Dominguez (1990) and von Hagen (1989b).

10. Note that the German reaction to a Dutch interest rate innovation is of the same order of magnitude as the Dutch response to a German innovation. This result is consistent with De Grauwe's (1988) observations of interest rate links between Germany and the Netherlands.

11. The ECU weights used here are 0.104 for Belgium, 0.032 for Denmark, 0.221 for France, 0.395 for Germany, 0.013 for Ireland, 0.11 for Italy, and 0.125 for the Netherlands.

12. Eichengreen (1989) argues that the United Kingdom in the classical gold standard and the United States in the Bretton Woods system, rather than acting as hegemons, performed similar coordinating functions.

6

The EMS and
Central Bank Cooperation

The cooperative interpretation of the EMS regards the system as an arrangement to foster policy coordination among central banks. It rests on the proposition that monetary policy in one country has spillover effects on other countries. As already noted, the builders of the EMS regarded policy coordination as an essential goal of the EMS arrangement. In this chapter, we analyze the cooperative interpretation in more detail.

6.1 Central Bank Cooperation:
Theoretical Foundations

We use a simplified version of our Chapter 3 model to demonstrate the main points of the cooperative interpretation. The model is streamlined in three ways: we neglect the bond market and assume that money is the only financial asset; we assume that the European economies (of Germany and Italy) are perfectly symmetric in the sense that the parameters of of supply and demand functions for labor, output, and money are the same in both countries; and, finally, we disregard policymaking in the United States, which amounts to assuming that U.S. monetary policy is unchanged, whether or not the European countries coordinate their policies. The simplified model is summarized in Table 6.1.

To understand the international linkages of stabilization policies in the model, consider the example of a negative supply shock ξ, such as an oil price rise, affecting both European countries. In the absence of a policy reaction, this shock leads to an increase in the output price levels, driving down the real wages and offsetting the initial employment effects. But a central bank with a preference for price stability will react with a restrictive monetary policy to stabilize the price level at the cost of some reduction in employment. The domestic monetary contraction leads to an appreciation of the domestic currency, which in turn raises the foreign price level and thus works against the foreign central bank's attempt to contain inflation. By assumption, the foreign central bank faces the same policy problem and responds in the same way, so that its actions raise the price level in the home country and induce the domestic central bank to reinforce its monetary contraction. With their independent monetary policies, the two central banks ignore this interdependence. In the resulting equilibrium, neither currency appreciates because the two policies offset each other. However, the two central banks overreact to the original shock—both could be better off with less restrictive monetary policies, achieving the same degree of price stability at a lower employment cost.

In contrast to this scenario of competitive appreciation (or devaluation in the case of a positive supply shock), a different spillover arises from a relative demand shock, η. Such a shock raises the demand for German

TABLE 6.1   The Simplified Model

(6.1) *Production Functions*

$$y_1 = y_1^n + (1-\alpha)n_1 + \xi;$$
$$y_2 = y_2^n + (1-\alpha)n_2 + \xi.$$

(6.2) *Demand for Labor*

$$w_1 - p_1 = -\alpha n_1 + \xi;$$
$$w_2 - p_2 = -\alpha n_2 + \xi.$$

(6.3) *Supply of Labor*

$$w_1 = P_1^e;$$
$$w_2 = P_2^e.$$

(6.4) *Demand for Output*

$$y_1 = \phi^{-1}q + \beta y_2 + (1-\beta)y_1 + \phi^{-1}\eta;$$
$$y_2 = -\phi^{-1}q + \beta y_1 + (1-\beta)y_2 - \phi^{-1}\eta.$$

(6.5) *Money-Market Equilibrium*

$$m_1 - p_1 = y_1 - y_1^e;$$
$$m_2 - p_2 = y_2 - y_2^e.$$

---

output and lowers the demand for Italian output. The German central bank reacts with a monetary contraction that causes the mark to appreciate. At the same time, the Italian central bank reacts with a monetary expansion causing the lira to depreciate. In this scenario, the actions each central bank takes work to the other's benefit; with independent monetary policies, however, the central banks do not realize this mutual benefit and underreact to the relative shock. Again, coordination would make both countries better off—the same degree of price stability could be obtained with less employment variation.

The reduced-form solutions for the two policy target variables, employment and the consumer price level, are now

(6.6) $$n_1 = m_1 - m_1{}^e; n_2 = m_2 - m_2{}^e;$$

$$q_1 = m_1 - (1 - \alpha)(m_1 - m_1{}^e) + \varepsilon(m_1 - m_1{}^e - (m_2 - m_2{}^e)) - \xi + \beta\eta;$$

$$q_2 = m_2 - (1 - \alpha)(m_2 - m_2{}^e) + \varepsilon(m_2 - m_2{}^e - (m_1 - m_1{}^e)) - \xi - \beta\eta;$$

where $\varepsilon = \beta^2\phi\,(1 - \alpha)$. We assume that the two central banks, lacking an agreement to coordinate their monetary policies, use their money supplies as policy instruments. Each bank maximizes its preference function on the basis of knowledge about the current realization of the exogenous shocks, given what it knows about the policy of the other. The resulting Nash equilibrium[1] is

(6.7) $$m_1 = (\alpha + \varepsilon)(k_n\xi - h_n\beta\eta); m_2 = (\alpha + \varepsilon)(k_n\xi + h_n\beta\eta);$$

$$q_1 = -\sigma(k_n\xi - h_n\beta\eta); q_2 = -\sigma(k_n\xi + h_n\beta\eta);$$

where $k_n = 1/(\sigma + \alpha(\alpha + \varepsilon))$, and $h_n = 1/(\sigma + (\alpha + 2\varepsilon)(\alpha + \varepsilon))$.

There are two ways to evaluate this equilibrium; they correspond to alternative interpretations of the policy problem. One is to assume that an agreement for policy coordination has to be chosen before the actual shocks are experienced. Alternative arrangements are then evaluated in terms of the *expected utility* they yield. This is appropriate if reaching an agreement to coordinate is time-consuming or involves significant transaction cost. The other method is to assume that a policy regime is adopted after the realization of the shocks. A set of given shocks is then taken as the initial condition for coordination, and alternative arrangements are evaluated in terms of the *realized utility* levels given these shocks, as in Begg and Wyplosz (1987) or Hughes-Hallet and Minford (1989, 1990). In the context of evaluating the EMS, the second procedure seems rather unsatisfactory. It poses the question about the future of a cooperative arrangement, once the initial conditions have been sufficiently improved upon.[2] Furthermore, the formation of an arrangement like the EMS seems to be too involved and politically too visible to be purely ad-hoc. Therefore, we follow the first alternative.

The Nash equilibrium yields the expected utility levels

(6.8) $\qquad E2U_{1n} = -(\sigma + (\alpha + \varepsilon)^2)\sigma(k_n^2\sigma_\xi^2 - 2\beta k_n h_n \sigma_{\xi\eta} + h_n^2\beta^2\sigma_\eta^2);$

$\qquad E2U_{2n} = -(\sigma + (\alpha + \varepsilon)^2)\sigma(k_n^2\sigma_\xi^2 + 2\beta k_n h_n \sigma_{\xi\eta} + h_n^2\beta^2\sigma_\eta^2),$

where $\sigma_{\xi\eta}$ is the covariance of the two shocks.

In a cooperative arrangement between the two central banks, in contrast, the money supplies are chosen to maximize the joint preference function $U_1 + U_2$:[3]

(6.9) $\qquad m_1 = \alpha k_c \xi - (\alpha + 2\varepsilon)h_c\beta\eta; \; m_2 = \alpha k_c \xi + (\alpha + 2\varepsilon)h_c\beta\eta;$

$\qquad q_1 = -\sigma(k_c\xi - h_c\beta\eta); \; q_2 = -\sigma(k_c\xi + h_c\beta\eta),$

where $k_c = 1/(\sigma + \alpha^2) < k_n$ and $h_c = 1/(\sigma + (\alpha + 2\varepsilon)^2) > h_n$. The expected utility levels are

(6.10) $\qquad E2U_{1c} = -\sigma\{k_c^2\sigma_\xi^2 - 2(\sigma + \alpha(2\varepsilon + \alpha))k_c h_c\beta\sigma_{\xi\eta} + h_c^2\beta^2\sigma_\eta^2\};$

$\qquad E2U_{2c} = -\sigma\{k_c^2\sigma_\xi^2 + 2(\sigma + \alpha(2\varepsilon + \alpha))k_c h_c\beta\sigma_{\xi\eta} + h_c^2\beta^2\sigma_\eta^2\}.$

Cooperation does not imply a fixed exchange rate here. In fact, the optimal cooperative policies demand a change in the nominal exchange rate whenever there is an asymmetric demand shock: The solution for the exchange rate in the cooperative equilibrium is $s = (\sigma - (\alpha+2\varepsilon)^2 - 2\alpha(\alpha\beta - \varepsilon))h_c\eta$. Comparison of the cooperative strategies (6.9) with the noncooperative ones (6.7), shows that the monetary response to the common supply shock ξ decreases and the response to a relative demand shock η increases.

Both central banks unambiguously gain from cooperation if there is only one source to the stabilization problem—that is, if there are only common supply shocks ($\sigma_{\xi\eta} = \sigma_\eta^2 = 0$) or only relative demand shocks ($\sigma_{\xi\eta} = \sigma_\xi^2 = 0$) affecting the two economies. (The same holds for a common, symmetric demand shock or relative supply shock.) This result is complicated if the common supply shock and the relative demand shock are correlated ($\sigma_{\xi\eta} \neq 0$). Equations (6.8) and (6.10) indicate that the expected utility levels depend critically on the sign of the covariance of the two shocks; equations (6.7) and (6.9) show why this is so.

With a negative covariance, Italy expects its reactions to common supply shocks and relative demand shocks to offset each other; this requires less monetary variance and consequently entails less variation in employment. For example, a negative supply shock, which demands a monetary contraction, would tend to be accompanied by a shift of aggregate demand away from Italian output, which by itself dampens inflation. Germany, in contrast, expects that its reactions to these shocks reinforce each other. Under the plausible condition that $(\alpha + \varepsilon) < 2$, Italy unambiguously gains from cooperation if the covariance is negative, but Germany may be worse off than in the Nash equilibrium (6.8), if $\sigma_{\xi\eta}$ is large in absolute value.[4] The situation is reversed when the covariance is positive. The correlation between the common supply shock and the relative demand shock thus creates a distribution problem for the two countries: Cooperation may result in a utility loss relative to the Nash equilibrium for one country, although the two together benefit from it. Under such circumstances, the losing partner will not adhere to cooperation unless it is adequately compensated.

6.2 The EMS as a Surrogate for Cooperation

A second and even more severe problem with cooperation is that it is not incentive-compatible for the individual countries. To see this, consider the marginal utility of a German monetary expansion, when Italy plays the cooperative strategy (6.9) and if we assume $\eta = 0$ for simplicity:

$$(6.11) \qquad \left. \frac{U}{1m} \right|_{m = m^* = \alpha k_\varsigma \xi} = \sigma \varepsilon k_c \xi .$$

For example, in the presence of a negative supply shock, the German authorities can improve their outcome by deviating from the cooperative monetary strategy. To this end, they would adopt a more restrictive policy and enjoy the disinflation benefit of the ensuing appreciation of the DM. Of course, the Italian central bank faces a similar temptation. There is a conflict between the individual and the common interest, a problem familiar from cartel theory. This makes the cooperative solution nonviable, unless the participants' policy actions can be monitored closely.[5] Canzoneri and Gray (1985) argue that cheating is relatively easy in the international context, given the complexity of the national policy processes and the ambiguity of the definitions of policy variables such as "money."

The cooperative interpretation of the EMS says that, by pegging the exchange rate at a predetermined level, the two countries together may improve over the Nash solution and reap at least some of the benefits from cooperation.[6] Fixing the exchange rate then is a restricted form of cooperation, a surrogate for full, unrestricted cooperation with a flexible exchange rate. Since exchange rates are easy to monitor, cheating would be immediately discovered. Therefore, fixing the exchange rate is a viable strategy. To illustrate the point, assume that Italy commits to pegging the DM/lira rate. Germany chooses the money supply given this constraint. The resulting equilibrium has

$$(6.12) \qquad m_1 = \alpha k_c(\xi - (1 - \varepsilon\theta)\beta\eta); \; m_2 = m_1 + \theta\beta\eta;$$

$$q_1 = -\sigma k_c(\xi - (1 - \varepsilon\theta)\beta\eta); \; q_2 = q_1 + (1 - \varepsilon\theta)(1 - 2\beta)\eta;$$

and

$$(6.13) \qquad E2U_{1e} = -\sigma k_c(\sigma_\xi^2 - 2(1 - \varepsilon\theta)\beta\sigma_{\xi\eta} + (1 - \varepsilon\theta)^2\beta^2\sigma_\eta^2);$$

$$E2U_{2e} = - [\sigma k_c\sigma_\xi^2 + 2\sigma\alpha k_c(2\,\zeta - \beta^2\theta)\sigma_{\xi\eta} + (\sigma\zeta^2 + \alpha^2(\zeta - \beta^2\theta)^2)\sigma_\eta^2];$$

where $\theta = 1/(\alpha\,\beta + \varepsilon)$ and $\zeta = \beta\theta(1 - \alpha^2 k_c\beta)$. Comparing (6.13) with (6.9), we find that the fixed rate arrangement can be preferable to the Nash solution for both countries. In fact, it is identical to the cooperative equilibrium if the relative shock plays no role ($\sigma_\eta^2 = 0$).[7] More generally, there is greater improvement of the fixed rate solution over the Nash solution the less important the relative shock is compared to the common shock. This is not surprising, if we recall that adjustment to the relative shock is facilitated by an appreciation of the DM.

The distribution of the gains from the arrangement now depends on the variance of the relative demand shock and, again, on the covariance of the two types of shocks. If the covariance is positive, Germany is likely to fare even better with a fixed exchange rate than with full coordination. The reason is that fixing the exchange rate forces Italy to respond in a relatively more expansive way to a positive relative demand shock than otherwise and thus take a larger share in the adjustment to this shock. A large positive covariance will eventually make the fixed rate arrangement unacceptable for Italy, whereas Germany would still prefer it over the Nash equilibrium. The situation is reversed, of course, if the covariance is negative. This implies that the distribution of the gains is not automatically in favor of the dominant country that determines money growth in the arrangement.[8]

Going back to the reduced-form solutions (6.6), one can see that any deviation from the basic symmetric structure of the model will produce an effect similar to that created by the relative demand shock variable in the present setup. Such a deviation may consist of shocks impacting the two economies in different ways, or it may entail structural hetero-geneities (that is, different parameter values in the supply and demand functions of the model). In view of this generalization, the essence of our discussion is that fixing exchange rates performs the better as a surrogate for central bank cooperation the less important are asymmetries between participating economies that cause differing impacts of the exogenous shocks on output, prices, or employment and that call for differing optimal policy responses. In other words, the more asymmetric the participating economies, the more important becomes the loss of the $N - 1$ degrees of freedom relative to the gain from coordinating monetary policies.

Even if the expected utility from cooperating in the EMS is larger than what the members expect from noncooperation, there remains the possibility that once the EMS has been created, a large asymmetric shock occurs, making the distribution of the actual gains unacceptable for a member. The EMS has two instruments to deal with this problem and prevent the system from falling apart. One is the institution among the members of transfer payments, which facilitates a compensation of those who lose by those who benefit from the arrangement. The various credit mechanisms described in Chapter 2 are important in this respect. In addition, the greater emphasis on intramarginal intervention can be interpreted in this way, because the inclusion of intramarginal intervention in the general financing of interventions shifts a greater part of the adjustment onto the hard-currency countries of the EMS. The other important institution is the possibility of realignments. A parity realignment restores temporarily the lost degrees of freedom in the joint response to a given shock. Because all members are involved in the realignment decision, the action cannot be interpreted as noncooperative behavior. Instead, a realignment allows for the cooperative use of all degrees of freedom when the pressures from asymmetric shocks become too large. Anecdotal evidence from the EMS suggests that realignments have indeed been determined in a cooperative way (Padoa-Schioppa 1988; Ungerer 1990). This view of realignments underscores the argument, made by the early proponents of the EMS, that realignments are not a sign that policy coordination in the EMS has failed.

6.3 Policy Coordination with Imperfect Information

The preceding discussion assumes that the monetary authorities have perfect information about all relevant variables when they plan their optimal policies. In reality, central banks cannot observe all shocks immediately and directly. Instead, they observe goods and asset prices that convey imperfect information. Recent literature has shown how exchange-rate arrangements can be used to cope with problems of imperfect information (e.g., Boyer 1978; Aizenman and Frenkel 1985; Glick and Wihlborg 1990; von Hagen and Neumann 1990). This research shows that the exchange-rate regime determines the "LM curve" and consequently its stability characteristics. Furthermore, exchange-rate policies alter the information content of goods and asset prices and therefore affect the private sector's ability to infer imperfectly observed shocks.

This literature rests on the paradigm of a small open economy pegging the exchange rate to the currency of a large country. In the case of economies of similar size, for which strategic interaction plays an important role, imperfect information has additional, strategic aspects. Here, we illustrate its role with an example of "private" information.

Domestic central banks do not generally have access to the information systems of foreign central banks. Therefore, it is plausible to assume that central banks have private information about the state of their countries' economies that is not accessible to other central banks. To model this assumption, we rewrite the aggregate demand functions as

$$(6.14) \qquad y_1 = \phi^{-1}q + \beta y_2 + (1-\beta)y_1 - \phi^{-1}\eta_1,$$

$$y_2 = -\phi^{-1}q + \beta y_1 + (1-\beta)y_2 + \phi^{-1}\eta_2,$$

with $E\eta_1\eta_2 = 0$.[9] We assume that the German central bank knows η_1, but has no information about η_2. For the Italian central bank, the situation is reversed. Both central banks know the value of the common shock ξ, but cannot observe the foreign central bank's current money supply. For simplicity, we let $\xi = 0$.

According to a popular argument, arrangements for international policy coordination serve the purpose of facilitating the exchange of private information among policymakers. This reasoning is based on the conjecture that independent policies based on imperfect information lead to inferior equilibria. The first-order conditions for the present policy game are now

$$(6.15) \quad m_1 = h_c(\alpha + \varepsilon)(\varepsilon E_1 m_2 - \beta\eta_1/2); \ m_2 = h_c(\alpha + \varepsilon)(\varepsilon E_2 m_1 - \beta\eta_2/2).$$

Here, E_1 and E_2 denote the expectations of the German and Italian central banks. Because $E_1\eta_2 = E_2\eta_1 = 0$, and the expected Italian policy can only be a reaction to $E_2\eta_1$ or η_2, $E_1 m_2 = 0$. This yields the optimal policy $m_1 = -(\alpha + \varepsilon)\beta h_c\eta_1/2$. The Italian optimal policy can be found accordingly.

The Nash equilibrium with asymmetric information has

$$(6.16) \qquad E2U_{1a} = -\sigma h_c \beta^2 \sigma_{\eta_1}^2/4 - (\sigma + \alpha(\alpha + \varepsilon))^2 h_c^2 \beta^2 \sigma_{\eta_2}^2/4;$$

$$E2U_{2a} = -\sigma h_c \beta^2 \sigma_{\eta_2}^2/4 - (\sigma + \alpha(\alpha + \varepsilon))^2 h_c^2 \beta^2 \sigma_{\eta_1}^2/4.$$

It can be shown that $EU_{1a} < EU_{1n}$, and $EU_{2a} < EU_{2n}$. The information asymmetry worsens both central banks' outcomes. Thus, there is a potential gain for both from exchanging information, even without their playing cooperative strategies. However, the simple exchange of information does not work. Because the realizations of η_1 and η_2 determine the distribution of the utility levels, both central banks have an incentive to overstate the true size of their domestic shocks as a means of increasing the foreign central bank's part of the adjustment to the shock. Consequently, central bank officials would rationally perceive the information obtained from other central banks as not credible.[10]

Pegging the exchange rate in this context is a mechanism to transmit information indirectly. If, as in the preceding examples, the Italian central bank commits to fixing the DM/lira rate, the German optimal policy becomes $m_1 = -\alpha(1 - \varepsilon\theta)\beta\eta_1/2(\sigma + \alpha^2)$, while the Italian policy is still $m_2 = m_1 + \theta\beta(\eta_1 + \eta_2)$. The exchange-rate peg allows the Italian authorities to react to η_1, which they are unable to do otherwise, and prevents their Nash reaction to η_2, which is unknown to the German authorities. The resulting equilibrium has

$$(6.17) \qquad E2U_{1E} = -\sigma k_c (1 - \varepsilon\theta)^2 \beta^2 \sigma_{\eta_1}^2 - (1 - \varepsilon\theta)^2 \beta^2 \sigma_{\eta_2}^2;$$

$$E2U_{2E} = -\{\sigma(\theta - (\alpha + \varepsilon)h_c)^2 + \alpha^2(\theta(1 - \beta) - (\alpha + \varepsilon)h_c)^2\}\beta^2 \sigma_{\eta_1}^2/$$
$$4\sigma + \alpha^2(1 - \beta)^2\}\beta^2\theta^2\sigma_{\eta_2}^2/4.$$

It can be shown that the fixed rate equilibrium unambiguously yields an improvement for Germany. The outcome for Italy is less clear-cut; the fixed rate is preferable, if the variance of the Italian demand shock is large relative to the variance of the German shock, and if the parameter ε is large relative to the parameters α and σ.[11]

To summarize, fixing exchange rates is a suboptimal coordinating strategy because of the implied loss of degrees of freedom. On the other hand, agreements to fix exchange rates have the advantage of specifying rules of coordination that are easy to monitor internationally and that therefore give rise to viable arrangements. Depending on the nature and relative size of the shocks, fixing exchange rates may be preferable to full cooperation from the point of view of a bank seeking feasibility and stability of the arrangement. Information imperfections and asymmetries give rise to further incentives for policy coordination through fixed exchange rates.

6.4 Policy Coordination in the EMS:
A Simulation Exercise

So far, we have limited our analysis to the very restrictive case of a two-country world in which money is the only financial asset. In this section, we use a richer version of our model to investigate further the qualities of the EMS as a surrogate for central bank cooperation. Going back to the model formulated in Section 3.3, we now include three countries in the analysis: Germany, Italy, and the United States. This allows us to analyze the EMS as an agreement that does not include all countries. The relevance of this extension comes from the fact that an EMS outsider, like the United States, will generally pursue different optimal policies in the presence of the EMS than otherwise and thus possibly change the desirability of central bank cooperation in the EMS. Furthermore, we now include bonds as additional assets in the model. We use the assumption that bonds are tradeable internationally; capital flows thus become another channel of international spillovers of monetary policy. Finally, we focus in this section on the consequences of the EC's current "Single Market Program."

The simple, two-country model used previously indicates that fixed exchange rates are equivalent to optimal policy coordination among two symmetric economies affected by a symmetric shock. Our expanded analysis raised two primary questions: First, how robust are the welfare gains from fixed exchange rates when the symmetry assumption is relaxed? Second, how will the qualities of the EMS as a cooperative arrangement change as a result of the Single Market Program, which we assume to carry major structural changes in the economies as capital and labor are reallocated and competition becomes more effective in the integrated market?

The approach we follow in this section is similar in spirit to the analysis of Basevi et al. (1988). We use numerical simulations to evaluate the consequences of stochastic asymmetries among the members for the performance of central bank strategies. Stochastic asymmetries occur when the immediate impact of a stochastic shock differs across countries. The simulations are helpful, because the closed-form solutions of the model are too complex to provide straightforward insights. By designing a set of simulation exercises that mimic the expected structural changes resulting from the Single Market Program, we intend to gain some insights into the future stability and desirability of the EMS.

Stochastic Environments

Our model has five aggregate shocks affecting the three economies, two on the supply side (ξ_i) and three on the demand side (η_j) (see Table 3.1). By an appropriate choice of the parameters a_{ij} and c_{ij} of the aggregate production and demand functions, we can generate the stochastic asymmetries of interest for our simulations. Let $A = [a]_{ij}$ be the (3x2) matrix specifying the impact of the two supply shocks ξ_1 and ξ_2 on the production functions of the three economies, and let $C = [c]_{ij}$ be the (3x3) matrix specifying the impact of the three demand shocks. For our simulations, we use the following parameterizations:

$$(6.18) \qquad A = \begin{pmatrix} 1 & 1 \\ a_{21} & 1 \\ 0 & 1 \end{pmatrix} \quad C = \begin{pmatrix} 1 & 0 & 0 \\ c_{21} & 1 & 0 \\ c_{31} & 0 & 1 \end{pmatrix}.$$

Note that changes in the impact parameters a_{21}, c_{21}, and c_{31} can be interpreted in terms of the covariance matrix of the composite structural aggregate supply disturbances $u_i = a_{i1}\xi_1 + \xi_2$ and the structural aggregate demand shocks $v_j = c_{j1}\eta_1 + c_{jj}\eta_j$, $j > 1$, and $v_1 = \eta_1$.

The second column of matrix A specifies that ξ_2 affects all three countries in the same way. Thus, ξ_2 is a "global supply shock" common to the three countries, the kind of shock previously analyzed. A first type of stochastic asymmetry is created by the first column of this matrix. It specifies ξ_1 as a "European supply shock" with direct effects only on Germany and Italy. The impact of this shock may differ for Germany and Italy, depending on the value of the parameter a_{21}. This setup is useful in analyzing the effects of a EMS policy coordination in the presence of asymmetric supply shocks, which are likely to arise in the process of market integration.

On the demand side, we consider two types of stochastic asymmetries. The first is a "European demand shock," which affects only Germany and Italy directly. In this scenario, $c_{31} = 0$, and the choice of c_{21} specifies how differently the shock affects Italy compared to Germany. This permits us to study the importance of relative demand shocks among the EMS members, as in the previous section. The second is a "U.S.-German demand shock," for which we set $c_{21} = 0$ so that it has no direct effect on Italy; the parameter c_{31} determines how differently the shock affects the United States compared to Germany. A special case of the U.S.-German demand shock is given by $c_{31} = -1$, which is a perfect negative correlation of its impact on Germany and the United States. With such an assumption, we find the model behaves as in the case of exogenous shift in private investors' portfolios from dollar-denominated assets to DM-denominated assets, or vice versa.[12] Giavazzi and Giovannini (1987), among others, argue that a major goal of the EMS is to spread out more evenly the effects of such shifts among the participating economies. The U.S.-German demand shock therefore permits us to study the importance of such shifts for the coordination of policies in the EMS.

Model Calibration

To simulate policy scenarios, we need to specify the numerical values for some of the model's basic parameters. Table 6.2 summarizes the parameter values used in the baseline version of the model. Note that the parameterization of the two European economies is symmetric, whereas the U.S. economy has different parameter values. To obtain an empirically plausible set of parameters, we start from long-run elasticity estimates in Taylor's (1988) multicountry model for our three countries. For Germany and Italy, we use the average of the two countries' parameter estimates to preserve the symmetry of these two economies. Where necessary, first derivatives are transformed into elasticities using annual data for 1974–1984, the period that underlies Taylor's estimation. The use of long-run elasticities is justified, because our model has no explicit short-run dynamics. For our purpose, the most important aspect of these parameter values is to obtain empirically plausible responses in prices, interest rates, and exchange rates to the exogenous shocks and to monetary policy actions.

TABLE 6.2 Parameter Values for the Symmetric Baseline Model

Parameter	Germany	Italy	US	Parameter	Germany	Italy	US
α	.634	.634	.682	θ	.0213	.0213	.0473
ρ	.486	.486	.645	γ	.144	.144	.079
β_{ij}				ϕ_{ij}			
Germany	.720	.229	.057	Germany	—	.223	.10
Italy	.229	.720	.057	Italy	−.223	—	.10
US	.057	.057	.890	US	.00	.00	—

Source: Author's data

Taylor provides estimates of the income and interest elasticities of aggregate consumption and investment. To translate these parameters into the income and interest elasticities of aggregate output demand required by our model, we multiply Taylor's elasticity estimates by the average 1974–1984 shares of consumption and investment in national income.[13] To derive the expenditure shares β_{ij}, we first approximate β_{ii} as one minus the share of total imports in national income. Next, the share of total imports of each country is allocated between the remaining two countries of the model on the basis of the ratio of their actual average import shares over 1981-1987.[14] The resulting estimates obviously overstate the importance of, say, Italy's market share in German imports. However, our procedure provides a convenient way to reconcile empirical estimates with the natural limitations of a three-country model. Finally, the real exchange-rate elasticities of output demand are approximated by the weighted sum of Taylor's estimates of the terms of trade elasticities of export and import demand, the weights being the shares of exports and imports in national income.

Monetary Policy Strategies and Regimes

Central bank strategies to maximize the objective functions are defined by the choice of a policy instrument. With flexible exchange rates, we assume that all three central banks adopt monetary control strategies— they use the domestic money supplies as their policy instruments. To model the EMS, we assume that the Banca d'Italia pegs the DM/lira exchange rate, while the Bundesbank and the U.S. Federal Reserve System (the Fed) adopt monetary control strategies. The full solution of the model is obtained by optimizing the utility functions with respect to the relevant policy instruments and subject to the constraints of equations (3.1) through (3.7).

Policy regimes are defined by the rules of international policy coordination. We distinguish three different regimes. One is the "Nash" regime with flexible exchange rates, in which the three central banks pursue independent monetary control strategies, taking as given the policies in other countries. Alternatively, we consider two forms of EMS policy coordination, an "asymmetric" and a "symmetric" EMS. In the former, the Banca d'Italia fixes the DM/lira rate; while the Bundesbank unilaterally maximizes its preference function without regard to the effects of its policy on the EMS partner. The asymmetric EMS thus embeds the popular notion of a hegemonic Bundesbank in the EMS. In the symmetric EMS, Italy again pegs the DM/lira rate, but the German money growth rate is set so as to take account of its spillover effects on the Italian policy targets.

The Baseline Simulations

As previously discussed, the desirability of international policy coordination depends critically on the significance of the international spillovers of monetary policy. To describe their importance in the model, we define the monetary spillover index. The spillover index, K_{ij}, between two countries, i and j, is the negative ratio of the coefficients of country j's and country i's money supplies in the reduced-form equation for country i's consumer price index,

(6.19) $K_{ij} = -(dQ_i/dM_j)/(dQ_i/dM_i).$

The larger K_{ij}, the more important is the impact of the foreign country's monetary policy on country i's price level. With the baseline parameterization, the index is $K_{12} = K_{21} = 0.62$ between the two European countries, $K_{13} = K_{23} = 0.26$ between the United States and Europe, and $K_{31} = K_{32} = 0.18$ between Europe and the United States. The baseline parameterization thus has the plausible characteristic that cross-country effects are more important in Europe than between Europe and the United States.

Part A of Table 6.3 reports the differences between Germany's and Italy's best policy responses under the Nash regime and the other two regimes, part B the welfare improvements of the EMS regimes over the Nash outcomes. Four different shocks are considered in each part of the table. The upper panel has the responses to a negative world supply shock. As was the case in the two-country model, the Nash policies here are too restrictive. Coordination leads to less contractive policies. Note that the symmetric EMS yields a smaller improvement over Nash than the asymmetric EMS. This result delivers an important message about the design of decisionmaking rules in the EMS. By forcing the German monetary authorities to respond explicitly to the Italian interests, the system may actually lose relative to the asymmetric case. That is, the assumed hegemony of the Bundesbank may benefit all participants.

The second panel of the table adds a European supply shock $\xi_1 = -1$ to the previous situation and compares the outcomes for three different values of the impact parameter a_{21}. If the shock affects both European countries symmetrically ($a_{21} = 1$), the differences in the money supply changes between the Nash regime and its alternatives become larger, but the relative welfare improvements are the same. Things change as a_{21}

TABLE 6.3 Baseline Policy Simulations

Part A: Difference in Money Growth Between Coordinated Policy and Nash Regime

	World Supply Shock	
	Asymmetric EMS	*Symmetric EMS*
Germany	.50	.17
Italy	.50	.17

	European Supply Shock					
	$a_{21}=1$		$a_{21}=.5$		$a_{21}=-1$	
	A	S	A	S	A	S
Germany	.85	.28	.60	.19	−.15	−.07
Italy	.85	.28	.32	−.09	−1.30	−1.65

	European Demand Shock					
	$c_{21}=1$		$c_{21}=.5$		$c_{21}=-1$	
	A	S	A	S	A	S
Germany	.43	.14	.19	-.02	−.52	−.50
Italy	.43	.14	−.13	-.34	−1.82	−1.80

	U.S.–German Demand Shock					
	$c_{31}=1$		$c_{31}=.5$		$c_{31}=-1$	
	A	S	A	S	A	S
Germany	.22	−.09	.09	−.14	−.31	−.27
Italy	−.43	−.74	−.57	−.79	−.96	−.92

Part B: Relative Welfare Improvements Over Nash Regime

	World Supply Shock	
	Asymmetric EMS	*Symmetric EMS*
Germany	.21	.11
Italy	.21	.11

	European Supply Shock					
	$a_{21}=1$		$a_{21}=.5$		$a_{21}=-1$	
	A	S	A	S	A	S
Germany	.21	.11	−.02	−.10	−5.20	−5.21
Italy	.21	.11	.26	.07	−1.06	−.95

Note: A = asymmetric EMS, S = symmetric EMS.

(continues)

TABLE 6.3.   Baseline Policy Simulations *(continued)*

Part B: Relative Welfare Improvements Over Nash Regime

| | European Demand Shock | | | | | |
| | $c_{21}=1$ | | $c_{21}=.5$ | | $c_{21}=-1$ | |
	A	S	A	S	A	S
Germany	.21	.11	−.46	−.58	−3.80	−3.80
Italy	.21	.11	.07	−.14	−1.04	−1.02

| | U.S.–German Demand Shock | | | | | |
| | $c_{31}=1$ | | $c_{31}=.5$ | | $c_{31}=-1$ | |
	A	S	A	S	A	S
Germany	−.79	−.91	−1.38	−1.52	.31	.29
Italy	−.02	−.23	−.14	−.33	−1.33	−1.23

Note: A = asymmetric EMS, S = symmetric EMS.

begins to decline.   The EMS regimes become more contractive with $a_{21} = 0.5$ and more so when $a_{21} = -1$. At the same time, the stochastic asymmetry alters appreciably the distribution of the welfare gains from coordination. With $a_{21} = 0.5$, the EMS yields an improvement for Italy, but not for Germany. Both fixed exchange-rate regimes become unacceptable for Germany and Italy when $a_{21} = -1$.

Similar findings emerge from the third panel. Here we add a European demand shock, $\eta_1 = 1$, to the world supply shock and compare the outcomes for three different values of c_{21}. Again, the relative welfare improvements are the same as in the first panel if the shock affects the two European countries equally ($c_{21} = 1$), although the difference between the coordinated and the Nash policy responses is smaller. As the impact of the shock on Italy declines, the EMS policies become more restrictive than the Nash policies. Coordination in both EMS regimes is unfavorable for Germany. Italy suffers a welfare loss under the symmetric EMS. However, the asymmetric EMS is favorable to Italy, if $c_{21} = .5$ and unfavorable if $c_{21} = -1$. Again, the alleged hegemony of the Bundesbank turns out to be beneficial to Italy.

The final panel considers a U.S.-German demand shock of unit size. The fixed exchange-rate arrangements perform differently than before. With a positive effect of the shock on the United States the symmetric and the asymmetric EMS yield worse outcomes than the Nash solutions for Germany and Italy. But if the shock affects the United States in the opposite direction, Germany gains in both fixed exchange-rate systems. This is consistent with the conjecture that Germany has a preference for the EMS when there are significant shifts in the relative demand for German and U.S. assets. However, the German interest in the EMS in this case runs counter to the Italian preference for flexible exchange rates.

The Robustness of the Welfare Gains from Coordination

These results underscore the importance of the symmetry assumption for the desirability of policy coordination in the EMS. They imply that the robustness of the welfare benefits from EMS coordination to stochastic asymmetries is a critical aspect of the cooperative interpretation of the EMS. The less robust its benefits are, the more likely the EMS results in a welfare loss for at least one participant (if asymmetries are empirically significant). But as long as the member countries can withdraw freely and unilaterally from the system, the EMS cannot survive if it leaves one or more members with lower welfare levels than those achievable under Nash equilibrium. Realizing that it could fare better with an independent policy, the losing member would revert to the Nash strategy. Consequently, the degree of asymmetries is critical for the stability of the arrangement. We now evaluate the robustness of the gains of the two EMS regimes in more detail.

Let the realization of the world supply shock be $\xi_2 = -1$, which guarantees benefits from the EMS if no other shocks occur. To measure the robustness of the welfare benefits from coordination in the presence of, say, a European supply shock, we compute the range of values of this shock for which coordination yields a benefit to both Germany and Italy. This range can be found by simulating the model with a given parameterization, but with different realizations of the shock, and identifying those simulations in which the German and Italian utility levels increase relative to their Nash levels. We call this range the maximum acceptable range (MAR) for the European supply shock. By definition, a realization of the shock outside its MAR means that at least one country is worse off in the EMS. The system would therefore break down when such a realization occurs. Thus, the smaller the MAR, the less robust are the benefits from coordination, and the less stable is the EMS regime.

MARs for the European demand shock and the U.S.-German demand shock are defined in a similar way. Given the world supply shock, the MAR for each shock is a function of the relevant impact parameter a_{21}, c_{21}, or c_{31}, which determines the degree of stochastic asymmetries among the European countries. Therefore, by varying the parameters a_{21}, c_{21}, and a_{31}, we can show how a changing degree of asymmetry affects the robustness of the benefits from the EMS. Note that the size of the MARs and their midpoints depend on the realization of the world supply shock. Although the location seems of little interest, the MARs should therefore be interpreted as indicating the relative size of the three shocks compared to a global shock, which the EMS can support.

To calculate the MARs, we take values of a_{21}, c_{21}, and c_{31} over the interval from –1.0 to 1.0, proceeding in increments of 0.1. The European supply shock, the European demand shock, and the U.S.-German demand shock are each given values between –1.5 to 1.5, also in increments of 0.1. Figure 6.1 shows the values of MARs from the simulations using the baseline model and changing values of import expenditure share. The line marked with "." refers to the asymmetric case, the "+" line to the symmetric case. The pair of lines closest to 0.23 refer to the baseline model. Both types of fixed exchange-rate regimes support only very small MARs for all three types of shocks. The smallest ranges occur for the European demand and supply shocks when their impact on Italy is exactly opposite to the impact on Germany ($a_{21} = -1$, or $c_{21} = -1$). Under such

FIGURE 6.1 MARs With Rising Import Expenditure Shares

A. European Supply Shock

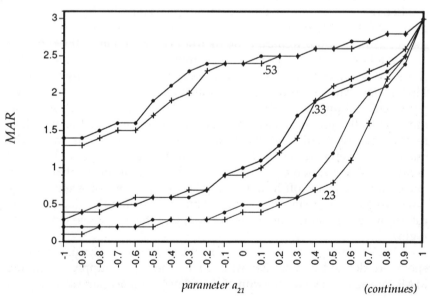

parameter a_{21} (continues)

FIGURE 6.1   MARs With Rising Import Expenditure Shares *(continued)*

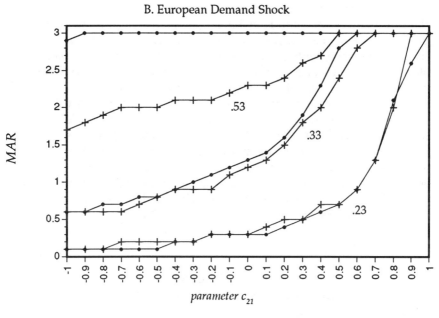

B. European Demand Shock

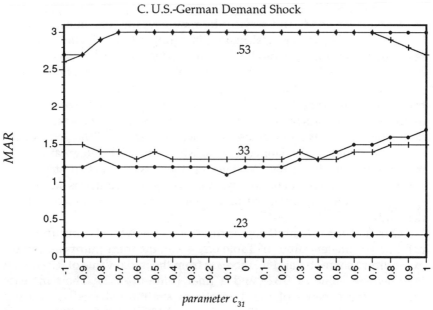

C. U.S.-German Demand Shock

MAR = maximum acceptable range
a_{21}, c_{21}, and c_{31} determine the asymmetry of the shocks

conditions, the EMS is viable if European demand shocks are no greater that 10 percent of the current global shock. The asymmetric EMS is viable if European supply shocks are up to 20 percent of the global shock, and the symmetric EMS again is viable if European shocks do not exceed 10 percent of the global shocks. Thus, the benefits from coordination in the fixed rate arrangements disappear even in the presence of relatively small shocks if the member countries are affected differentially. The robustness of the EMS to European shocks improves gradually but slowly as the shocks become more symmetric. Only if a_{21} and c_{21} exceed 0.5 can the system support European shocks that equal the size of the global shock. In contrast, the robustness to U.S.-German demand shocks does not change with the impact parameter c_{31}. Note that the MARs of the asymmetric EMS are larger than the MARs of the symmetric EMS with respect to the European shocks, unless the impact parameters approach unity. This indicates that in the baseline simulations, the asymmetric design of the decisionmaking processes in the EMS raises the robustness of the system.

6.5 Policy Coordination in the EMS and the Process of European Integration

The EC's Single-Market program aims at completing integration of the markets for goods and services by removing the remaining nontariff barriers to trade and financial market integration through elimination of regulations prohibiting cross-border business in financial services. In the context of our analysis, we hypothesize that the program will bring about two major structural changes in the European economies. First, intra-EC trade will increase and a larger share of total expenditures will be spent on European imports by the member countries. Second, financial markets deregulation is bound to increase the interest elasticity of the demand for money as it did in the United States, when financial deregulation was implemented in the 1980s. We take up these issues in two steps, first considering the consequences of increasing expenditure shares on imports (price elasticities of demand) and then interest elasticities of money demand.

Our first set of simulations proceeds as follows. Starting from the baseline parameter values of Table 6.2, we let the intra-European import expenditure shares b_{12} and b_{21} increase from the initial value of 0.229 to an intermediate value of 0.329 and a final value of 0.529. Their increase comes at the expense of the domestic expenditure shares b_{11} and b_{22}, which decline from 0.72 to 0.62 and then to 0.42. That is, our paradigm of trade integration is trade creation as opposed to trade diversion, i.e., substituting European imports for U.S. imports. As a result of these changes, the monetary spillover index between the European countries, K_{12}, goes from 0.62 to 0.79 and 0.96; the spillover of U.S. monetary policy on Europe goes from 0.18 to 0.09 and 0.02. Trade integration increases the importance of the intra-European spillover and diminishes the importance of the U.S.-European spillover.

In the second set of simulations, we start again from the parameter values of Table 6.2 and let the interest elasticities of money demand change from the initial value of −.0223 to −.1123. Again, the monetary spillover index between the two European countries increases from 0.62 to 1.16. However, the coefficient between the United States and Europe moves in the same direction, from 0.18 to 0.31. Financial integration, unlike trade integration, increases the importance of spillover between the European countries and between Europe and the United States.

Figure 6.1 shows the MARs with increasing European import expenditure shares, increasing interest elasticities. Again, "." lines refer to the asymmetric EMS and "+" lines to the symmetric EMS. The central message of the figures is that the structural changes increase the MARs for all shocks and thus increase the scope for beneficial policy coor-

FIGURE 6.2 MARs With Rising Interest Elasticity Money Demand

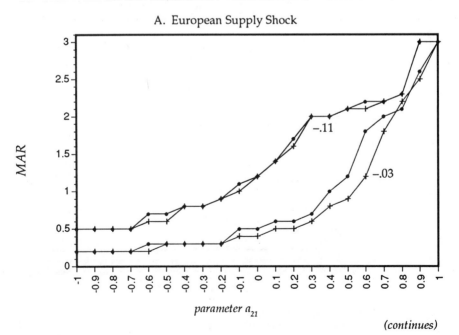

A. European Supply Shock

(continues)

FIGURE 6.2 MARs With Rising Interest Elasticity Money Demand *(continued)*

B. European Demand Shock

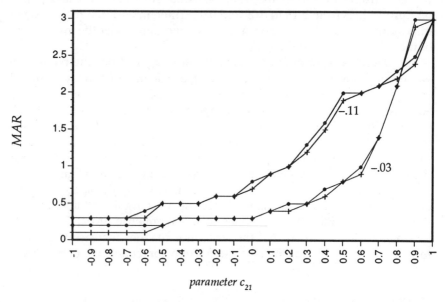

C. U.S.-German Demand Shock

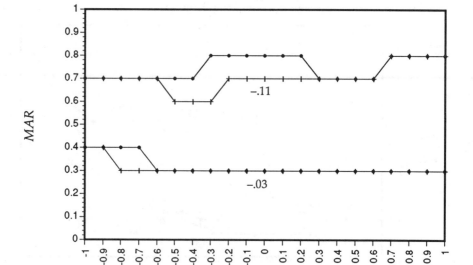

MAR = maximum acceptable range
a_{21}, c_{21}, and c_{31} determine the asymmetry of the shocks

dination. There are, however, some marked differences between the two sets of simulations. Higher import expenditure shares raise the MARs considerably for both EMS regimes and all three types of shocks. With large import expenditure shares, the robustness of the asymmetric and the symmetric EMS to European supply shocks is about the same; however, the symmetric EMS is remarkably more robust to European demand shocks. Financial integration has a much smaller effect on the robustness of the EMS. The MARs, although rising with the much higher interest elasticity of money demand, remain small. As before, however, the robustness of the two EMS regimes becomes more similar as the interest elasticities increase.

EMS Policy Coordination and the Role of Side Payments

These simulations indicate that the scope for welfare-improving policy coordination is severely limited by stochastic asymmetries. As already noted, there are three possible reasons for this observation: The first was raised by Rogoff (1985c) and Canzoneri and Henderson (1988, 1991 ch. 3). A coalition of a subgroup of players may have a worse set of equilibrium outcomes than independent players have individually because the outsiders' optimal response to the coalition is different from their optimal response to noncoordinated policies. The second is that fixing exchange rates may be a bad rule for cooperation because of the loss of desirable degrees of freedom in the adjustment to asymmetric shocks. The final explanation is that the distribution of the gains from coordination becomes uneven in the presence of asymmetries, so that one country may lose from coordination when the other gains.

These three possibilities have very different policy implications. In the first case, the best reaction of the group is to return to independent policymaking or to include the outsiders in the arrangement. In the second case, it would be necessary to regain the lost degrees of freedom, either by loosening the exchange-rate constraint—for example, allowing frequent realignments—or by trying to achieve cooperation with flexible rates. In the third case, coordination is beneficial to the group, but the partners need to solve the distribution problem; because no change in the basic design of EMS policy coordination is required, it is of interest to find out how important the distribution problem is for the robustness of the EMS compared to the other two potential sources of instability.

In the general context of game-theoretic analysis, the problem of distributing the gains from cooperation can be solved by introducing side payments—that is, by allowing the winning partner to transfer a part of its welfare gain to the losing partner and induce it to keep the arrangement. This may sound very technical at first, but the EC and the EMS do have institutional provisions facilitating transfer payments among the members. Regional development programs in the Community, as well as the credit mechanisms of the EMS with their implicit subsidies, can be interpreted as versions of side payments; they are institutions created to compensate members for possible disadvantages of EMS membership. Thus, the concept of side payments is not an unrealistic one in our context.

Even without modeling the exact nature of such side payments and how they are implemented, it is clear that a necessary condition for side payments to stabilize the EMS is that coordination increases the sum of the participants' utilities. Otherwise, either both partners lose or one gains exactly what the other loses, and there is no room for side payments to uphold the arrangement. To see how side payments change the robustness of European policy coordination, we determine the maximum ranges the various shocks in the model can take so that policy coordination in the EMS increases the sum of the German and Italian utility functions. We call these ranges the maximum acceptable ranges with side payments, MARSP. Again, the smaller the MARSP for a given type of shock, the less robust are the welfare benefits from coordination for the group as a whole, and the more likely coordination breaks down even with side payments.

Figures 6.3 and 6.4 report the values of MARSP for the three types of shocks and the changes in the two structural parameters; in essence these two figures are the exact counterparts of Figures 6.1 and 6.2. Like MARs, MARSPs decline as the impact effects of the European supply and demand shocks become more asymmetric. A comparison of these simulations with the corresponding ones without side payments reveals the importance of side payments in overcoming the limits of policy coordination. It should be noted that the reported results do not indicate the direction of the side payments. From the baseline simulations in Table 6.3, we know that depending on the size, sign, and type of the shock, payments can either go to Germany or Italy.[15]

The baseline simulations tell us that for a European supply or demand shock, the MARSPs of the asymmetric EMS exceed the corresponding MARs by a factor of three; the MARSPs of the symmetric EMS exceed the corresponding MARs by a factor of six if the shock affects Germany positively and Italy negatively. Thus, side payments contribute positively to the robustness of the gains from coordination. Even so, however, the ranges remain fairly small: as long as a_{21} and c_{21} are negative, the European shocks must not significantly exceed the global shocks, and they must remain much smaller if the two parameters approach negative one. The more equal the effect of the shocks in both countries, the smaller is the increase in MARSPs relative to MARs. Thus, the potential of side then

FIGURE 6.3 MARSPs With Rising Import Expenditure Shares

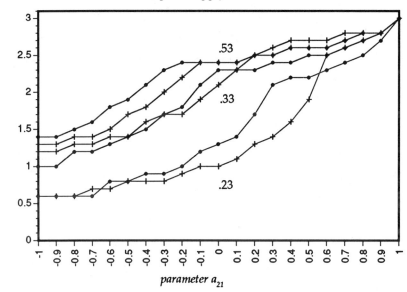

A. European Supply Shock

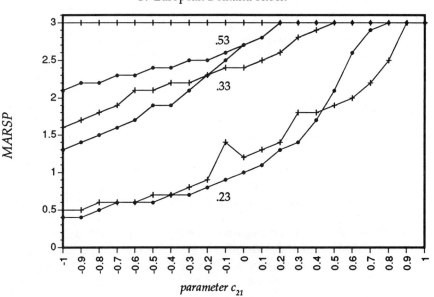

B. European Demand Shock

(continued)

FIGURE 6.3 MARSPs With Rising Import Expenditure Shares *(continued)*

C. U.S.-German Demand Shock

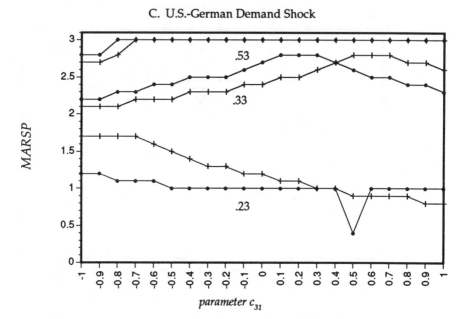

parameter c_{31}

MARSP = maximum acceptable range with side payments
a_{21}, c_{21}, and c_{31} determine the asymmetry of the shocks

payments to increase the robustness of the EMS seems rather limited. This potential is greatest in the case of U.S.-German demand shocks. In the baseline simulation, MARSPs exceed MARs by a factor of about three for both EMS regimes. In conclusion, the call for transfer mechanisms in the EMS is justified most of all on the basis of the assumption that most European shocks are weakly or negatively correlated, or that shocks originating outside the EMS and affecting only one EMS country are the dominant source of disturbances.

MARSPs rise as the import expenditure shares and the money demand interest elasticities increase; the implications of deeper economic integration are therefore qualitatively similar to those for the system without side payments. Figure 6.3 reveals that with higher import expenditure shares under the two demand shocks, the ranges of the symmetric EMS and the asymmetric EMS become more similar and approach the maximum value of three. We can interpret this result to mean that increasing goods market integration eliminates the importance of side payments in the presence of asymmetric demand shocks. The same is not true for European supply shocks. Here, MARSPs first rise and

FIGURE 6.4 MARSPs With Rising Interest Elasticity Money Demand

A. European Supply Shock

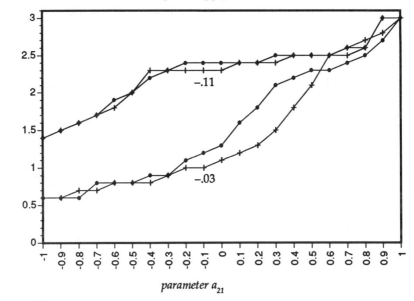

parameter a₂₁

B. European Demand Shock

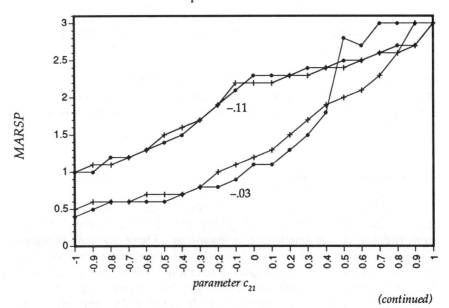

parameter c₂₁

(continued)

FIGURE 6.4 MARSPs With Rising Interest Elasticity Money Demand (continued)

C. U.S.-German Demand Shock

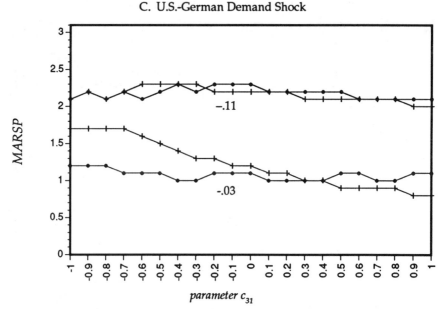

MARSP = maximum acceptable range
a_{21}, c_{21}, and c_{31} determine the asymmetry of the shocks

decline with trade integration. Comparing Figure 6.1 with Figure 6.3, we find side payments are useful to stabilize the EMS with modest trade integration. However, with very deep integration, MARSPs fall back to the levels of MARs, indicating that the distribution problem loses relevance. Figures 6.2 and 6.4 suggest that deeper financial market integration lowers the importance of side payments, although less so than with trade integration.

Other Simulation Results

Hughes-Hallett and Minford (1990) present simulation exercises to demonstrate the impact of EMS policy coordination on the economic performance of the participating countries. These authors compare alternative policy paths, which have the same starting year, to reduce inflation and stimulate output growth over a fixed time horizon. Hughes-Hallett and Minford (1989) and Minford (1988) present simulations of two-year monetary expansions in individual EMS countries. The simulations are performed using the Liverpool multicountry model, which includes Germany, France, Italy, and the United Kingdom as ERM members, together with a number of outsiders. Hughes-Hallett and Minford compare noncooperative and cooperative regimes in which exchange rates are with an EMS in which Germany unilaterally determines money growth for all participants and realignments occur in fixed, predetermined intervals. EMS exchange rates are allowed to fluctuate within margins of ±3 percent.

Mindford and Hughes-Hallett's simulations produce welfare gains from the EMS that are small and badly distributed among the participants. The distributional problem can be alleviated by weakening Germany's assumed dominant position in an "equal shares" coalition or one that is required to yield at least the same welfare as do uncoordinated policies for all members. The authors conclude that EMS policy coordination achieves little and seems difficult to sustain, because the gains are easily offset by additional adverse shocks. It remains unclear, however, to what extent their results depend on their peculiar specification of the EMS. Apart from treating the United Kingdom as a member of the ERM, they treat realignments unrealistically. The assumed fixed periodicity of realignments contradicts the historical record (see Table 2.3) as well as Begg and Wyplosz's (1987) theoretical result that the timing of realignments is an important strategic variable in the type of policy problems considered. In the Liverpool model, the anticipation of a realignment triggers increases in contract wages and prices that lead to a real appreciation of the currency and a loss of competitiveness, hence output and employment, before the realignment takes place. In this setup, monetary policy in the EMS countries other than Germany has perverse effects: real interest rates and exchange rates rise, and output falls in response to a monetary expansion. These effects can be alleviated by imposing capital controls that cut the link between domestic and foreign interest rates.

Hughes-Hallett and Minford (1989) use the same model to evaluate how the EMS copes with country-specific shocks to the real exchange rate or the demand for money, or with a shock common to all, such as higher oil prices. They compare noncooperative and cooperative policies under floating rates with a noncooperative EMS dominated by the Bundesbank and a cooperative EMS with joint decisionmaking. The results are rather negative for the EMS: coordination improves upon the noncooperative EMS in only one case, and even there the group's gains are negligible. But in view of the preceding theoretical analysis, these negative results are not entirely surprising. We have seen that the quality of exchange-rate management as a surrogate for cooperation depends crucially on the relative importance of asymmetric shocks. The country-specific shocks considered by Hughes-Hallett and Minford are examples of rather large asymmetries, and the focus of the analysis on such shocks leads one to expect negative results.

6.6 Empirical Evidence of EMS Coordination

Padoa-Schioppa (1985a) and Ungerer (1990) argue that realignments have become the most important aspect of EMS policy coordination in practice. The members have gradually developed bargaining and joint decisionmaking procedures for realignments. More often than not, realignments have been combined with other measures of economic policy (Ungerer et al., 1986 Tables 6 and 10). However, realignments can at best achieve only retroactive coordination—a coordinated solution to policy incongruence committed in the past. During the second half of the 1980s, realignments have become much less frequent. Together with the dismantling of capital controls, this is often interpreted as evidence for closer advance coordination in the EMS (Giavazzi and Spaventa, 1990), which is more in the spirit of the cooperative interpretation.

Beyond such general assessments, the policy coordination in the EMS is hard to evaluate empirically. The literature has proposed to measure coordination in terms of the convergence and correlation of EMS central bank operating targets, such as money growth and money-market interest rates. Rogoff (1985b) and Ungerer, et al. (1986) are skeptical about policy coordination in the EMS because money growth rates in the participating countries showed little convergence in the first half of the 1980s and have remained low since then (Russo and Tullio 1988). In contrast, Weber (1990) reports that money supply shocks have become more symmetric in the EMS, an observation that is consistent with closer coordination of monetary expansions. But this evidence is difficult to interpret, because coordination may well require divergent monetary developments depending on the nature of the underlying shocks.

The evidence on EMS interest rate comovements is more favorable to the hypothesis of policy coordination in the EMS. Ungerer et al. (1986) report that the correlation of money-market rates between Germany and the smaller EMS countries increased between 1979 and 1985. Russo and Tullio (1988) use principal components analysis to show that interest rate movements in the EMS countries increasingly depend on a common factor explaining more than 75 percent of the cumulative variance. Kirchgässner and Wolters (1991) perform regression analysis showing that EMS interest rates have become more interactive in the 1980s and find that EMS interest rates followed a common trend in the sense of being cointegrated in the 1980s but not in the 1970s. Weber (1990, 17) separates symmetric from asymmetric interest rate movements in the EMS and shows that the symmetric component dominated in the 1980s. If money-market rates are viewed as the main operating targets in the EMS countries (see Chapter 5), these results give credence to the hypothesis that the EMS has fostered policy coordination.

6.7 Conclusions

In this chapter, we have analyzed the cooperative interpretation of the EMS. The essence of this view is that fixing exchange rates serves as a surrogate for more complete, welfare-improving cooperation among central banks. The main advantage of an exchange-rate arrangement as a cooperative device is that the agreement is easy to monitor. This mitigates the threat to the stability of central bank cooperation arising from the conflict between individual and collective interest. But this advantage comes at the expense of losing the degree of freedom that exchange-rate flexibility provides in the adjustment to asymmetric shocks. As a result, the desirability of the EMS and the distribution of the welfare gains it achieves depend critically on the relative size of asymmetric and symmetric shocks and on the correlation pattern between these two.

Our simulations underline this critical role of stochastic asymmetries in determining the benefits from policy coordination in the EMS. The numerical results, though naturally suffering from the limitations of model simulations, suggest several generalizations. First, asymmetries among the participating countries strongly reduce the scope for policy coordination on the basis of fixed exchange rates. Second, economic integration among the participants of an exchange-rate system raises the robustness of the gains from coordination. Our results indicate that trade integration contributes more to robustness than does financial integration, although this particular finding may result from the rather narrow aspects of financial integration we have considered. Our results suggest that economic and financial deregulation in the Single-Market Program promises to strengthen monetary policy coordination in the EMS.

It seems plausible to assume that asymmetric demand and supply shocks in Europe arise predominantly from independent monetary and fiscal policies in the individual countries, including government inter-ventions in individual markets to regulate market forces or to redistribute income. If this is true, the Single-Market process will have two consequences for the importance of stochastic asymmetries. In the short run, stochastic asymmetries will become more important as idiosyncratic market interventions are removed. In the long run, stochastic asymmetries will lose importance as greater mobility of goods, services, and productive factors reduce the scope and incentives for independent market intervention. The results in this chapter indicate that the robustness of monetary policy coordination in the EMS will first deteriorate and then improve as a consequence. This suggests that any attempt for more complete coordination or for making the EMS a tighter constraint should be postponed until the Single Market has been achieved.

Third, our results indicate that alternative rules of decisionmaking in the EMS exhibit different robustness properties. The asymmetric EMS, in which a dominant Bundesbank alone directs monetary policy, is more robust to European supply shocks and less robust to European demand shocks than is a symmetric EMS, in which monetary policy is planned cooperatively. As trade integration proceeds, the two arrangements become more alike in their robustness to European supply shocks, but the greater robustness of the symmetric EMS to European demand shocks remains. The expected progress with the Single Market thus makes collective decisionmaking increasingly desirable. This may explain why the demands to overcome an alleged Bundesbank hegemony have grown stronger since the Single-Market program was started.

Finally, we have investigated the role side payments play in overcoming the problem of the unequal distribution of the welfare gains from EMS policy coordination in the presence of asymmetries. Although side payments can improve the robustness of the EMS, our results show that trade integration is even more effective to alleviate the distribution problem. Together with the earlier results, this suggests that the European countries should spend more time and effort to advance the integration process than to implement and administer side payments. Such payments produce the greatest benefit when shocks originate outside the region and affect fully only one member. But if this were the case, the desirability of fixed exchange rates among the EC countries—and ultimately one currency—would be very much in doubt in the first place.

Notes

1. A Nash equilibrium is the outcome of a strategic game in which each party maximizes its objectives by taking the actions of the other party (or parties) as given. A Nash equilibrium is deemed to be the optimal noncooperative decision.

2. Wyplosz (1988) argues that several members asked for changes in the institutional design of the EMS in the mid-1980s because the system had by then fulfilled the role of overcoming the inflationary environment of the late 1970s.

3. More generally, the cooperative game entails the maximization of the joint preference function $aU + (1 - a)U^*$, $0 < a < 1$, where "a" is determined in a bargaining process.

4. The condition $\alpha + \varepsilon < 2$ ensures that $(\sigma + (\alpha + \varepsilon)^2) k_n h_n < (\sigma + \alpha (\alpha + 2\varepsilon)) k_c h_c$. The condition holds unless the real exchange-rate elasticity of aggregate demand is very small.

5. Note that international agreements to coordinate monetary policies lack effective enforcement mechanisms to keep countries from cheating.

6. See Canzoneri and Gray (1985), Canzoneri and Henderson (1988), Mélitz (1985), Laskar (1986), Fratianni and von Hagen (1990a). This situation must be distinguished from the case of one country adopting the exchange rate as the policy instrument.

7. Mélitz (1985) argues that the exchange-rate arrangement is superior to cooperation under such circumstances because it saves the cost of repeated bargaining over a joint policy otherwise.

8. In the EC, exchange-rate fixity is valued for its positive effects on the customs union and therefore constitutes an additional common good achieved in the arrangement. Preserving this common good will induce an EMS central bank to tolerate (at least temporarily) an outcome otherwise worse than the Nash equilibrium. Thus, in the presence of relative shocks among the participating countries, an exchange-rate peg may be a more stable arrangement than full coordination with flexible exchange rates.

9. The previous relative demand shock η is now the average of two shocks, one originating in each country, $\eta = (\eta_1 + \eta_2)/2$.

10. Note that in a repeated game context the incentive to overstate the domestic shock is limited only to the extent that the foreign central bank can monitor the true shock after the fact.

11. Note that ε depends on the degree of international economic integration between the two countries.

12. In the present model, the reduced-form effect of stochastic shocks to the individual money demand functions is similar to the effect of aggregate demand shocks.

13. The use of national income instead of GNP as a measure of aggregate demand is justified by the fact that our model neglects capital consumption.

14. Thus, for example, Germany's total import share of 27.8 percent is allocated between Italy (15.4 percent) and the United States (12.4 percent).

15. Our simulations also do not indicate the size of the side payments required to stabilize the EMS. We explore this issue in Chapter 9.

7

Exchange-Rate and Inflation
Uncertainty in the EMS

The December 1978 resolution of the European Council in Brussels described the purpose of the EMS as "establishing a greater measure of monetary stability in Europe" (see Chapter 2). According to Ungerer and his colleagues (1983), monetary stability has two aspects: internal stability (stability of cost and prices) and external stability (stability of exchange rates). The key word "stability" can be interpreted in a variety of ways. One is the stability of *levels*, that is, price stability and exchange-rate fixity. Chapter 2 looked at the performance of the EMS using this concept of stability. But stability can also be interpreted in terms of *conditional variance*, which we consider in this chapter. Specifically, we interpret "greater monetary stability" as being reduced variance of exchange rates and inflation rates around their expected values—that is, reduced exchange-rate and inflation uncertainty.

The cooperative view of the EMS implies that policy coordination reduces exchange-rate and inflation uncertainty and results in greater symmetry of variations in inflation rates. The interpretation of monetary stability in terms of uncertainty corresponds well with this view. Three issues are at stake. First, has the EMS reduced uncertainty about EMS exchange rates and EMS inflation? Second, given that EMS policymakers have often expressed concerns that intra-EMS exchange rates are destabilized by speculative capital flows between the United States and Germany, has the EMS been able to sever the link between EMS exchange rates and unexpected fluctuations in the DM/U.S. dollar rate? Finally, to what extent has the EMS achieved greater symmetry of inflation rates?

7.1 Modeling Exchange-Rate
and Inflation Uncertainty

We define exchange-rate and inflation uncertainty in terms of conditional variances: exchange-rate (inflation) uncertainty increases if the variance of the one-period-ahead exchange-rate prediction error increases.[1] Similarly, we use conditional covariances between EMS and non-EMS exchange rates (the covariances of their respective prediction errors) to measure the link between non-EMS rates and EMS rates. In this section, we explain our methodology to test for changes in uncertainty.

Our analysis is based on Engle's (1982) Autoregressive Conditional Heteroskedasticity (ARCH) approach to modeling time-variant conditional variances and covariances. ARCH models build on the notion that the conditional second moments of a time series follow a dynamic process that can be represented in a parametric model. Two characteristics of ARCH models make them attractive for our purposes. First, they are compatible with the common observation that exchange-rate distributions are leptokurtic.[2] Second, the specification of a parametric model for the conditional variances gives rise to straightforward hypothesis testing for variance stability.

Let x_t be a mean-stationary stochastic process and $E(x_t | I_{t-1})$ its conditional expectation given the information set I_{t-1}. Define $\xi_t = x_t - E(x_t | I_{t-1})$ as the one-period-ahead prediction error with a normal distribution. The ARCH model stipulates that the conditional variance of x_t, $\sigma_t^2 = E(\xi_t^2 | I_{t-1})$ follows an autoregressive stochastic process:

$$(7.1) \qquad \sigma_t^2 = \sigma_0^2 + \sum_{i=1}^{n} \beta_i \xi_{t-i}^2,$$

with $\beta_i \geq 0$, $i = 1, \ldots, n$. Intuitively, equation (7.1) says that the conditional variance of x increases following one or several large prediction errors. That is, large prediction errors raise the probability of further large errors, but large errors are less likely following small errors. This specification accommodates the observation that large (and small) exchange rate changes tend to be clustered over time. Stability of the variance process requires that the characteristic equation

$$(7.2) \qquad 1 - \sum_{i=1}^{n} \beta_i \lambda^i = 0$$

has no roots $|\lambda_i| \geq 1$. From (7.1), we obtain the unconditional variance of the prediction error as

(7.3)
$$E(\xi_t^2) = \sigma_\xi^2 = \sigma_0^2 / (1 - \sum_{i=1}^{n} \beta_i).$$

The variance in (7.3) is the steady-state solution of the conditional variance of the process $(x_t) = (x_0, x_1, ..., x_T, x_{T+1}, ...)$, given a sequence of information sets $(I_{t-1}) = (I_{-1}, I_0, ..., I_{T-1}, I_T, ...)$. We focus on this variance as the basic measure of uncertainty about (x_t).

Let $\hat{\xi}_t$ be an estimated prediction error of x_t from an econometric forecast model. The parameters of the variance model (7.1) can be estimated by regressing $\hat{\xi}_t^2$ on a constant and its own lags. If the likelihood function of ξ_t is separable in the parameters of (7.1) and the parameters of the conditional expectation, $E(x_t | I_{t-1})$, least-squares estimates are asymptotically consistent and normal.[3] Consequently, we can apply Wald or LaGrange multiplier tests for changes in these parameters.[4]

Consider the following ARCH regression as an example:

(7.4)
$$\hat{\xi}_t^2 = \sigma_0^2 + \sigma_1^2 D_t + \beta_1 \hat{\xi}_{t-1}^2 + \beta_2 D_t \hat{\xi}_{t-1}^2 + v_t,$$

where D_t is a dummy variable with $D_t = 0$, $t < t^*$, and $D_t = 1$, $t \geq t^*$. From this regression, a test that the long-run solution (7.3) of the conditional variance of x_t has decreased after t^* involves a test of the hypotheses $H_1: \sigma_1^2 < 0$, $H_2: \beta_2 < 0$, or both. Of course, the composite parameters $(\sigma_0^2 + \sigma_1^2)$ and $(\beta_1 + \beta_2)$ must still be positive. Variations of (7.4) form the basis of our analysis of uncertainty in the EMS.

Time-varying conditional covariances between two stochastic processes can be defined in an analogous way.[5] Thus, let (y_t) be a mean-stationary stochastic process with expectation $E(y_t | I_{t-1})$, and let $\theta_t = y_t - E(y_t | I_{t-1})$ be the normally distributed prediction error. Let $h_t = \theta_t \xi_t$. The autoregressive conditional covariance (ARCC) process is

(7.5)
$$\sigma_{\eta\xi,t} = \gamma_0 + \sum_{j=1}^{m} \gamma_j h_{t-j},$$

where again we require stability of the characteristic equation. As earlier, the unconditional covariance of the error process is

(7.6)
$$\sigma_{\theta\xi} = \gamma_0 / (1 - \sum_{j=1}^{m} \gamma_j),$$

the steady-state solution for the conditional covariance of (x_t) and (y_t). Our tests of changes in covariances are based on regression equations like (7.4), which involve estimates of the residual product h_t.

7.2 Nominal and Real Exchange-Rate Uncertainty in the EMS

In this section, we first consider the conditional variance processes of nominal DM exchange rates of four EMS and four non-EMS currencies: the Belgian franc, the French franc, the Italian lira, the Dutch guilder, the U.S. dollar, the Canadian dollar, the Japanese yen, and the pound sterling. All exchange rates are weekly London quotations reported by the Harris Bank, *Foreign Exchange Weekly Review*. DM rates were derived from U.S. dollar rates on the assumption that triangular arbitrage holds. The sample period spans January 1977-October 1988. We define the following subsamples: "Pre-EMS" from January 1977 to March 9, 1979; "EMSI" from March 16, 1979, to April 1, 1983; and "EMSII" from April 8, 1983, to October 14, 1988. The split of the sample is motivated by the observation that the more significant changes in EMS inflation trends have occurred after the realignment of March 1983, which also marked the end of the Mitterrand experiment in France (see Chapters 2 and 3).

A major problem in the analysis of exchange-rate uncertainty is the treatment of realignments. Realignments are by definition discrete events that should be distinguished from the daily variation of exchange rates between realignments because their probability distribution is necessarily different. Their contribution to exchange-rate uncertainty in the EMS therefore deserves special attention. Clearly, realignments cannot be expected with certainty because the system then would be exposed to speculative attacks (Wyplosz 1986). Casual inspection of market predictors such as forward rates, on the other hand, shows that realignments are not totally unexpected (Collins 1988). Our strategy is to assume a worst-case scenario for the EMS in which all realignments are completely unexpected. Computing exchange-rate uncertainty under this assumption yields an empirical upper bound of the true uncertainty in the EMS. To the extent that realignments are partly anticipated, our assumption biases the comparison of exchange-rate uncertainty in the EMS to pre-EMS uncertainty against the EMS. It follows that if the upper bound is found to be below pre-EMS levels, the same must be true for the true uncertainty level.

Let $s_{i,t}$ be the logarithm of the DM exchange rate of currency i (DM per unit of currency i). It is generally accepted that nominal exchange rates follow random walks. Hence, we assume

(7.7) $$\Delta s_{i,t} = \alpha_{it} + \xi_{it},$$

where α_{it} is the stochastic process generating the realignments and ξ_{it} is the process of weekly innovations. We assume $E(\xi_{it} | I_{t-1}) = E(\xi_{it}\alpha_{it} | I_{t-1}) = 0$ and the worst scenario, $E(\alpha_{it}) = E(\alpha_{it} | I_{t-1}) = 0$. To obtain estimates of the realizations of α_{it}, we first regress $\Delta s_{i,t}$ on a set of eleven realignment dummies. The estimate of the process $\alpha_{i,t}$ has zeros except on dates immediately following a realignment. On realignment dates, we define the dummy coefficient as the realization of $\alpha_{i,t}$. Correspondingly, the estimated variance of α_{it}, $\sigma_{\alpha i}^2$ is

(7.8) $$\hat{\sigma}_{\alpha i}^2 = T^{-1} \sum_{t=1}^{T} \hat{\alpha}_{it}^2.$$

Our estimates of the exchange-rate innovations ξ_t are obtained by subtracting the estimated realignment process from the actual change in the exchange rate. They are used to estimate and test the ARCH specification. Table 7.1 displays the steady-state conditional variances of weekly DM rates of EMS currencies, together with the estimated variances of the realignment process. The p-values in this table indicate the marginal significance levels of rejecting the relevant hypothesis of stability of the conditional variance process. The table shows that the conditional variances of weekly fluctuations between realignments has decreased in three of four cases in EMSI, the exception being the Belgian franc. However, if we take the variance estimate of the realignment process into account, the EMS in its first phase has reduced uncertainty only for the lira, but it may have increased uncertainty for the Belgian and French francs. In contrast, exchange-rate uncertainty has been reduced in all four cases during the second phase.

The first part of Table 7.2 shows the corresponding steady-state solutions of the conditional variances of non-EMS DM rates along its main diagonal. Here, we find that uncertainty greatly increased for the U.S. dollar, the yen, and the pound during the first EMS phase. In the second phase of the EMS, there is a further increase in uncertainty about the U.S. and the Canadian dollar rates but a reduction in the uncertainty about the yen and the pound exchange rates. A comparison of Table 7.1 and the second part of Table 7.2 reveals that the EMS has strongly reduced uncertainty about DM exchange rates inside the system, but—with the possible exception of the DM/yen rate—exchange-rate uncertainty with regard to nonmember currencies has increased.

The upper half of Table 7.2 reports the conditional covariances of weekly DM exchange-rate changes of member and nonmember

　　　　　　　　Exchange-Rate and Inflation Uncertainty in the EMS

TABLE 7.1 Conditional Variances of Weekly DM Nominal Exchange Rates

	Pre-EMS	EMSI		EMSII	
	σ_ξ^2	σ_α^2	σ_ξ^2	σ_α^2	σ_ξ^2
Belgium	1.30	1.72	2.03	0.59	0.09
p			0.017		0.053
France	2.56	1.57	1.81	0.82	0.03
p			0.002		0.001
Italy	5.68	2.45	0.15	1.40	0.07
p			0.001		0.001
Netherlands	1.00	0.86	0.16	0.78	0.00
p			0.069		0.001

Note: Subperiods are pre-EMS January 3, 1977, to March 9, 1979; EMSI March 16, 1979, to April 1, 1983; EMSII April 8, 1983, to October 14, 1988. σ_ξ^2 is the steady-state solution of the ARCH model; σ_α^2 is the variance of the realignment process. Both apply to weekly percentage changes of DM rates times 10. p is the marginal significance level of rejecting stability of the variance process in the relevant subperiod.

Source: Fratianni and von Hagen (1990c).

currencies; evidently, the EMS has changed the stochastic link between them. Of particular importance is the strong decline of the covariance between DM rates of EMS currencies and the DM/U.S. dollar rate. This is consistent with the hypothesis that the EMS has weakened the effects of speculative capital movements between dollar- and DM-denominated assets on EMS exchange rates. Similar results hold (with the exception of the Belgian franc) for the conditional covariances between DM rates of EMS currencies and the DM/Canadian dollar, DM/yen, and DM/pound sterling exchange rates.

Triangular arbitrage implies that we can use the information of Tables 7.1 and 7.2 to calculate the conditional variance of all exchange rates of the five EMS currencies with the four non-EMS currencies. Specifically, let $s_{ij,t}$ denote the logarithm of the exchange rate of EMS currency i with non-EMS currency j. The arbitrage condition $\Delta s_{ij,t} = \Delta s_{j,t} - \Delta s_{i,t}$ implies

(7.9) $\qquad E((\Delta s_{ij,t})^2 \mid I_{-1}) = E[(\Delta s_{i,t}) + (\Delta s_{j,t}) - 2 \Delta s_{i,t} \Delta s_{j,t} \mid I_{-1}],$

where $E((\Delta s_{i,t})^2 \mid I_{t-1})$ is the conditional variance of the DM price of

TABLE 7.2 Conditional Covariances of Weekly DM Nominal Exchange Rates

	United States			Canada			Japan			United Kingdom		
	Pre-EMS	EMSI	EMSII	Pre-EMS	EMSI	EMSII	Pre-EMS	EMSI	EMSII	Pre-EMS	EMSI	EMSII
EMS												
Belgium	1.56	1.27	0.99	1.25	1.10	0.40	0.80	1.31	0.30	1.20	1.30	0.80
p		0.045	0.013		0.036	0.041		0.001	0.145		0.001	0.018
France	3.42	1.44	1.00	2.90	1.30	0.47	3.20	0.89	0.10	3.10	1.40	1.10
p		0.011	0.011		0.001	0.001		0.028	0.001		0.001	0.003
Italy	7.86	3.79	2.88	5.40	2.20	0.47	3.10	2.50	1.00	7.90	3.50	3.10
p		0.001	0.028		0.001	0.034		0.117	0.034		0.001	0.001
Netherlands	1.80	1.26	0.78	1.11	1.15	0.05	0.80	0.90	0.10	1.80	1.30	0.70
p		0.179	0.478		0.267	0.040		0.118	0.195		0.234	0.001

Note: Subperiods are pre-EMS January 3, 1977, to March 9, 1979; EMSI March 16, 1979, to April 1, 1983; EMSII April 8, 1983, to October 14, 1988. Covariances are steady-state solutions of ARCC estimates. All covariances are multiplied by E + 5. Exchange rates are defined as DM per unit of foreign currency. p is the marginal significance level of rejecting stability of the covariance process in the relevant subsample.

Source: Fratianni and von Hagen (1990c).

(continues)

TABLE 7.2 Conditional Covariances of Weekly DM Nominal Exchange Rates (continued)

	United States			Canada			Japan			United Kingdom		
	Pre-EMS	EMSI	EMSII	Pre-EMS	EMSI	EMSII	Pre-EMS	EMSI	EMSII	Pre-EMS	EMSI	EMSII
Non-EMS												
United States	15.60	21.8	28.7	—	—	—	—	—	—	—	—	—
P		0.050	0.012									
Canada	17.20	15.60	27.30	19.20	17.70	27.00	—	—	—	—	—	—
P		0.117	0.069		0.074	0.068						
Japan	3.90	11.70	9.10	—	—	—	12.30	21.80	12.20	—	—	—
P		0.006	0.002					0.001	0.060			
United Kingdom	8.50	7.10	5.70	—	—	—	—	—	—	8.00	16.20	13.00
P		0.041	0.521								0.047	0.109

Note: Subperiods are pre-EMS January 3, 1977, to March 9, 1979; EMSI March 16, 1979, to April 1, 1983; EMSII April 8, 1983, to October 14, 1988. Covariances are steady-state solutions of ARCC estimates. All covariances are multiplied by E + 5. Exchange rates are defined as DM per unit of foreign currency. p is the marginal significance level of rejecting stability of the covariance process in the relevant subsample.

Source: Fratianni and von Hagen (1990c).

currency i and $E(\Delta s_{i,t} \Delta s_{j,t} | I_{t-1})$ is the conditional covariance of the DM price of currency i and currency j. Based on (7.9), we calculate the steady-state conditional variances of EMS to non-EMS currency exchange rates (such as the lira per dollar rate) and compute the changes in the EMSI and EMSII subperiods relative to the pre-EMS period. Table 7.3 shows the results, together with the relative changes in the steady-state values of the conditional variances of the DM exchange rates, excluding the variances resulting from realignments.[6]

The key message of Table 7.3 is that the EMS has reduced exchange-rate uncertainty between member currencies at the expense of greater exchange-rate uncertainty between member and nonmember currencies: Lower "internal" uncertainty has been accompanied by higher "external" uncertainty. This holds especially for the second EMS phase, and most strongly with respect to the U.S. dollar.

To consider "internal" exchange-rate uncertainty in more detail, let $a_{ij,t}$ denote the logarithm of the exchange rate between two EMS currencies, i and j, both different from the DM. Using the triangular arbitrage condition again we have:

TABLE 7.3 Relative Changes in Conditional Variances
of Weekly DM Exchange Rates

	EMSI					EMSII				
	Germany	United States	Canada	Japan	United Kingdom	Germany	United States	Canada	Japan	United Kingdom
Belgium	0.32	0.52	-0.04	0.74	1.22	-0.55	0.98	0.48	0.02	0.73
France	-0.39	0.81	0.04	1.55	1.31	-0.68	1.43	0.68	0.49	1.67
Germany	-0.40	-0.08	0.77	1.03	—	0.73	0.40	-0.01	0.63	—
Italy	-0.57	1.99	0.12	0.63	—	-0.75	3.37	0.68	-0.02	1.88
Nether-lands	-0.14	0.55	-0.09	0.78	1.67	-0.22	1.15	0.49	1.29	0.09

Note: Relative changes are defined as the differences between EMSI (EMSII) and pre-EMS conditional variances divided by the pre-EMS conditional variances. Conditional variances of EMS rates other than DM are computed from Tables 8 and 9.

Source: Fratianni and von Hagen (1990c).

$$(7.10) \qquad \frac{1}{6} \sum_{i=1}^{3} \sum_{j>i} E((\Delta a^2_{ij,t}) \mid I_{t-1}) =$$

$$\frac{1}{2} \sum_{i=1}^{4} E((\Delta s_{i,t})^2 \mid I_{t-1}) - \frac{1}{6} E((\sum_{i=1}^{4} \Delta s_{it})^2 \mid I_{t-1}).$$

The left-hand side of (7.10) is the average conditional variance of non-DM exchange rates in the EMS, such as the lira/French franc rate. The right-hand side shows how this average can be obtained from the sum of the conditional variances of the individual DM rates and the conditional variance of their sum. Comparing (7.10) before and after the EMS shows whether the reduced uncertainty about DM rates in the EMS was accompanied by a reduction, on average, of the uncertainty about other exchange rates in the EMS. Combining the estimates of Table 7.1 with the steady-state values of the sum of the conditional variances of the DM rates, we obtain estimates of the difference between the average variances (7.10) in the EMS and in the pre-EMS period:

EMSI	EMSII
0.20	− 0.21

Average uncertainty about non-DM exchange rates increased in the first four years of the EMS. Only in the second phase of the EMS was the average uncertainty reduced.

In summary, we find two distinct periods of EMS exchange-rate uncertainty. In its first phase, 1979 to early 1983, the EMS reduced uncertainty about nominal DM rates between realignments for three of the four currencies considered. However, we cannot reject the hypothesis that total uncertainty, which includes realignment uncertainty, remained the same or even increased. Furthermore, the reduction in DM-rate uncertainty was accompanied by higher uncertainty about non-DM rates in the EMS and about exchange rates with nonmember currencies. In the second phase, after March 1983, we find a general reduction of uncertainty about intra-EMS exchange rates, but this again was accompanied by an increase in uncertainty about exchange rates with outside currencies.

Next, we apply the same approach to the analysis of real exchange rates. We study DM rates for the same EMS members plus Denmark, for which the necessary data exist, and the same nonmembers as before. In this step, we employ monthly data from the *International Financial Statistics* published by the International Monetary Fund. All data are seasonally unadjusted. DM exchange rates are obtained from U.S. dollar rates; we assume again that triangular arbitrage holds. Real exchange-rate changes are defined with inflation differentials in terms of consumer price indexes. The net estimation sample runs from January 1983 to April 1988.

In contrast to nominal exchange rates, real exchange rates are not, in general, random walks. Hence, to obtain a prediction error for real rates, we must specify a forecast model. Following Rogoff (1985b), we specify empirical forecast models for the logarithmic differences of real exchange rates. Here we do not intend to test a structural model of real exchange rates; instead our models should produce forecasts based on available information. With a limited sample size, the number of regressors must, of course, also be limited; therefore, we chose a set of predictor variables that, under a variety of theoretical models, contain relevant information for real exchange rates vis-à-vis the DM: lagged first differences of the real exchange rates, a linear time trend, realignment dummies, lags of the differenced inflation, money growth and output growth differentials with Germany, lags of the differential average money and output growth rates between the EMS and our non-EMS countries, and lags of the logarithmic first difference in the DM/U.S. dollar real exchange rate. The lag structure was chosen to satisfy serial noncorrelation of the residuals. All data come from the *International Financial Statistics* tapes of the IMF. Money and output are measured as "reserve money" and "industrial production." The lag specifications are lags 1, 2, 3, and 12 of the real exchange rate; lags 1, 2, and 3 for inflation, money, and output growth differentials measured with reference to Germany; lags 1 and 3 for the remaining variables. All forecast models are tested for parameter stability after March 1979 to allow for parameter changes resulting from the inception of the ERM. The adjustment, if necessary, is done with interactive dummy variables.

Table 7.4 reports the steady-state values of the conditional variances of the DM real exchange rates in the EMS. There are no significant differences here between the two phases of the EMS. With the exception of the Belgian franc, real exchange-rate uncertainty after 1979 is significantly lower than in the pre-EMS period. This result remains true even if the variance of the realignment process is included.[7] The lower half of Table 7.5 shows that the behavior of real DM rates of non-EMS currencies is ambiguous. We find a significant increase in uncertainty about the real DM/U.S. dollar rate but reductions in uncertainty about DM/Canadian dollar rates and DM/pound sterling rates. No apparent change in the uncertainty about the real DM/yen rate is found. The upper half of this table, however, reveals that the covariances of real DM rates within and outside the EMS have been reduced significantly in most cases. The EMS has weakened the stochastic link of DM real exchange rates inside and outside the system.

Table 7.6 reports the relative changes of the conditional variances of

TABLE 7.4 Conditional Variances of Monthly DM Real Exchange Rates

	Pre-EMS	EMS	
	σ_ξ^2	σ_ξ^2	σ_v^2
Belgium	0.36	0.39	0.31
p		0.871	
Denmark	1.07	0.41	0.35
p		0.038	
France	1.73	0.28	0.54
p		0.001	
Italy	4.32	0.63	0.37
p		0.001	
Netherlands	0.67	0.15	0.07
p		0.001	

Note: Subperiods are pre-EMS January 1973 to February 1979; EMS March 1979 to March 1988. Variances σ_ξ^2 are steady-state solutions of ARCH models for monthly percentage changes in real rates net of realignment effects. p is the marginal significance level of rejecting the hypothesis of stability of the ARCH model. σ_v^2 is the variance of realignment effects. Exchange rates are measured as DM per unit of foreign currency. Real rates are defined with CPIs.

Source: Fratianni and von Hagen (1990c).

EMS real exchange rates. Again, we note a strong reduction of uncertainty about real DM rates of EMS currencies accompanied by a strong increase in the uncertainty about the real U.S. dollar rates of all EMS currencies. For the other non-EMS currencies, the results are more favorable. The table suggests moderate decreases in real exchange-rate uncertainty of EMS currencies vis-à-vis the Canadian dollar and the pound sterling, and no clear change vis-à-vis the yen.

Turning to the average conditional variance of real exchange rates among EMS currencies other than the DM, we find the difference between the EMS and the pre-EMS periods is –0.83. This indicates that the reduction of uncertainty about real DM exchange rates has been accompanied by a reduction on average of the uncertainty about other

TABLE 7.5 Conditional Covariances of Monthly DM Real Exchange Rates

	United States		Canada		Japan		United Kingdom	
	Pre-EMS	EMS	Pre-EMS	EMS	Pre-EMS	EMS	Pre-EMS	EMS
EMS								
Belgium	0.87	0.54	0.84	0.11	0.48	0.13	0.59	0.13
p		0.162		0.019		0.229		0.001
Denmark	0.75	0.30	0.74	0.19	0.57	0.12	–0.00	0.00
p		0.282		0.071		0.097		0.335
France	1.15	0.69	1.16	0.11	1.18	0.01	0.94	–0.04
p		0.030		0.047		0.013		0.031
Italy	3.46	0.93	2.75	0.45	1.59	0.33	2.30	0.28
p		0.009		0.009		0.16		0.007
Netherlands	0.91	0.10	0.87	0.05	0.43	0.20	0.46	0.05
p		0.001		0.006		0.009		0.068
Non-EMS								
United States	6.24	9.21	—	—	—	—	—	—
p		0.001						
Canada	5.07	3.06	6.22	4.42	—	—	—	—
p		0.007		0.006				
Japan	2.21	1.55	—	—	4.63	4.63	—	—
p		0.018				0.867		
United Kingdom	3.10	2.24	—	—	—	—	4.35	3.05
p		0.056						0.064

Note: Subperiods are pre-EMS January 1973 to February 1979; EMS March 1979 to March 1983. All covariances are steady-state solutions of estimated ARCC models and apply to monthly percentage changes of real exchange rates. p is the marginal significance level of rejecting stability of the ARCC process. Exchange rates are measured as DM price of foreign currency. Real rates are defined with CPIs.

Source: Fratianni and von Hagen (1990c).

TABLE 7.6 Relative Changes in Conditional Variances of Real Exchange Rates

	Germany	United States	Canada	Japan	United Kingdom
Belgium	0.08	0.75	−0.06	0.18	−0.10
Denmark	−0.62	0.55	−0.23	0.05	−0.36
France	−0.84	0.43	−0.20	0.23	−0.19
Germany	—	0.48	−0.29	0.00	−0.30
Italy	−0.85	1.19	−0.18	−0.20	−0.23
Netherlands	−0.78	0.80	−0.13	0.00	−0.29

Note: Relative changes are computed as the differences between EMS and pre-EMS conditional variances divided by pre-EMS conditional variances. Conditional variances of EMS rates other than DM are computed from tables 10 and 11.

Source: Fratianni and von Hagen (1990c).

EMS real exchange rates. The result remains valid if one includes the uncertainty resulting from realignments.

7.3 Realignment Uncertainty in the EMS

So far, we have simplified the treatment of realignments in the analysis of exchange-rate uncertainty by assuming that all realignments have been completely unanticipated. In this section, we look at the issue of realignment uncertainty in more detail. By definition, realignments are discrete events. Since the creation of the EMS, there has been considerable variation in length of the time intervals between realignments as well as in the size of the realignments. This demonstrates that the formation of realignment expectations involves two problems: the timing of the realignment and its size.

To stress the distinction between the timing and the size of realignments, we can think of exchange-rate anticipations in general as a product of anticipations about the discrete event of realignments and anticipations about exchange-rate changes given that a realignment takes place or does not. Formally, let there be two possible states of the world in each period: state R, in which a realignment takes place, and status N, in which no realignment occurs. Let $E^R_t s_{t+4}$ and $E^N_t s_{t+4}$ be the expected DM exchange rate of an EMS currency four weeks ahead in states R and N, respectively, and let $\beta_{t, t+4}$ be the subjective probability that market participants entertain at time t of state R occurring during the next four weeks. The unconditional expectation of the exchange rate four periods ahead—if it is unknown which state will prevail—is

$$(7.11) \qquad E_t s_{t+4} = (\beta_{t,t+4}) E^R_t s_{t+4} + (1 - \beta_{t,t+4}) E^N_t s_{t+4}.$$

Assuming that open interest rate parity holds in the Euro-currency markets and that the assets traded are perceived to be perfect substitutes, we can solve interest rate differentials for the expected exchange rate,

$$(7.12) \qquad E_t s_{t+4} = i_t - i^*_t + s_t.$$

Taking first differences yields

$$(7.13) \qquad E_t s_{t+4} - E_{t-1} s_{t+3} = \Delta i_t - \Delta i^*_t + \Delta s_t.$$

Table 7.7 reports these changes in expectations before and between realignments. The table is based on our weekly exchange-rate data together with weekly quotations of one-month Euro-deposit interest rates taken from the Harris Bank *Weekly Review*. Both are Friday closing quotations of bid rates in London. For France and Italy, exchange-rate expectations rise significantly before a realignment, indicating that the market anticipates the upcoming event. In contrast, changes in expected exchange rates are close to zero between realignments. The revision of expectations is larger in the second subperiod.

To get a sharper picture of the time pattern of changes in exchange-rate expectations, we regress the right-hand side of equation (7.13) on an intercept and two dummy variables: one, R_{-4}, captures the change in expectations in the four weeks preceding a realignment; an interactive one, $R_{-4} * EMSII$, allows for a change in the coefficient of the pre-realignment dummy after March 1983. In addition to these dummy variables, we employ simple time series models to account for the serial correlation structure of the residuals, which arises from the overlapping forecast horizons of the expectations in equation (7.13).

Table 7.8 reports the regression results. They confirm with more precision the message contained in Table 7.7. For example, the average annual expected devaluation of the DM/FF exchange rate was 0.66 percent between realignments and 4.58 percent before realignments. The structure of expectations did not change from EMSI to EMSII. Similar

TABLE 7.7 Weekly Changes of the One-month Expected DM Exchange Rate
(period averages percent per annum)

	Between Realignments	Four-Week Period Before Realignments
Period: March 16, 1979 to March 18, 1983		
Belgium	−1.42	−0.96
France	−1.15	−3.98+
Italy	−1.24	−4.87*
Netherlands	0.03	−1.26
Period: March 25, 1983 to January 9, 1987		
Belgium	−0.15	−1.65
France	−0.27	−4.30**
Italy	−0.56	−5.49**
Netherlands	−0.17	0.69

Note: +, *, and ** denote statistical significance at 10 percent, 5 percent, and 1 percent, respectively (two-tailed t distribution).

Source: Data adapted from Fratianni and von Hagen (1990b).

characterizations hold for the other countries covered in Table 7.8.[8] For France and Italy, the table suggests that market expectations change dramatically during the four weeks before a realignment occurs. For these two countries, the coefficient on R_4 multiplied by 11 (the number of realignments) is not statistically different from the cumulative changes in the bilateral central parities realized by the 11 realignments. This indicates that, on average, the size of the realignments was correctly anticipated. Furthermore, the finding of large changes in the expectations in the four weeks before realignments is consistent with the hypothesis that market participants anticipated the timing of realignments approximately correctly. This pattern did not change between EMSI and EMSII.

TABLE 7.8 Transfer Functions for Weekly Changes of the One-Month Expected Exchange Rate, March 16, 1979, to February 6, 1987 (percent per annum)

	Constant	R-4 Dummy	(R-4)*EMSII Interaction Dummy	AR1	MA1	MA2	MA3	SEE	DW	Q(12)
Belgium	−0.78 (2.33)	−0.03 (0.02)	−0.84 (0.44)	—	0.10 (2.01)	0.02 (0.37)	−0.12 (2.35)	6.43	2.00	11.09
France	−0.66 (2.47)	−3.92 (3.53)	0.12 (0.07)	—	0.04 (0.79)	0.08 (1.70)	0.06 (1.28)	6.18	1.99	14.40
Italy	−0.92 (3.58)	−4.57 (3.86)	0.35 (0.19)	−0.73 (5.93)	0.81 (7.48)	—	—	6.44	1.97	7.29
Nether- lands	−0.10 (0.67)	−0.99 (1.49)	1.91 (1.85)	—	0.45 (9.10)	−0.08 (1.56)	0.11 (2.27)	5.05	2.01	20.32

Note: R-4 signifies the four-week period before realignment; EMSII is a dummy equal to one for the period March 25, 1983, to February 6, 1987, and zero otherwise. AR and MA are autoregressive and moving average components. Q(12) is the Ljung-Box Q-statistic, which is treated as a Chi-square with 12 degrees of freedom. The levels of significance are 14.85 (25 percent), 18.55 (10 percent), 21 (5 percent), and 23.3 (2.5 percent).

Source: Data adapted from Fratianni and von Hagen (1990b).

Given the assumptions above, we can compute the unconditional exchange-rate expectation error from the data as

$$(7.14) \qquad s_{t+4} - E_t s_{t+4} = s_{t+4} - (i_t - i^*_t + s_t)$$
$$= s_{t+4} - E^R_t s_{t+4} - (1 - \beta_{t,t+4})(E^N_t s_{t+4} - E^R_t s_{t+4})$$
$$= s_{t+4} - E^N_t s_{t+4} + \beta_{t,t+4}(E^N_t s_{t+4} - E^R_t s_{t+4}).$$

It is plausible to assume that $E^N_t s_{t+4} > E^R_t s_{t+4}$ if the realignment entails a devaluation of the currency against the DM. Assume that the conditional forecast $E^R_t s_{t+4}$ and $E^N_t s_{t+4}$ are unbiased, and suppose that we collect data for the expectation error from all four-week periods before realignments, so that hindsight tells us the true state of the world was R. The second line of equation (7.14) tells us that the average unconditional exchange-rate forecast error should be negative in those periods, unless $\beta_{t, t+4} = 1$. Conversely, the average error between realignments should be positive, unless $\beta_{t, t+4} = 0$. That is, as long as there is uncertainty about the timing of realignments, the average unconditional forecast errors in the two selected samples will not be zero, even though the average conditional forecast errors are.

Table 7.9 reports the average unconditional forecast errors for our four EMS currencies. The average errors are positive between realignments and negative before realignments. The switch in sign is statistically significant for the Belgian franc, the French franc, and the Italian lira during EMSI and for the latter two during EMSII. Note that during the second period under consideration, the Dutch guilder realigned against the DM only once, and the Belgian franc was never realigned. Thus, Table 7.9 indicates that the markets perceived the central rates of the guilder and the Belgian franc during EMSII as credible in the sense that the probability of a realignment was very small. The French franc and the Italian lira, in contrast, were repeatedly realigned against the DM in both subperiods. For these two currencies, the average error is much smaller in absolute value between realignments than in the four weeks before realignments. The same observation holds for the Belgian franc in the first phase of the EMS. This difference in the absolute values suggests that markets perceived a very small probability of realignments at all instances except during the months before a realignment actually occurred. In contrast, the probability of a realignment rose during those four weeks, but it remained below one. Thus, even shortly before realignments, their timing remains uncertain.

Table 7.10 looks in more detail at the structure and significance of the forecast errors defined by equation (7.14) by regressing them on an intercept and the three dummy variables R-4, EMSII, and its interaction. The intercept indicates the average forecast error between realignments, and the intercept plus the coefficient on R-4 measures the average error in the four weeks before a realignment. As in the case of Table 7.8, the construction of the dependent variable implies serial correlation, which we capture with simple time series models. The results of this table corroborate the impressions of Table 7.9. For example, the average error for the French franc amounts to about –4 percent. This negative average forecast error stands in sharp contrast to a positive average error of approximately 14 percent in the prerealignment periods during EMSI and a negative average error of approximately 1 percentage point in the prerealignment periods of EMSII. Belgium behaves qualitatively like France. Italy does so only during EMSI; the prerealignment average forecast error of the lira during EMSII remains approximately 10 percent.

TABLE 7.9 Four-Week Forecast Error of Exchange-Rate Changes
(period averages percent per annum)

	Between Realignments	*Four-week Period Before Realignments*
Period: March 16, 1979, to March 18, 1983		
Belgium	1.72	−18.98*
France	2.93	−16.65*
Italy	6.08	−13.36*
Netherlands	0.29	−0.49
Period: March 25, 1983, to January 9, 1987		
Belgium	2.98	4.68
France	3.80	−10.54*
Italy	5.45	−10.77*
Netherlands	0.49	2.90

Note: * statistically significant at 1 percnet level (two-tailed t distribution).

Source: Fratianni and von Hagen (1990b).

The DM/guilder exchange rate shows a zero average forecast error throughout the EMS.

Rewriting equation (7.13) as

$$(7.15) \quad E_t s_{t+4} - E_{t-1} s_{t+3} = E^N_t s_{t+4} - E^N_{t-1} s_{t+3}$$
$$+ \beta_{t-1,t+3}(E^R_t s_{t+4} - E^R_{t-1} s_{t+3} - E^N_t s_{t+4} + E^N_{t-1} s_{t+4})$$
$$+ (\beta_{t,t+4} - \beta_{t-1,t+3})(E^R_t s_{t+4} - E^N_t s_{t+4}),$$

we can decompose the revision of expectations into two components: revisions of expected exchange rates for each possible state, R or N, and revisions of the probability of a realignment. Assume that shortly before realignments, changes in the realignment probability are the dominant source of revisions of exchange-rate expectations—that is, newly arriving information primarily concerns the timing of the next realignment, not so

TABLE 7.10 Transfer Functions for the Forecast Error of Exchange-Rate Changes, March 16, 1979, to February 6, 1987 (percent per annum)

	Constant	R-4 Dummy	EMSII	(R-4)*EMSII Interaction Dummy	AR1	MA1	MA2	MA3	SEE	DW	Q(12)
Belgium	2.44	−20.82	−0.26	28.72		−0.86	−0.79	0.75	6.46	2.07	13.04
	(1.68)	(8.90)	(0.13)	(7.42)		(25.97)	(21.46)	(22.69)			
France	4.15	−18.80	−2.59	15.55		−0.92	−0.65	−0.60	6.78	2.06	15.86
	(2.88)	(7.93)	(1.26)	(3.97)		(23.08)	(12.36)	(14.74)			
Italy	7.38	−17.78	−2.46	6.22		−0.23	−0.20	−0.13	17.44	2.00	1.80
	(3.63)	(3.94)	(0.87)	(0.85)		(4.49)	(3.88)	(2.48)			
Nether-lands	0.11	1.63	0.49	0.89	0.39	−0.96	−0.93	−0.82	5.51	2.03	9.07
	(0.12)	(-0.85)	(0.36)	(0.28)	(6.45)	(26.28)	(29.51)	(27.15)			

Note: R-4 signifies the four-week period before realignment; EMSII is a dummy equal to one for the period March 25, 1983, to February 6, 1987, and zero otherwise. AR and MA are autoregressive and moving average components. Q(12) is the Ljung-Box Q-statistic, which is treated as a Chi-square with 12 degrees of freedom. The levels of significance are 14.85 (25 percent), 18.55 (10 percent), 21 (5 percent), and 23.3 (2.5 percent).

Source: Data adapted from Fratianni and von Hagen (1990b).

much the exchange-rate level in either state. The revision (7.15) then is approximately

$$(7.16) \qquad E_t s_{t+4} - E_{t-1} s_{t+3} = (\beta_{t,t+4} - \beta_{t-1,t+3})(E^R_t s_{t+4} - E^N_t s_{t+4}).$$

Next, consider again the average unconditional forecast error (7.14). If the conditional exchange-rate forecast of a realignment is unbiased, the average expectation error around realignments is $(1 - \beta_{t,t+4})(E^R_t s_{t+4} - E^N_t s_{t+4})$. Consequently, the ratio of (7.16) to (7.14) is approximately equal to

$$(7.17) \qquad \frac{\beta_{t,t+4} - \beta_{t-1,t+3}}{1 - \beta_{t,t+4}} = \frac{-\Delta(1 - \beta_{t,t+4})}{1 - \beta_{t,t+4}}$$

Equation (7.17) yields an approximate measure of how quickly markets revise the probability that no realignment will occur during the four weeks ahead. For France and Italy, the countries showing significant changes in expectations around realignments, these average relative changes in the nonrealignment probability are

	EMSI	EMSII
France	−.24	−.41
Italy	−.36	−.51

Three observations are noteworthy: First, the revisions are in the correct direction—realignments become increasingly likely during the month before they occur. Second, the speeds of revision rise between EMSI and EMSII, indicating that markets adjust expectations more rapidly as the EMS ages. Finally, the relative changes are well below unity in absolute value. This result is consistent with stable learning processes.

To summarize, we find that realignments have not been completely unanticipated in the EMS. The data suggest that the size of realignments has been correctly anticipated on average. Furthermore, the evidence is consistent with the hypothesis that market expectations about the timing of realignments are rational and are correct on average. This means that our estimates of total exchange-rate uncertainty in the previous section have overstated the contribution of realignments. In this sense, the success of the EMS in reducing exchange-rate uncertainty within the group has likely been larger than previously stated. However, realignments remain a significant source of exchange-rate uncertainty in the EMS.

7.4 Inflation Uncertainty in the EMS

In this section, we investigate the impact of the EMS on inflation uncertainty. As in the analysis of real exchange rates, we start with a forecast of the inflation rate—measured in terms of monthly changes in the CPIs—to obtain estimates of the monthly prediction error. For this purpose, we regress a country's inflation rate on its own lags (1, 2, 3, 12), a trend, a constant, an EMS dummy variable, domestic money and output growth rates (lags 1, 2, 3), a basic commodity price index for industrial countries (lags 1, 2, 3), and EMS and non-EMS average inflation and money growth rates (lags 1 and 3). The set of regressors was chosen with the purpose of obtaining a list of domestic and external variables that, under a variety of open economy models for the EC countries, would have some explanatory power for domestic inflation. The lag structure had to be limited in order not to exhaust the number of degrees of freedom; in the construction of the empirical models, we eliminated lagged regressors if they were not significant and if the elimination did not lead to a violation of the serial noncorrelation of the estimated errors. The data come from the *International Financial Statistics* and are seasonally unadjusted. The net sample period spans from January 1973 to April 1988. The models were checked for shifts in parameter values after March 1979 and adjustments were made, when necessary, with interactive dummies.

Table 7.11 reports the results. Here, we consider the conditional variances of inflation rates together with the conditional covariances with average EMS inflation rates and average non-EMS inflation. Two principal messages emerge from the table. First, we observe a significant reduction of inflation uncertainty during the EMS period in four out of six EMS countries: Denmark, Germany, Italy, and the Netherlands.[9] Yet we also

TABLE 7.11 Conditional Variances and Covariances of Inflation Rates

	Pre-EMS	EMS	p_1	Pre-EMS	EMS	p_2	Pre-EMS	EMS	p_3
Belgium	5.74	5.71	0.31	0.59	2.00	0.045	1.03	1.37	0.071
Denmark	35.06	25.21	0.033	2.41	2.41	0.692	-2.77	0.30	0.036
France	4.34	4.34	0.887	1.83	1.83	0.746	1.93	0.73	0.159
Germany	5.46	3.14*	0.028	1.85	1.85	0.880	1.20	1.41	0.020
Italy	24.75	9.81	0.000	4.83	1.35	0.009	3.31	1.23	0.149
Nether-lands	11.54	4.91	0.000	1.20	1.20	0.848	1.37	1.3	0.420
EMS	2.74	2.74	0.180	—	—	—	1.88	1.42	0.013
Canada	8.40	5.01	0.061	0.13	0.07	0.079	1.05	1.06	0.423
Japan	60.38	18.58	0.002	7.36	0.01	0.000	12.97	4.26	0.037
United Kingdom	36.32	10.80*	0.035	3.71	3.71	0.210	3.18	3.96	0.065
United States	5.48	5.48	0.956	0.64	0.85	0.068	3.04	3.04	0.691
Non-EMS	5.91	4.54	0.187	1.88	1.42	0.013	—	—	—

Note: p_1, p_2, and p_3 are the marginal significance levels of rejecting the hypothesis of no change in the parameters of the variance and covariance models. Subperiods are pre-EMS 1974 to February 1979; EMS March 1979 to April 1988. * indicates shift in April 1983. Entries are variances and covariances of innovations in monthly percentage changes times 100 and are steady-state solutions of the estimated ARCH and ARCC models.

Source: Fratianni and von Hagen (1990c).

find significant reductions of inflation uncertainty outside the EMS—Japan, the United Kingdom, and to a smaller extent, Canada. Thus, the overall picture resembles the impression drawn in Chapter 2 from the discussion of trend inflation rates in the EMS and a group of nonmembers: Significant reductions of inflation uncertainty are no special characteristic of the EMS. This is compatible with the view previously expressed that both EMS and non-EMS countries were exposed to similar shocks and that the EMS had no particular effect on inflation performance.

The second important observation is that the conditional variances of the EMS and the non-EMS average inflation rates did not change significantly. The variance of the average inflation rate is the sum of the variances of the individual rates and their covariances. Because some of the individual variances decreased, the constant variance of the average implies that some of the covariances increased. Thus, unexpected inflationary shocks spread out more evenly among the members of each group. In other words, unexpected changes in inflation have become more symmetric within each group.

Weber (1990) reports a finding that corroborates this conclusion. He performs Aoki factorizations of inflation rates in the EMS.[10] He finds that symmetric inflation shocks dominate asymmetric shocks among the members. Although the conditional variances of symmetric shocks remained the same during the EMS period as before, the conditional variance of asymmetric shocks declined significantly in most cases. This suggests that the reduction in EMS inflation uncertainty stems primarily from a reduction in the variance of asymmetric shocks.

The final important observation from Table 7.11 is that the conditional covariance between the EMS and the non-EMS averages fell significantly after the inception of the EMS. This implies that inflation shocks originating outside the EMS have a smaller impact on the EMS countries than before; shocks affecting the EMS countries have a smaller effect on non-EMS countries.

7.5 Conclusions

Our results indicate that the EMS has achieved significant reductions of exchange rate uncertainty among member countries, particularly about the DM. Rogoff (1985b), Artis and Taylor (1988), Meltzer (1990), and Weber (1990) reach similar conclusions. Weber (1990) finds reduced variance not only of monthly changes in real exchange rates but also in annual changes. This indicates that the impact of the EMS has reduced uncertainty not only at high-frequency fluctuations but also at low frequencies—it has stabilized long-run exchange-rate movements.

An important question in evaluating this finding is whether the reduction in exchange-rate uncertainty has been achieved at the cost of increasing the uncertainty about other variables, such as short-term interest rates. Rogoff (1985a) reports that interest rate volatility had increased in the early phase of the EMS. Artis and Taylor (1988) examine the possibility of a "volatility transfer" from exchange rates to interest rates in the EMS, that is, an increase in the conditional variance of short-term interest rates that accompanies the decrease in exchange-rate uncertainty. Investigating monthly data of onshore and offshore interest rate changes for France, Italy, Germany, and the Netherlands, they conclude that the EMS did not bring about an increase in uncertainty about interest rates. Meltzer (1990) considers the possibility of rising variances of real stock prices, real interest rates, inflation, or unit labor cost in the EMS. He finds no indication of a volatility transfer in those directions.

In contrast to these studies, however, our results point to a trade-off between exchange-rate uncertainty about EMS currencies and exchange-rate uncertainty of EMS currencies against non-EMS currencies. The reduction in uncertainty about intra-EMS exchange rates has been accompanied by an increase in EMS uncertainty about the U.S. dollar, the Canadian dollar, the yen, and the pound sterling. This increase in external exchange-rate uncertainty has been relatively smaller for the DM than for the other EMS currencies. Recent studies have shown how, in a multicurrency world, an arrangement like the EMS may destabilize exchange rates between members and nonmembers (Canzoneri 1982; Marston 1985). Shifts in aggregate demand between a member and a nonmember may result in larger exchange-rate variation between other participants in the arrangement and the outsider than may occur under flexible exchange rates. In addition, an exchange-rate arrangement distributes the effects of financial shocks affecting a member and a nonmember (for example, speculative shifts in the demand for their monies) more evenly among the participants. This may explain the relatively better outcomes for Germany, which issues the only major international reserve currency in the EMS, in the uncertainty trade-off.

A similar trade-off emerges for real exchange rates. Here, the reduction of uncertainty about real DM rates in the EMS has been accompanied mostly by an increase in the uncertainty about U.S. dollar rates. Our result of a trade-off of external for internal nominal and real exchange-rate uncertainty is consistent with the common observation that the variance of effective exchange rates did not change for the EMS countries (Ungerer et al. 1986; Meltzer 1990). The trade-off has been more favorable for Germany than for the other members: U.S. dollar exchange-rate uncertainty increased less for Germany than for most other member countries. At the same time, the reductions in uncertainty about the Canadian dollar and pound sterling rates are larger for Germany than most other EMS countries.

In light of the cooperative interpretation of the EMS and its emphasis on stabilizing random fluctuations, the finding of reduced nominal and real exchange-rate uncertainty in the EMS can be regarded as an indication of successful, welfare-improving policy coordination. The traditional European belief that such reduced uncertainty promotes international trade and the functioning of the European customs union (see Chapter 2) implies further welfare consequences: It suggests that the reduction of internal exchange-rate uncertainty in the EMS should stimulate intra-EMS trade and yield additional welfare gains to the members. But the finding of a trade-off between internal and external exchange-rate uncertainty makes the overall welfare conclusion ambiguous, because it implies a potential reduction in trade between EMS members and nonmembers.

One may argue that the trade-stimulating effects of the EMS are likely to dominate if most of the international trade of its members occurs within the EMS. (Table 7.12 reports the share of intra-EMS exports in total exports to industrial countries for the EMS countries.) Two observations

TABLE 7.12 Relative Shares of EMS Exports (percent)

	Belgium	Denmark	France	Germany	Ireland	Italy	Netherlands	EMS
1975	77.2	32.2	64.6	56.5	27.5	63.2	74.9	63.1
1976	79.3	34.3	66.3	57.5	30.1	64.3	76.0	64.6
1977	77.1	37.3	64.9	55.4	32.8	62.7	76.1	63.1
1978	77.3	40.3	65.2	55.6	33.6	62.6	76.6	63.1
1979	76.2	40.8	65.0	55.9	34.9	62.3	76.4	63.3
1980	74.8	42.8	64.8	55.8	36.6	62.8	77.0	63.3
1981	73.8	39.8	61.8	54.6	35.5	59.3	76.2	61.5
1982	72.5	41.6	61.4	54.5	36.4	59.3	74.8	60.9
1983	71.7	41.5	60.3	52.3	36.4	58.3	74.5	59.6
1984	70.3	37.0	58.0	50.3	38.1	54.6	72.9	57.3
1985	70.2	36.7	57.0	48.7	38.6	53.1	72.8	56.1
1986	72.5	39.3	58.1	48.2	39.6	55.6	71.5	56.4
1987	72.8	40.5	58.0	48.7	41.1	55.4	71.0	56.5

Note: Relative shares are ratios of exports to EMS countries to total exports to industrial countries.

Source: Fratianni and von Hagen (1990c).

are noteworthy. First, in 1979, only Denmark and Ireland—at the time both relatively young members in the EC—had less than a 50 percent share of their exports in the EMS area. Germany's share was 55.9 percent; for the remaining countries it was well above 60 percent. This would suggest that the net welfare effect of the EMS, even if we account for possible losses in external trade, was positive at the inception of the EMS. Second, since 1979, trade growth among EMS countries has been generally slower than trade between member and nonmember countries, resulting in falling shares of intra-EMS trade.[11] This means that the welfare implications of the EMS became more ambiguous during the 1980s.

Our results about inflation uncertainty indicate that the EMS has changed significantly the empirical conditional covariance pattern of inflation rates. These empirical changes are consistent with each of the following three conjectures about the EMS:

1. Policy coordination within the EMS has reduced the burden of common external shocks borne by the EMS relative to that borne by non-EMS countries;

2. Policy coordination within the EMS has reduced the inflationary impact of shocks originating from the non-EMS group and has equalized its distribution among member countries;

3. Policy coordination within the EMS has reduced the variance of country-specific inflation shocks originating in the member countries.

The essence of these conjectures is that policy coordination within the EMS has changed the exposure of the member countries to unexpected inflation shocks. There is monetary convergence in EMS in the form of a more even distribution of *unexpected* inflation rates among the members, a result that supports the cooperative view of the EMS.

Notes

1. See Rogoff (1985b) and Artis and Taylor (1988) for a similar approach. Others have considered observed variability of exchange rates as the relevant criterion to evaluate the EMS (e.g., Artis 1987; Padoa-Schioppa 1985a; Ungerer, et al. 1983, 1986). From an economic perspective, conditional variances are more relevant because they reflect the private sector's forecasting problem.

2. A leptokurtic distribution has more probability mass in the tails than the standard normal distribution. See Diebold (1988), Diebold and Pauly (1985), or Artis and Taylor (1988) for applications of the ARCH model to exchange rates.

3. The likelihood function is called separable in the parameters of the variance model and the parameters of the conditional expectation if the latter does not depend on the former and vice versa.

4. For a discussion of the least-squares estimation of ARCH models see Weiss (1986). The likelihood function is separable if the forecast model for x_t does not contain the conditional variance process as the regressor, and if the variables contained in the forecast model for x_t are not included in the model for σ_t^2.

5. See, for example, Diebold and Pauly (1985).

6. The realignment effects increase the EMSI results, but leave EMSII virtually unchanged.

7. This result is consistent with Mussa's (1986) finding that the observed variability of real exchange rates is generally lower under fixed nominal rates.

8. We also investigated but rejected the possibility that the level of the expected exchange rate may influence its revision. The potential importance of the level occurs in cases when forecasts that have produced an "excessively" appreciated currency are likely to be followed by a string of forecasts going in the opposite direction.

9. Meltzer (1986) reports a reduction in German inflation uncertainty on the basis of Kalman filter estimates.

10. Let π_i and π_j be the inflation rates of countries i and j, respectively. Under an Aoki factorization, the variance of $(\pi_i + \pi_j)$ measures the variance of symmetric shocks; the variance of $(\pi_i - \pi_j)$ measures the variance of asymmetric shocks.

11. De Grauwe and Verfaille (1987) attribute this observation to the slowdown in real GNP growth in the EMS relative to non-EMS countries.

8

European Monetary Union

In Chapter 2 we noted that the movement for European monetary union (EMU) has gained momentum since 1988. Today its chances to succeed look brighter than ever before. We pointed out the intimate link between the movement for monetary union in Europe and the quest for political union: economic considerations alone do not fully explain the push for EMU, nor the opposition to it. Nonetheless, economic arguments remain important to evaluate the prospect of EMU and to assure that the institutions of the future union be designed in a way to foster the best economic outcome.

The literature on monetary integration has long been heavily influenced by the work of Mundell (1961), McKinnon (1963), and Kenen (1969) on optimum currency areas. Resting on the Keynesian paradigm of sticky prices and wages, they focus on how permanently fixed exchange rates change the ability of an economy to adjust to shifts in aggregate demand. But as Jürg Niehans has remarked, the concept of an *optimum currency area* is flawed because it lacks a well-defined criterion of optimality. More recent literature instead has taken a cost-benefit approach to monetary union and has discovered that there are more sources of costs and benefits than those implied by the Keynesian stabilization problem (Commission of the EC 1990; De Grauwe 1992). In this chapter, we follow the new approach and analyze the potential advantages and disadvantages of EMU. Our conclusion is that the costs and benefits depend crucially on the institutional design of the monetary union. With this in mind, we point out some important characteristics for a successful EMU.

8.1 The Costs and Benefits of European Monetary Union

The costs and benefits of European monetary union arise from three grounds, all of which have already been mentioned and discussed in the context of the EMS. The first is the use of a single medium of transactions and unit of account in the EC. For reasons discussed in Chapter 2, a single medium of exchange will be beneficial for the proper functioning of CAP and is complementary to the progress of trade integration in the EC. Apart from these benefits of deepening European integration, the use of one medium of exchange in the EC reduces transactions cost because businesses and consumers no longer have to exchange currencies and administer foreign currency portfolios.

It is difficult to quantify the potential savings of transactions cost resulting from EMU. Intra-EC trade in goods and services represents approximately 20 percent of Community GDP; intra-EC asset transactions are estimated to be a multiple of exports and imports of goods and services.[1] Bid-ask spreads on money conversion are quite high when they involve cash (2-5 percent), smaller for credit cards or Euro-checks, and smallest for interbank transactions (0.05-0.1percent). For lack of careful studies of the savings of transaction costs, we are left with educated guesses. Artis (1989) speculates that the transaction savings could amount to 1 percent of Community GDP, Gros and Thygesen (1990b) suggest a smaller figure of 0.25-0.5 percent, and the Commission of the EC (1990) has ventured a prediction of 0.13 percent.

There will be additional savings because with a unified medium of exchange, the price system will become more transparent, and opportunities for price discrimination will disappear. Thus, monetary union enhances competition, which is to the advantage of the consumer. Moreover, a monetary union can achieve economies of scale in the use of international reserves to stabilize exchange-rate fluctuations with nonmember currencies, at least if external shocks tend to offset one another (Laffer 1973; Christie and Fratianni 1978).[2]

The EC Commission argues that further benefits will accrue from the elimination of exchange-rate uncertainty, which would stimulate trade and investment. However, this is debatable. Economic theory yields no clear prediction about the trade and investment effects of reduced exchange-rate uncertainty, and the existing empirical evidence is equally equivocal.[3] Our analysis in Chapter 7 has shown that the system has achieved lower internal uncertainty at the cost of higher external uncertainty. This implies that the net benefits of reduced exchange-rate uncertainty resulting from EMU can go both ways. In total, the economic benefits from a unified medium of exchange appear fairly small.

The other two sources of cost and benefit from EMU are related to the future role and capacity of macroeconomic stabilization. There are two important questions to consider: Will the countries participating in EMU have to suffer a rate of inflation exceeding their current rates, and will the

EMU be able to deal successfully with exogenous shocks? Our discussion of the disciplinary and cooperative interpretations of the EMS has prepared the ground for an answer, though there is no simple yes or no to either question.

8.2 Central Bankers:
Collusion Versus Competition

Perhaps the greatest challenge to EMU comes from the view that monetary union is a form of collusion among central bankers. As everyone knows from experience, collusion among producers in output markets reduces the force of competition and allows complacent suppliers to lower the quality of their products. In the same way, it is argued, collusion among central bankers would reduce monetary policy competition and reduce the quality of the policy outcome. The main measure of the quality of monetary policy is price stability, therefore, monetary union entails more inflation. This view has recently been argued by the British government (HM Treasury 1989, 9):

> Deciding now that monetary union has to have a single currency precludes debate and removes any role for the market in favor of a central plan. Moreover, by eliminating both competition and accountability from members' monetary policies, the Delors Report version of union risks producing a higher inflation rate in Europe—one in which performance approximates more to the average than to the best.

The gist of the competitive policy argument can be sketched as follows: In a world of free currency convertibility, capital mobility, and flexible exchange rates, central banks are subject to the pressures of international monetary policy competition. A high inflation rate of the prices quoted in one currency encourages the private sector to hold assets denominated in other, more stable currencies and to abandon the use of the inflationary currency as a medium of transactions. Consequently, the central bank's benefits from inflation—namely revenues from seignorage and the ability to conduct stabilization policies—are reduced. In contrast, a low-inflation central bank is rewarded by an increasing use of its currency. Competition of monetary policies therefore exerts an important disciplinary force on central bankers and prevents them from inflating too much.

According to this view, the creation of a monetary union reduces the degree of competition. By fixing the relative prices of their currencies or by issuing a common currency, central bankers eliminate opportunities for choice. As a result, the threats and rewards from competition disappear. Monetary union destroys the discipline of policy competition and thereby worsens the quality of the product—that is, it results in higher average inflation (Vaubel 1980, 1989a; Dowd 1988; HM Treasury 1989).

Advocates of monetary policy competition reject monetary union because it limits competition that otherwise guarantees the largest degree of price stability. This negative assessment of monetary union rests critically on three assumptions. First, each central bank can pursue a credible low-inflation policy independently of others under competitive circumstances. Second, collusion among the members of the monetary union reduces the degree of effective competition in the international arena. Third, individual incentives to inflate are the same for each central bank in the monetary union; collusion only reduces the cost of high inflation and the reward for low inflation. The important question is how valid these assumptions are.

Credibility of Low-Inflation Policies

Governments generally cannot make credible advance commitments to optimal low-inflation policy rules because in practice there is no formal punishment for breaching those commitments. We saw in Chapter 4 that the nonenforceability of policy announcements creates a bias toward inflation. Equilibrium inflation is positive although it generates no output or employment gains, because a zero- or low-inflation policy rule is not time-consistent and its announcement, therefore, is not credible.

The inflation bias and the lack of credibility stem from the lack of an effective commitment mechanism for the monetary authority, which is a deficiency in the political institutions. The bias arises from the struggle between elected politicians, who are mostly concerned with using monetary policy to ensure levels of output and employment favorable for reelection, and central bank officials, who are more concerned with price stability. Effective commitment is necessary because price stability is a long-run goal of monetary policy, which in the short run conflicts with the opportunity to use monetary surprises to achieve real effects of monetary policy. The more the central bank has to give in to political pressure, the less credible is its commitment to price stability and the higher is the inflation rate.

O'Flaherty (1990) and Fratianni, von Hagen, and Waller (1991), among others, formalize this view and interpret the relation between the monetary authority and the government as an agency problem: The central bank executes monetary policy on behalf of the government. The crucial point is that the quality of monetary policy is a function of the relationship between the agent and the principal. This relationship is characterized by the agent's incentives to use monetary policy in serving the short-run, political goals of the government. The more the agent's own well-being—salary, perquisites, and power—depends on the political fate of the current government, the more likely is it that monetary policy will be dominated by short-run considerations. Two extreme solutions are possible: a highly "dependent" central bank, subservient to government's wishes, and a highly "independent" central bank oblivious to any short-run political considerations. The theory of credibility implies that the trend inflation rate increases with the short-run orientation of monetary policy. The conclusion is that central bank independence is a prerequisite of price stability; indeed, the optimal monetary arrangement calls for complete monetary independence.

The credibility problem implies that the quality of domestic monetary policy is endangered by the lack of a commitment mechanism and the influence of politicians on the central bank, factors that change the implications of central bank collusion. Collusion, in the form of fixed exchange rates or monetary union, can remove monetary policy from politically dependent domestic authorities and delegate it to a more independent foreign or European authority. This is, of course, the essence of the disciplinary interpretation of the EMS, according to which high-inflation countries, like France and Italy, have used the EMS to submit their policies to the authority of the Bundesbank (Chapter 4). By fixing their exchange rates with the DM, these countries have adopted the Bundesbank's low-inflation policy and gained additional credibility for their own new commitment to price stability. The fixed exchange rate relieves these central banks from some of the political pressures and thus lowers their inflation bias.

The same argument can be made with regard to a monetary union, provided the common monetary authority is credible in its commitment to price stability. Thus, central bank collusion in a monetary union can yield in principle a better monetary policy, at least for some countries. There are those who argue that this is not a benefit unique to monetary union because other domestic commitment mechanisms can be designed (e.g., Minford et al. 1991), but the fact is that many European countries have not been able, for political reasons, to create domestic monetary institutions committed to price stability.

How, then, would the EMU perform as a commitment mechanism for price stability? Our discussion in Chapter 4 showed that to achieve an effective commitment mechanism, one must lower the political benefit a government derives from embarking on inflationary policies. A monetary union is clearly more promising in this regard than the EMS, because a country that would want to inflate would have to secede from the union, issue once more a national currency, and reinstate a domestic monetary authority. The political cost of such a step would surely be much higher than the cost of obtaining a realignment in the EMS. In addition, a formal withdrawal would most likely take some time and, thus, eliminate much of the surprise element that is so critical to obtaining the benefits from inflation. Thus, even if the disciplinary view of the EMS remains dubious, a case can be made for successful commitment to price stability in an EMU. On the other hand, just as Germany has in the EMS, a monetary union will have a credibility disadvantage in comparison to an independent national central bank because of a flatter EMU Phillips curve (Chapter 4). This is because a monetary union, like the EMS, eliminates the penalty of a depreciation that stems from monetary expansion.[4]

Finally, one should note that the EMU monetary authority would have the strategic advantage of facing an opposition of up to twelve governments, whereas a national authority faces only one government. As long as elections are not synchronized and there are national idiosyncrasies in the timing of business cycles, the political interests of the individual governments are likely to differ and the resulting political pressures are likely to neutralize each other to some extent. This would leave the EMU monetary authority with more freedom to follow its own preferred policy. It is noteworthy in this context that Germany and Switzerland are both characterized by monetary authorities confronted with a relatively decentralized system of fiscal authorities, whereas the U.S. Federal Reserve System is faced by a fiscally strong federal government. The better Swiss and German inflation performances of recent decades support the hypothesis that central banks can achieve a greater degree of price stability when there is no strong central government. Provided that EMU central bank officials share similar preferences for low inflation, this improved strategic position raises the attractiveness of monetary union. As a corollary, monetary union appears again to be a more attractive delegation device than an EMS under the leadership of the Bundesbank, which, after all, is not entirely independent from the German government (Neumann and von Hagen 1992).

To summarize, credibility considerations tell us that given the institutional deficiencies of the current, national monetary arrangements, EMU has a good chance of raising the quality of European monetary policy. Its effectiveness and preferability to both the EMS and independent monetary policies rest critically on the design of the European central bank, in particular on the extent to which this institution will be independent from European governments.

The Seigniorage Incentive to Inflate in a Monetary Union

The credibility argument focuses on the attempt to use monetary surprises for short-sighted, politically motivated goals. Another important incentive for inflation comes from the opportunity to generate government revenue by lowering the real value of government debt and financing government deficits. To illustrate the point, Tabellini (1988) analyzes a two-period model of strategic conflict between a central bank and its government. The central bank identifies with the public interest in price stability, whereas the fiscal authorities, elected politicians, behave like Buchanan's "Leviathan"—they care only about public expenditures. The fiscal authorities want to extract as much seigniorage from the central bank as possible, but they are limited by its willingness to monetize government debt. The greater the power of the fiscal authority over the central bank (the degree of fiscal dominance), the lower is its cost of financing a given government deficit. Inflation becomes a positive function of the volume of debt outstanding and the degree of fiscal dominance. Again, the conclusion is that central bank independence is a condition for low inflation.

A related branch of the public finance literature views inflation as part of a nation's tax system. Contrary to the conventional view of inflation as an inefficient source of government revenue, this literature argues that in a world with transaction and distortionary costs in collecting taxes, inflation becomes part of a second-best tax structure (Klein 1978, 81). Its optimal rate is obtained at the point where the marginal social costs of raising revenues through inflation and through other distortionary taxes are equal to each other (Mankiw 1987; Gros 1990).

To illustrate the argument, let t_y be the distortionary tax rate on income, m_y the ratio of base money to income, b_y the ratio of debt to income, g the ratio of government expenditures to income, π the inflation rate, π^e its expectation, and z and v the weights of the tax and inflation distortions in the authorities' instantaneous welfare function, U. If we take the ratio of government expenditures to income g^* as given for the financing decision, the optimal inflation rate and the optimal tax rate are derived as the results of maximizing the government's preference function (8.1a) subject to the budget constraint (8.1b),

(8.1a)
$$L = -\int [U(z t_{ys}^2 + v \pi_s^2) \exp(-rs)]ds$$

and

(8.1b)
$$g + (r - (\pi - \pi^e)b_y = t_y + \pi m_y,$$

where r is the real interest rate. Note that in a steady state, unanticipated inflation is zero. The optimal tax and inflation rates must obey the first order condition

(8.2) $zt_y(m_y + b_y) = v\pi.$

The optimal steady-state inflation rate is

(8.3) $\pi = (g^* + rb_y)[m_y + v/(z(m_y + b_y))]^{-1}$

The larger the marginal collection cost ratio z/v, the lower the base-money velocity, and the higher the debt ratio, the larger is a country's optimal inflation tax.

     To evaluate the seigniorage aspect of EMU, we assume that in the monetary union, delegates of all countries represent their different national interests and tax systems when they decide on the common inflation rate. This is clearly a too-pessimistic view of the European central bank officials, but it provides a convenient way to evaluate the outcome of the most pessimistic scenario, in which the European monetary authority will have to find a compromise between the fiscal interests of its members. Table 8.1 shows the 1988 values of t_y, m_y, and b_y for most of the EC countries. When we assume for simplicity that the values of the unobservable marginal collection cost ratio z/v are equal for all members, these data allow us to calculate the preferred inflation rates of the individual members relative to Germany's preferred rate. We infer that all representatives have target rates in excess of the German target. Unless the Bundesbank can set the EMU inflation rate unilaterally, the European monetary authority is bound to target a higher rate than the lowest one achieved in the EC in the late 1980s. Delegates of Belgium, Greece, and Italy would have higher target rates than those of France, Germany, and the United Kingdom. Taking the debt-income ratio as a basic measure of a government's fiscal strength, we see from the table that the less fiscally strong a EMU member, the higher the target inflation rate it would prefer for the monetary union.[5] This corroborates Tabellini's (1988) conclusions. Assume a rule of one-country-one-vote: Spain would be the pivotal voter in the European monetary authority, and the EMU inflation rate would be one-third higher than the preferred German inflation rate.

     But there is no reason to believe that the EMU members would want the same target inflation rate for the union that they would like for themselves when they conduct independent monetary policies. The reason is a familiar free-rider problem. In a monetary union, seignorage accrues to the common monetary authority, and all countries share its revenues. This implies that an individual country can effectively tax citizens of

TABLE 8.1 Taxes, Monetary Base, Debt, and Inflation Rates

	Tax Rate (t_y)	Monetary Base (m_y)	Net Debt (b_y)	$t_y(m_y + b_y)$
		(as a proportion of GDP)		
		1988 values		
Belgium	0.460	0.077	1.233	0.603
Denmark	0.605	0.041	0.246	0.174
France	0.489	0.066	0.243	0.151
Germany	0.443	0.100	0.235	0.148
Greece	0.362	0.200[a]	0.644	0.305
Italy	0.401	0.150[a]	0.879	0.413
Netherlands	0.543	0.087	0.554	0.348
Spain	0.381	0.220	0.299	0.197
United Kingdom	0.391	0.033	0.387	0.164

	Relative Inflation Target[b]	H_E	H_Y
Belgium	4.07	−6.70	−0.24
Denmark	1.18	−0.20	−0.15
France	1.02	−0.04	−0.09
Germany	1.00	−0.12	0.22
Greece	2.06	0.23	0.19
Italy	2.79	0.77	0.48
Netherlands	2.35	−4.33	0.35
Spain	1.33	—	0.54
United Kingdom	1.11	−0.04	−0.15

[a] Indicates 1987 values.
[b] Compared to the German rate.

Source: OECD, *Economic Outlook* N. 45 data diskettes for net debt; IMF, *International Financial Statistics* for the monetary base; and European Commission, *European Economy*, Supplement A, N. 2, July 1989, for average tax rates.

other countries through a higher union inflation rate. When this is taken into account, the preferred union inflation rate for each country becomes

(8.4) $\pi_E = (g^* + rb_y)[(\theta m_E + v/(z(\theta m_E + b_y))]^{-1}$,

where m_E is the base-money to income ratio for the entire union and θ is the ratio of a country's share of EMU seignorage to the country's share of EMU income. A country's preferred union inflation rate is higher than the country's preferred steady-state inflation rate with independent policies if

(8.5) $H = (m_y - \theta m_E)(v/z - (m_y + b_y)(\theta m_E + b_y)) < 0$.

The term $(m_y - \theta m_E)$ represents the change in the country's seigniorage tax base as a result of joining the union. It is negative when the country obtains more seigniorage for a given inflation rate inside the union than it would domestically—that is, when free riding occurs. Given the data in Table 8.1, the term $(v/z - (m_y + b_y)(\theta m_E + b_y)$ is likely to be positive.[6] Consequently, a country prefers a higher common inflation rate than its own independent one if it can increase its inflation tax base in the union. The only distribution scheme causing the inflation incentives to be the same with and without EMU is with $\theta = m_y/m_E$, which means that seigniorage is distributed among the union members according to their shares in the monetary base of the EMU.

Table 8.1 displays values of H under two alternative distribution schemes for union seigniorage. H_E distributes seigniorage according to countries' weights in the ECU based on January 1987 par values. Given the 1988 tax and inflation rates, condition (8.4) is satisfied for almost all countries. Only Italy and Greece, the two relatively high-inflation countries, would desire a lower union inflation rate than their preferred independent rate. More significant, the lowest-inflation countries—Germany, Belgium, and the Netherlands—would have the strongest preference to raise the union inflation rate above their own. With such a distribution scheme, EMU would most likely produce higher average inflation than independent policies. In comparison, H_y assumes that seigniorage is distributed according to each country's share in regional real income. Here the outcome is more favorable to a lower union inflation; in particular, low-inflation Germany and the Netherlands as well as Italy and Greece would prefer lower union inflation. Assume again a democratic voting scheme: the pivotal voter this time would be Greece, which would desire a lower inflation in the EMU than under independent policies.

The important conclusion from this exercise is that the long-run inflation rate in an EMU depends critically on the way seigniorage is distributed among the members. This is independent of the institutional arrangement by which seigniorage is actually collected and distributed.[7] An inadequate distribution scheme provides incentives for an inflation-biased union. The normative implication is that the seigniorage distribution scheme should be engineered in such a way as to bias the outcome toward low union inflation.

To provide a means for settling on a particular target inflation rate, the rules of the EMU must specify a mechanism allocating voting power to each member. The results of this section indicate that the optimal design of the voting mechanism should be considered together with the design of a seigniorage distribution scheme. A low EMU inflation rate can be achieved by allocating the majority of the votes to the fiscally strong countries, which have a strong preference for price stability, while compensating the fiscally weak countries with the largest shares in seigniorage revenue. In this way, seigniorage considerations would not distort the incentives of fiscally disciplined countries toward more inflation, and the interests of fiscally profligate countries would not carry enough weight in raising the union's inflation rate. Both groups could be persuaded to agree to such a rule because the fiscally weak countries are compensated for their loss of voting power with more seigniorage revenue, whereas the fiscally strong countries gain influence at the cost of some revenues.

A Deflation-Biased Monetary Union?

Most of the literature on central bank competition sounds a fear that a monetary union would raise inflation, but there is an opposing view that starts from the claim that the EMS has a built-in deflation bias because of the Bundesbank's dominant role. For example, Katseli (1987) argues that in the EMS

> Domestic central banks have chosen to lose some of the "economic effectiveness" of domestic monetary policy and accept the leadership of the Bundesbank rather than face the erosion of their political autonomy by national governments (p. 28).

> Given West Germany's consistent preferences towards low inflation and a balance-of-payments surplus, choosing to be the follower on an international scale lowered the political capital required domestically to lobby for and maintain an anti-expansionary policy stance (pp. 28-29).

The uniform deflationary bias in macroeconomic policy during the 1980's can be explained only with reference to the institutionalization of a hierarchical and supranational system of decision making which over-represents specific domestic interests in the negotiated outcome (p. 30).

According to this view, the EMS is a "club" of central bankers run by the Bundesbank. To gain membership in the club, policymakers in other countries must act in line with the German authorities. Central bankers are believed to represent the interests of capital owners more than the interests of labor and to find it worthwhile to pay the price of subservience to the Bundesbank to gain independence from their own expansionist, national governments.[8] Consequently, the EMS has a deflation bias that goes against the economic interests of labor and the governments in the EMS countries. An EMU built on the EMS would likely be equally dominated by the Bundesbank and have the same deflation bias.

Membership in such an arrangement would hurt particularly the weaker economies in the EC. Therefore, EMU would have to be bolstered by significant regional redistribution schemes in the EC, which would hold it together and compensate those regions that suffer dispro-portionately from the consequences of deflation.[9] The central Community budget would have to grow rapidly to gain the necessary resources. This call for redistributive policies in an EMU has found a formal underpinning in the EC's Social Charter adopted in 1989. Oddly enough, instead of curtailing the alleged power of the central bankers' club, the Social Charter creates more clubs by strengthening the Brussels bureaucracy at the expense of national governments.

As for the empirical basis of the ostensible deflation bias of the EMS, we noted in Chapter 2 that EMS disinflation in the 1980s has not been any more pronounced than disinflation in other parts of the industrialized world. The central claim of the club-view adherents thus lacks empirical support. It is true that real growth has been slower and unemployment higher in the EMS countries, but this can hardly be debited to the monetary authorities. The burgeoning literature on "Eurosclerosis" and hysteresis points to supply-side considerations as the main culprit. For example, Todd (1984) argues that (tax-induced) increases in the relative cost of labor and capital led businesses to substitute capital for labor without expanding employment. The EC Commission (1984) speaks of structural labor market disequilibria resulting from imperfections and rigidities that prevented adjustment to external shocks. Lawrence and Schultze (1987, 42) summarize:

Most of the rise in unemployment stems, we believe, from two sources with unknown relative importance: hysteresis effects in the determination of wages . . . and increasing structural rigidities. . . . Europe's sustained experience with high and rising unemployment may have led to protective mechanisms and rigidities that helped perpetuate the unemployment.

In the same volume, Krugman (1987, 72) adds: "An unrepentant Keynesian, observing Europe's unemployment, would call for massively expansionary government policies. One of the surprising features of the European intellectual scene is that such unrepentant demand-siders are nowhere to be found." Krugman's assessment implies that the EMS did not impose "conservative" aggregate demand policies on a "liberal constituency," but delivered what the constituency wanted.[10] In conclusion, the claim of a deflation bias is unwarranted.

Monetary Union and the Degree of Effective Policy Competition

The competitive view of monetary policy objects to monetary unification because it restricts competition among monetary policy makers. Vaubel (1989a) elaborates on this point by referring to Hirshman's principles of "exit" and "voice" (Hirshman 1970). *Exit* is the ability to invest in assets denominated in different currencies. *Voice* is the voter's ability to disapprove of erroneous monetary policies through the ballot box. EMU dilutes voice because collusion among policymakers makes political responsibilities more diffuse and eliminates the demonstration effect that a successful monetary policy in one country has on other countries. In the context of monetary union, exit is a more powerful principle than voice, because elections are decided over multiple issues. But even in the competitive scenario, exit is limited by the fact that citizens of one country are forced to use their home currency for certain transactions, such as tax payments.

To what extent would EMU limit the power of exit? One important issue is how large the EMU is relative to the remaining nonmember economies. Central bank collusion in an EMU clearly restricts some competition of monetary policy, but it does not create an international monopoly. Exit opportunities will remain through the availability of non-EC currencies such as the U.S. dollar, the Swiss franc, and the Japanese yen, to name a few. Monetary policies in non-EC countries can still impart "good lessons." The effectiveness of exit does not require the largest possible number of individual policies, just as competition in goods markets can prevail even if the number of firms is not very large.

On the other hand, EMU promotes the elimination of barriers to competition by favoring the dismantling of exchange and capital control vis-à-vis nonmembers. The Community has proposed and begun the dissolution of such controls with respect to all countries as part of the process of financial integration. In a monetary union, their reimposition, although legally possible, would likely be subject to the consent of all members and therefore be removed at least partly from the discretion of national politicians.[11] By opening individual financial markets to more outside competition, EMU actually strengthens the force of and opportunities for exit.

8.3 Exchange-Rate Union or Currency Union?

The current debate over EMU is still undecided between the two forms the monetary union can take: an exchange-rate union, in which exchange rates are permanently fixed but different national monies continue to exist, and a currency union, in which only a European money circulates. The *Delors Report* envisions that exchange rates will eventually be irrevocably locked and the ESCB will take full responsibility for monetary policy in the Community. The report also favors the adoption of a single currency and hopes that national currencies will be replaced by a single currency. But the committee did not outline the mechanism that would make possible the withering away of national currencies.

Exchange-rate unions offer the advantages of preserving existing currencies and the "brand names" they have earned in the market, softening the objections of groups that feel threatened by the introduction of a common currency, and leaving open the possibility of undoing the union at some future date. This possibility, however remote it might be, is an inherent source of uncertainty (Artis 1989). Moving from an exchange-rate union to a currency union adds to the savings of transactions costs connected with the sale and purchase of several monies; thus, the transactions-cost benefits of a currency union will be greater than the benefits of an exchange-rate union.

Furthermore, by removing the possibility of countries opting out of the EMU easily, a currency union deepens financial market integration. Consider the rates of return on two imperfectly substitutable assets under flexible exchange rates:

(8.6) $R - R^* = Es_{t+1} - s_t + RP,$

where R and R^* are the market yields, s is the spot exchange rate, E is the expectations operator, and RP is a risk premium. We saw in Section 7.3 that interest rate differentials in the EMS have remained sizable, even after the last realignment in 1987. In addition to the risk premium, these differences reflect the probability and the expected size of future realignments. An exchange-rate union would not set the expected exchange rate equal to the spot rate because the governments retain an "escape clause." Individuals would realize that the notion of "irrevocably fixed" exchange rates has no practical meaning and expect, instead, that with some positive probability, governments will use the escape clause in the future. As a result, interest rate differentials will always be larger in an exchange-rate union than in a currency union; the effect will be higher real cost of borrowing and capital market distortions for those countries whose governments are considered more prone to the use of the escape clause than others.

Gros and Thygesen (1990a, 25) and Bini-Smaghi (1990) illustrate this point with the example of the Netherlands and Germany. According to Gros and Thygesen, Dutch economic policy closely mirrored Germany policy from 1983 to 1989, and the exchange rate between the guilder and the mark remained very stable, as if the two countries belonged to a de facto monetary union. Yet Dutch interest rates significantly exceeded German interest rates. More recent data confirm these observations. Between March 1987 and May 1990, yields on three-month Euro-guilder deposits exceeded the yield on Euro-mark deposits by 67 basis points. The guilder suffered a forward discount of 61 annual basis points vis-à-vis the DM, whereas in fact the guilder appreciated by 7 basis points.[12] In other words, it would have been appreciably more profitable to invest in guilder-denominated assets than in DM-denominated assets and forgo the hedge in the forward market. Given the Dutch government's intention to keep the fixed exchange rate with the mark, this suggests a sizable benefit from moving to one currency.

Does a currency union, then, imply that interest rates equalize? The answer is no. First, a currency union does not eliminate the risk premium. Borrowers will continue to enjoy different degrees of creditworthiness in the currency union. In particular, interest rates on public debt will continue to reflect differences in the fiscal strength of national governments and their perceived ability to serve their debt obligations, unless markets come to believe that the EMU will be the ultimate guarantor of all public debt. Regional real rates of return will continue to reflect real rates of appreciation and depreciation of one area against others, factors that of course remain possible in a currency union.[13] To summarize, the move from an exchange-rate union to a currency union will reduce but not eliminate interest rate differentials.

The credibility argument for monetary unification entails another benefit from moving to a currency union. Having a common currency rather than the traditional national currencies makes it more difficult to withdraw from the union than it is to adjust exchange rates in an exchange-rate union. That is, the currency union raises the price of reneging on the commitment to an EMU devoted to price stability. In this way, a common currency would allow the EMU to achieve a lower credible long-run inflation rate than would an exchange-rate union.

The move from an exchange-rate union to a currency union entails two potential costs: loss of seignorage revenues and loss of monetary sovereignty. It follows from the previous discussion of seignorage that an individual country may gain or lose seignorage, depending on the rules of revenue sharing the union agrees upon. The loss of monetary sovereignty is, of course, simply the other side of eliminating the escape clause that remains in the exchange-rate union. The value of this clause depends primarily on the nature of the shocks hitting the member countries and the ability of the currency union to cope with these shocks. Our discussion of the cooperative interpretation of the EMS implies that this ability is greatest in the face of very severe asymmetric demand and supply shocks, and that it diminishes with the provisions of side payments or redistributional schemes within the union. Later we show that the fiscal arrangements play a major role in this regard. Continuing economic integration works in favor of the currency union by reducing the destabilizing power of asymmetric shocks.

8.4 The Role of Fiscal Policy in a Monetary Union

EMU is not a matter of monetary policy alone. Many authors have pointed to the important fiscal policy implications of monetary unification in the EC.[14] Such implications arise mainly from two grounds: first, as previously discussed, government revenue from money creation in a monetary union is determined by collective decision or a common central bank and shared among the members of the union; second, a monetary union deprives individual members of monetary policy as an independent tool for stabilization and thus enforces a particular class of solutions to the "assignment problem," that is, the assignment of specific policy goals to the fiscal and monetary branches of economic policy.

Fiscal Discipline in a Monetary Union

Apart from the implications of sharing seignorage, a monetary union creates a potential avenue for using public debt to shift the incidence of taxes from domestic citizens to citizens of other countries.[15] Counting on the solidarity among the members of the union, a government may be tempted to issue debt in excess of the levels deemed sustainable in the absence of a union, expecting that the monetary union will come to its rescue in the case of a liquidity crisis rather than let it face bankruptcy or expose its citizens to large tax increases. Such rescue operations would tax citizens of other member countries either explicitly or, because monetizing the debt would increase EMU inflation, through a higher inflation tax on moneyholders (Lamfalussy 1989). The combination of solidarity and joint seignorage collection in a monetary union therefore works against the fiscal discipline of its members. The resulting threat to the EMU's monetary stability has led many to call for formal fiscal restraints on individual government budgetary policies as a necessary condition for EMU.

The *Delors Report* (1989), for example, speaks of "effective upper limits on budget deficits of individual member countries" and "the definition of the overall stance of fiscal policy over the medium term including the size and the financing of the aggregate budgetary balance" (para. 33). It regards fiscal restraints as one of the "basic elements" of an "economic union in conjunction with a monetary union" (para. 25) and concludes that fiscal restraints, such as balanced budget provisions or ceilings on deficits, are required to guarantee the soundness of fiscal policies in the union.

The implicit contention that the moral hazard problem is a consequence of the monetary regime is a basic flaw in this argument. The moral hazard problem is the outflow of closer international coordination and integration. Recent experience with the debt of developing and Eastern European countries is clear evidence of this. Industrial countries agreed to reschedule and forgive debt, irrespective of the exchange-rate arrangement linking debtor and creditor nations. Solidarity, not monetary union, is the source of bailouts. Certainly, EMU will raise the solidarity among the members. But to attribute the moral hazard problem to the monetary union itself is misleading.

At the same time, there are forces at work in a monetary union that enhance fiscal discipline and work against the negative incentive effect. Reputational considerations suggest that excessive debt is incurred by governments with direct access to the printing press. As already argued, joining a monetary union with an independent monetary authority eliminates such access and reduces deficits and debt (Goodhart 1989). The assured independence of the common monetary authority can indeed be regarded as an institutional substitute for fiscal restraints. EMU has no need for fiscal restraints if monetizing public debt by the common central bank is firmly precluded. In this regard, the call by the Delors Committee for fiscal restraints suggests that it already saw the independence of the future European central bank as a lost cause.

The pricing of default or inflation risk in the international capital markets is the main countervailing force against the adverse fiscal incentive. If public debt holders demand sufficiently large risk premiums in response to frivolous budgetary policies, the cost of issuing debt rises when nonsustainable levels are reached, making such policies unattractive from the government's point of view. The practical importance of the threat therefore depends critically on the efficiency of capital markets in assessing and pricing risk. Indeed, the *Delors Report* (para. 30) justifies its call for formal fiscal restraints with the explicit contention that markets do not price risk properly:

> To some extent market forces can exert a disciplinary influence. . . . However, experience suggest that market perceptions do not necessarily provide strong and compelling signals and that access to a large capital market may for some time even facilitate the financing of economic imbalances. . . . The constraints imposed by market forces might either be too slow and weak or too sudden and disruptive.

The report concludes that governments must rectify a market failure with an administrative rule. Again, we note that the market failure argument does not pertain solely to monetary integration; it arises with independent monetary policies as well. A monetary union—in which international interest rate differentials are clouded by exchange-rate expectations— would raise the visibility of risk premiums embedded in interest rate differentials and, thus, would enhance the efficiency of market forces (Council of Economic Advisors to the German Minister of Economics 1989).

On the other hand, there is no reason to assume a priori that fiscal restraints imposed by the Community would be more effective than market forces. Public choice theory suggests that national policy makers would seek and find ways to circumvent such rules, if doing so serves their political interest. At the same time, the rules and the enforcement mechanisms designed by the Community would emerge from a political process at the Community level that would not necessarily reflect the best economic rationale.[16] Historically, the performance of the Community in enforcing common rules has been rather poor (Mortensen 1990, 69). To get an impression of how effective formal restraints are in fostering fiscal discipline, we present some experience from the United States, where almost all states are subject to such rules.

Fiscal Restraints in the United States

Formal fiscal restraints exist in the United States in the form of statutory or constitutional balanced budget requirements and limitations on state debt. With the exception of Vermont, all states have some form of balanced budget requirements (BBRs), ranging from the simple provision that the governor has to submit a balanced budget (12 states) to the explicit ban on carrying over a deficit into the next fiscal year (29 states). There are 32 states with state debt limits in the form of nominal limits percentage limits relating to state funds, tax revenues, taxable or state property, or total appropriations; 38 states have debt limits of this kind, or special legislative restrictions such as a referendum requirement to create debt, or both.

A recent study by the Advisory Commission on Intergovernmental Relations (ACIR 1987b) provides an index of the stringency of the legal constraints implied by the BBRs. The index ranges from 0 (no requirement) to 10, with a distribution that is heavily skewed toward the higher values—36 of the 50 states have a ranking of 9 and 10. The index has a weak negative correlation with state debt per capita levels and debt-income ratios but no apparent correlation with debt growth. Higher fiscal stringency seems to give incentives to states to change their debt mix toward more nonguaranteed debt, a way to circumvent fiscal restraints.[17]

For a more formal assessment, we have grouped the states by degree of fiscal stringency: low (index value 0 to 4), medium (5 to 8) and high (9 and 10). Table 8.2 shows the average of the four indicators of fiscal performance for these groups. States with high BBR stringency have a significantly lower average state debt per capita than do states with low stringency. The only other significant difference is how debt is allocated between fully guaranteed and nonguaranteed debt. Here the evidence is clear: debt limits do make a statistical difference in the choice of debt mix.

The risk of a central bank bailing out an insolvent government treasury depends even more on the probability of particularly deviant fiscal behavior than on average fiscal performance. To see how fiscal restraints change this probability, we have isolated the three largest observations for each of the four indicators. The three states with the fastest debt growth and the largest ratios of nonguaranteed to guaranteed debt fall into the group with the highest stringency index and with formal debt limits. Two of the three states with the largest per capita debt and debt-income ratios, respectively, also belong to the group with the highest fiscal stringency and formal debt limits.[18]

The lesson we draw from this simple empirical exercise is that fiscal restraints do little to change average fiscal performance and do not significantly lower the probability of extreme outcomes. This broad conclusion is in line with the more detailed evidence provided in other studies.[19] Despite the obvious fact that the United States differs structurally and institutionally from the EC, this evidence casts doubt on the promise that formal fiscal restraints can enhance fiscal discipline in a European monetary union and reduce the monetary authority's risk of

TABLE 8.2 Fiscal Restraints and Fiscal Performance of States
in the United States (1985)

		Debt Limits 1		Debt Limits 2		BBR Stringency Index		
		Yes	No	Yes	No	Low	Medium	High
Debt per capita ($)	Aver.	1203.5	1290.1	910.7	2267.7	1576.6**	1723.5	919.2
	std. dev.	1904.0	775.0	654.8	2813.3	406.7	2714.8	752.8
Debt/ income ratio (percent)	Aver.	9.4	9.3	7.5	15.1	11.1	11.9	7.7
	std. dev.	11.5	5.8	5.2	16.6	4.4	16.0	5.7
Debt growth (percent)	Aver.	4.5	2.9	4.2	2.9	4.1	2.7	4.5
	std. dev.	4.2	3.0	4.2	2.1	4.1	2.1	4.4
Debt mix (percent)	Aver.	3.5*	2.6	3.5**	2.5	1.9**	2.0**	4.0
	std. dev.	2.3	1.5	1.9	0.8	0.2	1.2	2.6

Note: Debt Limits 1 are nominal debt limits and percentage limits relating to state funds, taxable property, tax revenues, or total appropriations. Debt Limits 2 add to Debt Limits 1 special legislative requirements. Aver. and std. dev. denote group average and standard deviation; * and ** denote statistical significance of a t-test for equal means at 5 percent and 1 percent, respectively.

Source: von Hagen (1991a).

acting as a lender of last resort. However, to the extent that they induce governments to engage in off-budget activities, fiscal restraints lower the information content of published government finance data, thus making it harder for the capital markets to perform efficiently. In conclusion, one should not trust too much in the ability of binding rules to rectify alleged market failures in restraining the growth of government debt.

Fiscal Stabilization and International Transfers

In line with traditional views of the optimal currency area (e.g., Kenen 1969), the changing nature of the assignment problem has led to the proposition that a viable EMU requires a significant centralized budget to absorb transitory, idiosyncratic shocks to individual member economies. This argument is closely related to the cooperative interpretation of fixed exchange rates: in the monetary union, monetary policy can still be used to stabilize aggregate shocks that affect all members of the union equally, but individual countries cannot use monetary policy to respond to idiosyncratic shocks. With a common currency, real exchange-rate adjustment to such shocks must operate through changes in regional prices and wages. But because prices and wages are sluggish, adjustment is too long and creates unnecessary disequilibria in the output and labor markets. Because monetary policy can no longer be used autonomously in the various parts of the union, fiscal policy has to play the role of equilibrating regional differences in the fluctuations of output and employment.

Suppose a recessionary demand shock hits the Netherlands but no other EC member directly. With flexible exchange rates the guilder would soon depreciate, and the resulting real depreciation would raise export demand and help the Dutch economy recover from the shock. In a monetary union, in contrast, relative price changes—and therefore the recovery—would be slow. More rapid adjustment could occur either by regional movements of labor and capital or by using Community fiscal policies to direct a greater portion of EC aggregate demand toward Dutch output (for example, by reducing the Dutch burden of taxes to the EC or by increasing EC public spending in the Netherlands). But for the transactions costs involved, factor movements are inefficient responses to transitory regional shocks. Specifically in the context of EMU, migration is rendered difficult by language and cultural differences and may even be considered politically unacceptable as a means of adjustment (Doyle 1989). This leaves Community fiscal policy as the main mechanism for absorbing such shocks.

The lack of adequate fiscal instruments would expose the EC to prolonged spells of regional economic disparities unrelated to the underlying trends of regional development, causing strain and dissatisfaction with the EMU and undermining its proper functioning. In view of this danger, the chairman of the committee in the *Delors Report* (1989, 89) argues:

[I]n all federations the different combinations of federal budgetary mechanisms have powerful "shock-absorber" effects, dampening the amplitude either of economic difficulties or of surges in prosperity of individual states. This is both the product of, and the source of the sense of national solidarity which all relevant economic and monetary unions share.

Sachs and Sala-i-Martin (1989) and Eichengreen (1990) point to the

U.S. experience to corroborate this view. Sachs and Sala-i-Martin contend that the U.S. federal fiscal system responds to regional shocks by offsetting about one-third of impact effects through counteraction tax and transfer payments. That is, a region suffering a real income loss of one dollar relative to the union is compensated by 35 cents of transfer payments and lower federal taxes. They and Eichengreen conclude that an EMU without a sufficiently large fiscal apparatus would be detrimental. However, von Hagen (1992) shows that the estimates presented in Sachs and Sala-i-Martin are biased upward, because they do not separate transitory from permanent regional shocks. This distinction is drawn properly in the empirical evidence, which shows that the U.S. fiscal system offsets only around 10 percent of a transitory regional shock, a finding confirmed by Atkeson and Bayoumi (1991). Masson and Taylor (1991) present evidence for Canada showing a similar, relatively small role of the federal fiscal system in dealing with regional shocks.

The call for a sizable centralized fiscal budget to stabilize transitory regional shocks in an EMU goes back to the MacDougall Report (Commission of the EC 1977), which estimated that a budget of about 5 percent of the Community's GNP would be required for a viable EMU. The *Delors Report* (1989, para. 30) judges that a central budget of that size is politically not feasible in the near future and therefore calls for greater coordination of fiscal policies among the members to achieve the same purpose. Recently, Begg and Wyplosz (CEPR 1989, 23) and Williamson (1990) have proposed allocation of a common unemployment insurance system in Brussels as a minimal fiscal setup.[20]

It is worth pointing out again that the type of economic disturbance in question is transitory shocks with asymmetric effects across the EC. Even in the presence of transactions cost and sluggish prices, relative price changes and factor movements guided by market signals remain efficient responses to permanent changes in a region's relative income. On the other hand, the EC may—and does—wish to use fiscal and other policy tools to reduce permanent income differences in the Community in the same way as national governments do, independent of its monetary regime. The MacDougall Report indicated that central governments tend to redistribute resources among regions in a permanent way. For example, between 1971 and 1973, the relatively poor regions of Italy received net public finance inflows averaging between 7.8 and 28 percent of their gross regional product. At the same time, their regional current-account deficits varied between 14.8 and 42.3 percent. In contrast, the relatively rich regions had net public finance outflows between 4.4 and 11.1 percent, compared with current account surpluses of 10.9 to 15.3 percent (Commission of the EC 1977, 33). Private capital flows obviously did not fully match current-account imbalances. Permanent regional redistribution is not the critical issue in the debate over EMU. Furthermore, shocks with symmetric effects across the EC would not require exchange-rate adjustment in the absence of EMU and can be dealt with using the common monetary policy in the EMU. Therefore, the debate over fiscal policy implications of EMU focuses specifically on transitory regional shocks.

A fiscal system to cope with such shocks can be implemented in two ways. The first one operates via government spending and has been advocated by the MacDougall Report. The EC would allocate a sufficiently large fiscal budget in Brussels, which would allow its central administration to direct funds to areas of relatively weak economic performance. Because the budget would be funded by all members, the necessary degree of income redistribution would be achieved by an appropriate regional distribution of EC spending. The MacDougall Committee concluded that in view of the size of regional shocks and the central government budgets commonly available for such purposes, EMU remained unfeasible without a Community budget of at least 5 to 7 percent of Community GNP. The *Delors Report*, and Lamfalussy (1989) in one of the contributions to its appendix, follow the same approach, but argue that the EC is not politically ready to accept such a large Community budget. Instead, close coordination of national budgets is required to serve the same purpose.

It is important to understand, however, that a fiscal redistribution system can work alternatively on the government revenue side and without any need for centralized government spending. Income redistribution to equilibrate regional shocks can be achieved through a Community-wide income tax and transfer system. The system would have to be designed such that relatively depressed regions are taxed less heavily than relatively prosperous regions (for example, by progressive income taxation) and would have to facilitate the transfer of tax revenues from the latter to the former. As in other federal systems, such as Germany, regional income redistribution can be achieved through rules of sharing taxes collected at the federal level among the individual member states. In combination with national institutions such as unemployment compensation, the tax system would execute automatic transfers among regions, without requiring any appropriations and spending authority at the Community level or coordination of national spending policies.

From a political-economy point of view, however, the two alternatives are not equally desirable. Increasing the Community budget means increasing the power of the central administration both in comparison to the national governments and to the EMU monetary authority. It raises the payoff for and encourages lobbying at the central administration and creates new opportunities for logrolling and influence peddling. In light of the experience with government spending programs at the national level, the efficiency of centralized or coordinated spending to buffer transitory regional shocks is highly questionable, given the sluggishness of the political process and the well-known difficulty in ending regional subsidies. A redistributive tax system, in contrast, would not make the actual transfers subject to political discretion. In addition, it would leave the spending power with the national administrations. The theory of fiscal federalism suggests that national administrations would recognize better the priorities and needs of the individual member countries. Finally, tax-based redistribution with decentralized spending would favor competition among fiscal authorities and help preserve the independence of the common monetary authority.

In contrast, the drive toward building significant centralized spending power or, as a politically more promising substitute, the coordination of national fiscal policies in a monetary union can be regarded from a very different perspective. To develop this view, we assume that the Europe 1992 program is successful in promoting goods market and financial market integration; this will increase intra-EC trade and raise the share of exports and imports in each country's GNP. Financial market integration will tend to increase the international substitutability of financial assets within the region, particularly at the shorter end of the market. Thus, each economy becomes more open and more closely integrated in the regional capital markets.

The important implication of these trends is that national fiscal policy is likely to lose much of its power to control output and employment, even in the short run. Greater openness implies greater spillovers of aggregate demand between the economies and, hence, reduces government spending multipliers. National fiscal policy makers will therefore see their power and influence diminish as economic integration proceeds in Europe. Public choice theory suggests that these policymakers will seek ways to regain their leverage and restore the effectiveness of their policy instruments. Coordination of national policies and centralization of fiscal policy at the Community level are both promising strategies to achieve that goal. Both are in essence forms of collusion among fiscal policy makers, and both serve to increase the clout of fiscal policy relative to monetary policy in a monetary union. Both raise the probability of fiscal dominance of the monetary union that in turn tends to endanger its usefulness as a commitment mechanism for price stability. For this reason, greater fiscal coordination is not only unwarranted but counterproductive for the performance of an EMU.

The Delors Committee may have feared that uncoordinated fiscal policies in a monetary union would yield inconsistent fiscal activism at the national level and put a strain on the monetary system. The Committee's recommendation of coordination coupled with binding constraints on fiscal policies may be interpreted as an attempt to prevent such inconsistencies while limiting the clout of fiscal policy by imposing constraints. But there is little reason to follow this approach. The reduced effectiveness of fiscal policy resulting from integration and the greater competition national governments will face in the capital markets reduce benefits and raise economic cost of national fiscal activism. Greater economic integration and competition among national fiscal policies therefore tend to induce governments to adopt stable fiscal policies compatible with stable monetary policy in the union.[21]

Harmonization of Tax Systems

Recent literature has pointed to the potential damage national inconsistencies of tax systems can cause in an economic union.[22] Taxes on goods, services, and factors of production distort relative prices, triggering inefficient flows of goods, services, capital, and labor and producing regional trade imbalances. The EC governments have agreed to reduce differences in value-added tax rates, taxes on capital income, and the like as an important element of the unified internal market. Monetary integration reinforces the importance of this element in that exchange rates can no longer be used to rectify after-tax relative price and interest rate differentials and the resulting regional imbalances. One can go further: the harmonization of tax systems is itself a precondition of monetary unification as long as the union retains individual national currencies tied together through fixed exchange rates maintained by foreign exchange market intervention. Persistent trade imbalances resulting from inconsistent tax laws would undermine the sustainability of the union. A significant degree of harmonization is therefore indispensable in an EMU.

8.5 Institutional Requirements
for a Low-Inflation EMU

The monetary union can improve the average quality of monetary policy only if its institutional design facilitates credible precommitment to low-inflation policies. Three important requirements must be fulfilled: institutional independence, personal independence, and professional competence. First, the monetary authority must be fully independent from political pressure. Bade and Parkin (1987), among others, have shown empirically that there is a significant positive relationship between the degree of independence of monetary authorities and price stability. In turn, three conditions must be satisfied to obtain central bank independence (Neumann 1991). First, national and Community politicians cannot interfere with the conduct of monetary policy. In particular, the monetary authority must have full control over the assets and liabilities of its balance sheet. This excludes compulsory lending to public sector authorities and the monetization of public debt.[23] The example of the Bundesbank demonstrates that monetary control is possible even without resorting to open market operations of significant size. Balance-sheet autonomy also excludes allowing a government or the Community to impose exchange-rate policies. Recent experience with international policy coordination has shown that governments all too willingly engage in efforts to manipulate exchange rates without regard to the future inflation consequences (Funabashi 1988; von Hagen 1989b). Furthermore, the monetary authority must not be obliged to follow instructions by governments or Community authorities. This includes general clauses such as supporting EC economic policies that create opportunities for government officials to exert pressure on the monetary authority.[24]

The second condition is that central bank officials in the union must have personal independence, which entails a duration of appointment sufficiently long to shield them from the short-run orientation of electoral interests. There should be no reappointments because these might tempt central bankers to serve political interests to assure a second term. As a practical solution, Neumann (1991) proposes setting a minimum age for appointment to the central bank board and terms sufficiently long for the appointee to reach normal retirement age.

Personal independence also includes not requiring central bank officials to appear regularly in direct, public confrontation with national governments or the European Parliament. The U.S. example demonstrates how the need to report to political authorities on a regular basis creates incentives for central bank officials to bow to political pressures.[25] This does not exclude, of course, accountability of the central bank: the monetary authority must be audited and supervised to assure that its policies are conducted on sound banking and accounting principles.

Finally, central bank officials should be professionally competent to understand the role of money in the economy and be prepared to educate the public and the politicians about the limits of monetary policy. Consequently, salaries ought to be commensurable with those earned by top management in the private sector. Otherwise, there is a danger that central bank positions would be regarded primarily as stepping stones to more lucrative private sector jobs, in which case central bankers would be eager to seek good contacts with private interest groups. Wage increases during the term of office should be linked to performance, as is true in the private sector. For example, one could fix the nominal level of the salaries to enhance the achievement of price level stability. Even if these conditions were fulfilled, the monetary union need not provide an effective solution to the precommitment problem, so long as politicians can regain control over monetary policy relatively easily and at their discretion. Under such circumstances, the private sector would rationally foresee that politicians revert to discretionary monetary policies under politically opportune conditions. Indeed, the failure to identify plausible and significant costs of reneging on a preannounced, low-inflation exchange-rate target is one of the main reasons most credibility interpretations of the EMS in the literature remain unconvincing.

EMU as a commitment mechanism requires that the political cost of regime reversals be large enough to outweigh the potential for short-run gains. This brings in two further requirements. First, politicians must find it very hard and politically costly to change the statutes of the monetary authority, so that its independence is not subject to the discretion of the political sector. This could be achieved by elevating the monetary statute of the EC to the rank of constitutional law. Second, because the individual member states retain their formal sovereignty to withdraw from the union, their commitment to membership must be rendered credible by making withdrawal sufficiently costly to outweigh the potential short-run gains from leaving the union and returning (temporarily) to an independent and more inflationary monetary policy. As one means of increasing the cost of withdrawal, EMU membership should therefore have constitutional status in all member countries. Furthermore, the monetary union should have highly visible institutions such as a common central bank, so that voters would regard membership withdrawal as a loss of reputation of their country. Finally, the adoption of a common currency—instead of retaining the existing currencies and simply fixing exchange rates, as proposed by the *Delors Report*—would enhance the credibility of the EMU commitment by raising the cost of reverting to an independent monetary regime.

8.6 Conclusions

Monetary union is a form of collusion among central bankers. Although collusion is unambiguously bad if it is compared to an ideal competitive scenario of independent central banks, we have argued in this chapter that there are reasons why EMU could raise the quality of monetary policy in Europe. EMU would not create a monopolistic scenario because there will remain strong competitive forces in the international monetary policy arena. The positive impact of EMU stems from its potential as a mechanism for commitment to price stability, an instrument many countries may not have available domestically. The important task therefore is to design the structure of EMU so as to make it a credible institution. For that purpose it is paramount that the European monetary authority be independent of the political system in general and the fiscal authorities in particular. The autonomy of the European central bank can and should be strengthened by isolating its officials from the short-run orientation of electoral interests and by designing a remuneration structure that is linked to price level performance. The incentive structure in the future EMU monetary authority also suggests that voting rules and rules for distributing seigniorage revenue must be designed in a way to reinforce the incentives for low-inflation policies.

The proper functioning of a monetary union requires some degree of harmonization of tax laws to avoid incongruent distortions of relative prices. Furthermore, it may need provisions facilitating income redistribution among the members to buffer regionally diverse economic shocks. Both features can be achieved by an appropriate design of the tax system. Beyond that, there is no need for any greater coordination or centralization of government spending in the monetary union. Efforts in that regard may appear attractive for national fiscal policy makers because they are deemed to lose power as a consequence of greater integration. But fiscal coordination and centralization run contrary to the establishment of a low-inflation EMU because they weaken the relative strength and independence of the monetary authority.

Finally, we reject the call for fiscal restraints in an EMU. Imposing formal constraints on budget policies does not seem to be a more promising way to prevent unreasonable budget deficits than market forces. However, fiscal restraints invite politicians to seek ways to circumvent the budgetary rules and ultimately make the public control of government more difficult.

Notes

1. Artis (1989) estimates the multiple at 10.
2. The direct saving from the reduction in foreign exchange is bound to be small because monetary authorities hold interest-bearing assets.
3. See De Grauwe (1992) for an excellent discussion.
4. As De Grauwe (1992) points out, this disadvantage entails, in particular, that Germany will insist on shaping the monetary union such that the European central bankers will have even greater preference for price stability than their counterparts in the Bundesbank.
5. For a discussion, see, for example, Tanzi and Ter-Minassian (1987), Council

of Economic Advisors to the German Minister of Economics (1989), and Giavazzi (1989).

6. As one can readily verify by solving expression (8.1) for v/z and the values indicated in Table 8.1.

7. In practice, the redistribution is likely to take more indirect forms such as additional programs for regional policies or structural policies, which allow for revenue flows among the members without direct reference to seignorage. The *Delors Report* (1989, para. 32) mentions such policies among the institutional arrangements of EMU.

8. We showed in Chapter 5 that such a rigid notion of German dominance in the EMS is not empirically warranted.

9. The *Delors Report* (1989) indirectly acknowledges this point by calling for regional policies supporting the creation of EMU (paras. 14, 27). In contrast, the Council of Economic Advisors to the German Minister of Economics (1989) negates the need for regional redistribution as an inherent consequence of EMU. The Council argues instead that attempts to harmonize wages and social policies in an EMU would reinforce resource misallocations and calls for policies assuring wage and price flexibility.

10. The "Europe 1992" program can be regarded in this context as an experiment in deregulation to release many of the structural deficiencies of the EMS economies. The general intellectual climate indeed seems to have changed from Eurosclerosis to Eurooptimism in the second half of the 1980s. Mortensen (1990) notes that Eurosclerosis has deeply influenced the EC Commission, whose 1985 projection of GDP growth in the EC in the second half of the 1980s fell short of actual growth by a half percentage point per year.

11. Note that despite the common perception that capital and exchange controls will soon be fully dismantled in the EC, the relevant directives allow for their reintroduction if governments perceive that short-run capital movements cause significant strain in foreign exchange markets and disturb the conduct of monetary policy in a member country. See Bofinger (1989, 433) and Key (1989, 596). Such provisions do not rule out the return to restrictions.

12. Harris Bank (various issues).

13. See Stultz (1984) for an analysis of real exchange-rate viability and interest rates.

14. See, for example, *Delors Report* (1989), Branson (1989), Isard (1989), Bredenkamp and Deppler (1990), Eichengreen (1990), von Hagen (1990), von Hagen and Fratianni (1990, 1991), Commission of the EC (1990), Masson and Mélitz (1991).

15. As discussed earlier, this also implies that individual governments may agree to higher inflation rate in the monetary union than with independent monetary policies.

16. We do not mean to say, however, that public choice theory rejects fiscal rules for this reason. Many public choice economists indeed argue in favor of fiscal rules to correct the elected politician's incentive to spend in excess of tax revenues.

17. By setting up special authorities to manage state projects and creating nonguaranteed debt in their name instead of undertaking guaranteed, "full faith and credit" debt, states can avoid fiscal restraints.

18. For more details, see von Hagen (1991a).

19. See ACIR (1987b), von Hagen (1991a), Heins (1963), Abrams and Dougan (1986). ACIR (1987b) presents a regression analysis of the impact of BBR stringency on state deficit spending and finds only a weak negative effect.

20. See also Bank of England (1990a, 67) for a critical discussion.

21. Another impetus for greater fiscal centralization in an EMU results if EMU is understood to lead inevitably to the political unification of the Community. With political unification, the EC would have to provide basic public goods—a common defense, police, a justice system—that require an adequate Community budget. But apart from such political considerations, EMU does not require centralization or coordination of government spending.

22. See, for example, Isard (1989), Tanzi and Ter-Minassian (1987), and Vegh and Guidotti (1989).

23. Barro (1983) shows that a government's ability to monetize public debt is a further source of inflation bias.

24. The *Delors Report* (1989, para. 32) proposes such a clause, the effectiveness of which is mediated, however, by the conditionality of the monetary authority's commitment to price stability.

25. The *Delors Report* (1989, para. 32) proposes that the chairman of the EMU monetary authority shall report to the European Parliament and the European Council.

9

On the Road to Economic
and Monetary Union

This chapter focuses on the transition from the present EMS to a future European economic and monetary union (EEMU). Our discussion deals at length with the blueprint proposed by the EC's Committee on the Study of Economic and Monetary Union, the Delors Committee. The *Delors Report*, by virtue of the stature of the committee members, all top representatives of the central banks in the EC, and the fact that it was officially endorsed at the EC's Madrid Summit in 1989, has become the inevitable standard against which one must measure approaches to EEMU. We begin with a review of the report. Next, we compare the Delors strategy with several alternatives, including the one proposed by Her Majesty's Treasury (HM Treasury 1989). In section 9.3, we present a public choice interpretation of the Delors strategy, then follow that with a discussion of the main criteria for the choice of a strategy for EEMU. In Section 9.5, we develop a simple model of adjustment to central bank dominance to ascertain how far out of line the high-inflation countries of the EC still are in relation to the low-inflation countries. Section 9.6 reviews the current debate over how long the transition phase toward EEMU should be, and the final section presents some conclusions.

9.1 The *Delors Report:*
A Strategy for Monetary Union

The *Delors Report* consists of three main parts, one dealing with economic union, one dealing with the construction of EEMU, and one dealing with fiscal policy. The strategy it proposes rests on four principles: the EMS as the basis for monetary union (MU); parallelism, the principle according to which economic union (EU) and MU must progress simultaneously; gradualism, the principle that the MU must be built in a stepwise procedure; and a call for binding fiscal restraints on the member governments. In this section, we characterize the first three points with some critical passages from the report.

Economic Union

> The success of the internal market program hinges to a decisive extent on a much closer coordination of national economic policies. . . . This implies that in essence a number of the steps towards economic and monetary union will already have to be taken in the course of establishing a single market in Europe (para. 14).

> Economic and monetary union would represent the final result of the progressive economic integration in Europe (para. 16).

Monetary Union

The report defines monetary union as a

> currency area in which policies are managed jointly. . . . The single most important condition for a monetary union would, however, be fulfilled only when the decisive step was taken to lock exchange rates irrevocably (para. 22).

> The adoption of a *single currency* . . . might be seen . . . as a natural and desirable further development of the monetary union. . . . The replacement of national currencies by a single currency should therefore take place as soon as possible after the locking of parities (para. 23).

> A new monetary institution would be needed because a single monetary policy cannot result from independent decisions and actions by different central banks. . . . [This institution] should be organized in a federal form, in what might be called a *European System of Central Banks* (ESCB). . . . The System would be committed to the objective of price stability; . . . it should be independent of instructions from national governments and Community authorities (para. 32).

Gradualism

The achievement of EEMU would occur in three stages:

> Stage one represents the *initiation of the process* of creating an economic and monetary union (para. 50).

[It] would center on the completion of the internal market . . . would strengthen economic and fiscal policy coordination (para. 51).

[It] would include all Community currencies in the EMS . . . [but] realignments of exchange rates would still be possible (para. 52).

The *second stage* could begin only when the new Treaty had come into force (para. 55).

. . . While the ultimate responsibility for monetary policy decisions would remain with national authorities, . . . a certain amount of exchange reserves would be pooled . . . [and] regulatory functions would be exercised by the ESCB in the monetary and banking field in order to achieve a minimum harmonization of provisions (such as reserve requirements or payment arrangements) necessary for the future conduct of a common monetary policy (para. 57).

The *final stage* would commence with the move to irrevocably locked exchange rates (para. 58).

. . . with the ESCB assuming all its responsibilities as foreseen in the Treaty (para. 60).

. . . The Council of Ministers . . . would have the authority . . . to impose constraints on national budgets . . . to make discretionary changes in Community resources . . . and to apply . . . structural policies (para. 59).

Parallelism

An important claim in the report is that monetary unification and economic integration cannot fruitfully proceed independently of each other, an axiom the report calls the principle of "parallelism" (para. 42):

Economic union and monetary union form *two integral parts of a single whole* and would therefore have to be implemented in parallel (para. 21).

The reason for parallelism, however, remains vague. On the one hand, "achieving monetary union is only conceivable if a high degree of economic convergence is attained" (para. 21), a proposition no economist would deny. On the other hand, the report fails to establish why MU would be a necessary condition for EU:

The creation of a single currency area would add to the potential benefits of an enlarged economic area because it would remove intra-Community exchange rate uncertainties and reduce transactions cost. . . . At the same

time, however, exchange rate adjustments would no longer be available as
an instrument to correct economic imbalances within the Community . . . .
With parities irrevocably fixed, foreign exchange markets would cease to be
a source of pressure for national policy corrections when national economic
disequilibria developed and persisted. . . . Measures to strengthen the
mobility of factors of production and the flexibility of prices would help to
deal with such imbalances (para. 26).

The role of MU for EU is thus ambivalent; MU may add or subtract from
the benefits resulting from EU. As Goodhart (1989) notes, the loss of a
degree of freedom in adjustment would actually suggest maintaining
exchange-rate flexibility during the creation of EU. The report insists on
parallelism instead:

Community policies in the regional and structural field would be necessary
in order to promote an optimum allocation of resources and to spread
welfare gains throughout the Community (para. 29).

The additional constraint of imposing MU in the transition period raises
the need for market intervention at the Community level and thus works
against the spirit of deregulation embedded in the Europe 1992 program.
Parallelism as the guiding principle for construction of EEMU creates a
predisposition for bureaucratic intervention and centralized Community
decisionmaking. The only justification for this choice can be found in
Jenkins's (1978) speech: to avoid "loss of political support for developing
the Community further into economic and monetary union" (para. 42).

9.2 Alternative Strategies to Achieve EEMU

The fundamental choice concerning a strategy for monetary union
regards the sequence of the events. There are several ways to reach the
goal of EEMU. For a better understanding of the dynamic processes
involved, we compare several alternative strategies in Table 9.1. All
scenarios share the same ultimate objective, EEMU, and the same
beginning, full integration of the markets for goods and services. From
this starting point, the completion of EU requires *elimination of all remaining
constraints* in the financial markets that currently hamper the free flow of
capital within the EC. The steps leading to MU, in contrast, involve
introduction of new constraints on monetary policy making until a unified
monetary system is achieved. Thus, EU and MU are qualitatively different.
The purpose of the following discussion is to evaluate different ways of
timing the elimination and addition of constraints on the road to EEMU.

TABLE 9.1 Alternative Paths to EEMU

	EU		MU			COMMENTS
	Goods and Services	Capital	EMS	ECB	FR	
	Y					Starting point: Integrated goods markets
A1	Y	Y				Integrated goods and financial markets (Europe 1992)
A2	Y	Y		Y	Y	Monetary reform for EEMU
B1	Y	Y				Europe 1992
B2	Y	Y	Y			Centralized policy coordination with flexible exchange rates
B3	Y	Y		Y	Y	EEMU
C1	Y	Y				Europe 1992
C2	Y	Y			Y	Decentralized but coordinated policies (e.g., gold standard)
C3	Y	Y		Y	Y	EEMU
D1	Y		Y			Delors stage 1
D2	Y		Y	Y		Delors stage 2
D3	Y	Y		Y	Y	Delors stage 3 = EEMU

Note: FR means irrevocably fixed exchange rates.

Source: Fratianni and von Hagen (1990e).

Scenarios A, B, and C complete EU first. At this stage, the EC would consist of fully integrated and widely deregulated financial and goods markets, the notion of Europe 1992. National monetary policies remain autonomous and exchange rates flexible until EU is completed, allowing free adjustment of real exchange rates through nominal exchange-rate changes. After this stage, the question is when to impose the new constraints leading to MU. Scenario A proposes introducing MU in one act through a Community-wide monetary reform. This reform would simultaneously transfer all monetary policy authority to the newly created European central bank (ECB) and abolish all nominal exchange-rate variation among EC currencies. This "radical" option must be measured against a variety of alternatives that all achieve MU through a gradual process.

Scenarios B and C take different routes after the establishment of EU (B1 and C1). Step B2 adds an ECB, which would coordinate the monetary policies of the members. The ECB would be an independent institution run by representatives of all participating central banks. Its function would be to formulate consistent monetary policies for all members and to monitor their implementation. Policy coordination would occur with flexible exchange rates that allow the member countries to adjust to idiosyncratic shocks and to converge to a common monetary policy at different speeds. The fact that exchange rates are flexible does not imply that coordination is loose. It can consist of common policy rules, such as monetary targeting. Monetary policy would still be executed at the national level, leaving the national authorities with the freedom to choose their own operating regimes and instruments to implement the common strategy; however, the national authorities would be responsible to the ECB for successful implementation. Step B3 finally fixes all EC exchange rates, clearing the way for MU. At this point, the ECB is transformed into an independent monetary authority for the EC with the power to formulate and enforce monetary policy in the Community as a whole.

In comparison, scenario C rests on a system of decentralized policy coordination with fixed exchange rates. At stage C2, all participants commit to truly fixed exchange rates, but they retain their individual monetary authorities. This is comparable to the Gold Standard, although no metallic or commodity money is necessary to implement this step. Stage C2 does, however, require a well-specified "anchor" for monetary policy in the EC for determining the common inflation rate. Depending on the rules for intervention and sterilization, this role could be assigned to a dominant member or to an outsider by targeting the common exchange rate with an outside currency. Policymaking is decentralized, but each monetary authority must assure the fixity of the exchange rate. Step C3 then adds the ECB as the central policy authority, which assumes the full authority over EC monetary policy at this stage. Compared to scenario B, scenario C has the advantage that decentralized coordination is easier to implement and to monitor. On the other hand, scenario C imposes a tight constraint on exchange rates and therefore gives up flexibility in the adjustment to idiosyncratic shocks at an earlier stage than does scenario B.

In the Delors scenario, scenario D, the road to MU starts from an enlarged EMS including all EC members in the Exchange-Rate Mechanism (ERM). The ERM requires only a small degree of policy coordination because it explicitly permits discrete realignments of exchange rates and, hence, persisting differences in inflation rates among the member countries. The possibility of realignments, however, exposes the ERM to the danger of speculative attacks. The more likely a realignment, the more certain becomes the profit from speculating against the central banks' ability or willingness to maintain the parities. An increasing likelihood of a realignment, therefore, triggers speculative capital flows that force central banks to intervene and deplete their reserves and precipitate the realignment. In view of this threat, the ERM needs capital and exchange controls to survive. Indeed, despite the common perception that such controls are being fully dismantled in the EC, their reimposition remains possible under current EC regulations if short-run capital movements cause significant strain in foreign exchange markets and disturb the execution of monetary policy in a member country (Bofinger 1989, 433; Key 1989, 596). Therefore, stage D1 does not complete EU. Instead, EU and MU are both reached only in the final stage of the Delors strategy. In this sense, making the EMS the basis of MU leads one to accept parallelism.

The ECB is added to the EMS in stage D2, but its functions remain vague. The authority over monetary policy making still rests with the national authorities at this stage. Some aspects of central banking may be transferred to the ECB to give the new institution an opportunity to acquire the skills necessary in stage 3. In this way, the Delors strategy provides for the coexistence of central and decentralized decisionmaking, which is bound to create conflicts among the institutions. Finally, the transition from step D2 to step D3 implies the simultaneous abolition of capital controls, the ending of the EMS, the imposition of irrevocable fixed exchange rates, and the transfer of full monetary policy authority to the ECB. Compared to the alternatives, the move to stage 3 requires both the elimination of the remaining constraints on capital flows and the addition of new constraints to reach MU. The final step of the Delors strategy is therefore less evolutionary than the alternatives and carries the danger of disruptive developments.

Giovannini (1990a) proposes a variant of the Delors strategy aimed at overcoming some of its weaknesses. Giovannini accepts the Delors principles of parallelism and building EEMU on the EMS. His strategy is therefore a variant of scenario D; he adds four main elements to it. First, realignments should no longer be permitted, so that exchange rates would already be irrevocably fixed in stage 1. Second, the participating governments would declare their willingness to counteract turmoil in the foreign exchange and the money markets caused by speculative capital flows by speeding up the final implementation of EEMU. Third, Giovannini gives more content to the functions of the European System of Central Banks (ESCB) during stages 1 and 2. Specifically, the ESCB would consist of an Exchange-Rate Stabilization Authority (ERSA) concerned with maintaining intra-EMS parities, and a board of central bank governors, whose role would be to propose monetary policy strategies for the member countries and to watch over the operations of ERSA and the consistency of the national policies. The national authorities would still retain their domestic monetary policy instruments. Thus, as is true of the Delors strategy, the proposal lacks a clear separation of responsibilities. There are no provisions regarding the sterilization of ERSA foreign exchange market interventions, and the effective authority of the board over ERSA remains unclear. The proposal therefore shares with the *Delors Report* the weakness of setting up an uncertain institutional environment.

Finally, Giovannini proposes a currency reform at the beginning of stage 3, which would fix all bilateral EMS exchange rates to unity. He claims that such a reform would allow the ECU to become the common European currency without the instability connected with a parallel currency (Giovannini 1990a, 16): To convince the public that there is no remaining difference among national currencies, the symbol of the European Currency Unit (ECU) should be added to the currency notes of each member nation (for example, the new deutsche mark note would carry both the DM and ECU logos. It is not clear, however, that a cosmetic reform of this kind would convince people to abandon the well-known national currencies in favor of the new ECU. The ECU might simply become the thirteenth currency in the Community.

In November 1989, the British Treasury put forth an alternative strategy for EMU, the "evolutionary approach to EMU" (HM Treasury 1989), a variant of our scenario B. It accepts the enlarged EMS as a starting point, but envisions a stage 1 that focuses on the completion of EU rather than a strengthening of the ERM. Thus, stage 1 should include (para. 4) "the dismantling of longstanding barriers to the movement of people, goods and services, . . . the strengthening of competition policy, the liberalization of capital movements, the strengthening of coordination of economic and monetary policies, the inclusion of all currencies in the ERM on equal terms." In addition, restrictions barring the residents of one country from using another country's currency should be removed to strengthen currency substitution and competition. Gresham's Law would then work in reverse: Inflation-prone currencies would be driven out of circulation. The proposal rests on the belief that the completion of EU creates sufficient pressures on national monetary policies to enforce the convergence of inflation rates at a low level and eliminate exchange-rate variability. In particular, depreciating realignments would become politically and economically unattractive because they would undermine the credibility of a commitment to price stability. Furthermore, as the more inflation-prone currencies are threatened to be driven out of circulation, the monetary authorities' incentive for inflationary policies would diminish. The result would be an EU in which all participating currencies would be used interchangeably and in which there would be "more or less fixed exchange rates" (HM Treasury 1989, para. 23). The evolutionary approach does not lead to EEMU itself, but it would lay the sound foundations on which MU could be built, if the Community so wished.

The British proposal was amended shortly afterward by a second proposal that envisions the introduction of a strong parallel currency, the "Hard-ECU" (HECU). HECUs, issued and managed by the European Monetary Fund (EMF), would be the thirteenth Community currency. The HECU would participate in the ERM, but would never devalue against any participating currency at realignments. We have argued elsewhere (Fratianni et al. 1991) that the HECU scheme would not work for three basic reasons. First, the HECU would not strengthen EMS discipline over the current arrangement, because the HECU would only be as stable as the most stable national currency in the EMS.[1] This implies that its attractiveness as an alternative currency depends entirely on a considerable degree of realignment uncertainty in the EMS, which contradicts the vision of exchange-rate and price stability in the EC. Second, the "hard" properties of the ECU would force the EMF to suffer capital losses at realignments, which would have to be distributed among participating central banks and would induce the low-inflation countries to try to avoid realignments. Finally, there is doubt that HECUs could displace national currencies. Habit, custom, and switching costs, such as adapting automatic tellers, are strong externalities that favor the use of existing monies over the adoption of new ones.

Long before the current proposals, the All Saints' Day Manifesto (1975) rejected the idea of a sudden currency reform to reach EMU on the ground that it gave the people no choice in the matter. This political reservation is shared by the HM Treasury proposal, which criticizes the *Delors Report*'s penchant for bureaucratic and centralized solutions. The proposal in the manifesto is again a variant of our scenario B. It proposed the introduction of an inflation-proof money as an alternative to existing national monies. With a guarantee of a zero ex-post real rate of return governments could not penalize money holders and, therefore, could not profit from generating unanticipated rates of inflation. With such a parallel currency, the argument went, the cost of adjusting to a common inflation rate would be lower than if exchange rates were rigidly fixed at some date. The proposal required that the national monetary authorities follow money supply or quantity rules, that exchange rates among national monies be flexible, and that the conversion rate between the parallel currency and the national currencies be set by the authorities according to a crawling peg formula. Only when all national monies were replaced with the inflation-proof currency would the ECB gain control of its supply.

9.3 A Public Choice Interpretation of the Delors Proposal

We have pointed out that the Delors committee's approach to MU has a number of strategic deficiencies. The parallelism concept introduces a bias for centralized market regulation. The choice of the EMS as the base of MU increases the cost of learning and therefore biases the process toward premature completion while discouraging the formation of an independent monetary authority for the monetary union. Finally, the call for binding fiscal restraints is largely unjustified. In light of these conclusions, the question arises: What is the motivation underlying the Delors committee's proposal? Public choice theory leads to a club interpretation with central bankers pursuing their own interests.

We start by sketching how EU will change the environment for fiscal policy making in the Community. Assume that the Europe 1992 program is successful in the two important dimensions of goods market and financial integration. Stronger goods market integration will increase intra-EC trade and raise the share of exports and imports in each country's GNP. Financial market integration, independent of the type of exchange-rate regime, will increase the international substitutability of financial assets within the region, particularly at the shorter end of the markets. Thus, each economy in the region becomes more open and more closely integrated in the regional capital markets.

The important implication of these two trends for EU is that national fiscal policies are likely to lose much of their power to control national output and employment, even in the short run. First, as the literature on fiscal federalism remarks, greater openness reduces the traditional Keynesian spending multipliers as a larger percentage of the induced demand spills over to the rest of the Community. Second, standard open-economy macroeconomics, typified in the Mundell-Fleming model, predicts that when there are rigid prices, flexible exchange rates, and perfectly integrated capital markets, fiscal policy becomes ineffective in a small country, because the momentarily higher domestic rate of interest following a fiscal expansion induces capital inflows, an appreciation of the domestic currency, and a complete crowding out of net exports. Only if the country is large enough to affect permanently domestic and world interest rates will the bond-financed increase in government spending succeed in raising domestic output under flexible rates. In contrast, fiscal policy remains effective under fixed exchange rates, because its domestic interest rate effect creates a pressure for appreciation of the home currency and forces the monetary authority to expand the money supply (see, for example, Frenkel and Razin 1987).

Progress toward EU, therefore, implies a power reduction of the national fiscal policy makers. Public choice theory would alert us to expect fiscal policy makers to seek ways to restore their leverage. Given the completion of EU, there are two ways for them to do so. Coordination of fiscal policies among the EC members offers a first way to overcome the relative size problem and to gain market power in international capital markets. Although each individual country is relatively small, the combined size of their financial markets would be sufficiently large to sustain a coordinated fiscal expansion to raise world interest rates. Second, by fixing exchange rates among the Community countries, fiscal policy makers can exert power over the instrument that remains effective even with EU, namely monetary policy. The process of goods market and financial integration thus sets in motion two tendencies among finance ministries: a move toward coordination and a predisposition for fixed exchange rates. It is noteworthy in this respect that in the larger Community countries, the legal power to choose exchange-rate regimes rests with the ministries of finance, not with the central banks.

To the EC central bankers, these tendencies must appear as a serious threat to their political power and independence. According to standard macroeconomic analysis, the imposition of truly fixed exchange rates will degrade national monetary policy to a minor role.[2] Furthermore, fiscal policy coordination will reduce the relative power monetary policy has over fiscal policy. Our interpretation rests on the assumption that central bankers take these developments of fiscal policy as given. In designing the future EC monetary regime, these central bankers therefore have a strong incentive to select strategies that diminish the perceived danger of fiscal dominance.

Interpreting the strategy proposed in the *Delors Report* as a rational response of EC central bankers to this threat requires showing how the

Delors strategy, if adopted, would reduce such a threat. We focus on two elements. The first is the report's insistence on building MU on the foundations of the EMS. The critical point is that monetary policy making rests at the national level. Far from being a true fixed exchange-rate arrangement, the ERM explicitly allows for realignments and therefore requires only a small degree of policy coordination. The *Delors Report* is very clear in this respect. During stage one, it proposes to extend "the scope of central bank autonomy" (para. 52)—to strengthen the position of monetary policy makers vis-à-vis their governments—and to include all Community currencies in the ERM. The main common policy institution at this stage, the committee of central bank governors, would be charged only to formulate and express opinions and write an annual report (para. 52). Similarly, during stage two, the "ultimate responsibility for policy decisions would remain . . . with the national authorities" (para. 55). The final transfer of policy authority to the ECB would occur only in the final stage. In essence, the creation of the ECB within the existing EMS raises the probability that the national monetary authorities will see their interests represented in the ECB but simultaneously lowers the probability of building a truly supranational and independent ECB.

The weak coordination implied by the EMS need not rule out, of course, the possibility of having closer coordination take place for a prolonged period of time, should this serve the interests of the central bankers. The experience since 1987 has made this quite clear. Such coordination, however, is less evidence of a "new EMS" (Giavazzi and Spaventa 1990) than of the simple fact that the adoption of similar policies may occur even without much formal coordination. We conclude that the Delors strategy, though suggesting that the way to MU is best achieved through a gradual strengthening of the EMS, in fact minimizes the loss of policy authority of the national central banks during this process.

The other critical point is the report's call for binding fiscal rules in an MU. These rules are envisioned as a way to guarantee the independence of the ECB in the final stage of EEMU through "exclusion of access to direct central bank credit and other forms of monetary financing" and to limit the scope of independence of national fiscal policy (para. 33). The former has an obvious justification in a monetary union committed to price stability (para. 32). But as noted in Chapter 8, there is no evidence that quantitative limits on national budget deficits assure fiscal discipline. Our interpretation sheds some light on this issue. Referring to the authority of regional and national policy makers in macroeconomic management, the report states that "given their potential impact on the overall domestic and external situation of the Community and their implications for the conduct of a common monetary policy, such decisions would have to be placed within an agreed macroeconomic framework and be subject to binding procedures and rules" (para. 19). To put it more plainly, the mere fact that fiscal policies interfere with monetary policy is sufficient to justify restrictions on governments' scope for independent decisionmaking. Obviously, the Delors committee understood well the enhanced power of fiscal policy when monetary policy is bound by an exchange-rate constraint. The committee did not favor coordination over uncoordinated fiscal policies, but rather took the tendency for coordinated policies as given and wanted to place restraints to safeguard the leverage of monetary policy. It called for binding rules to limit the discretionary power of the fiscal authorities and shift the balance of power in the future EEMU toward the central bankers.

When the *Delors Report* is interpreted as a rational response of the EMS central bankers to the threat of fiscal dominance, it is easy to make sense of the peculiarities of the report's strategy for EEMU. Its inefficiencies and biases are the price for maintaining monetary policy making at the national level as long as possible. The likely result is an ECB consisting of a collection of national interests instead of a true Community institution standing above particular interests.

9.4 Choosing a Strategy for EEMU

Strategies for EEMU must be evaluated on the basis of four fundamental criteria—credibility, flexibility, effective institution building, and the end-game problem—which together determine the cost of transition to EEMU. We now develop these four criteria in detail and evaluate the strategic alternatives for EEMU on their basis.

Credibility

The essence of credibility of monetary policies is that policymakers must find the failure to meet the commitment to a particular preannounced monetary strategy (when it can later be revised) less attractive than to honor it. We have seen in previous chapters that unless a strategy is credible, private sector expectations will not change in a way consistent with it, and policymakers cannot induce the public to behave in the desired way. Without credibility, not only may the goal be unachievable, but the strategy itself may be suboptimal.

On the road to EEMU, the credibility problem is to convince the public that the authorities are firmly committed to the delegation of monetary policy to a common central bank and the permanent fixing of exchange rates, and that withdrawal from this goal will always be the least attractive option. No commitment is credible, of course, if the end itself is unattractive for the majority of the parties involved. But a desirable goal is not enough. EEMU may seem attractive today, but this may change in the future. Unexpected economic shocks and political events may occur that undermine its desirability.

The main advantage of our "radical" scenario A is that EEMU is a *fait accompli* at once, without ifs and buts. Reneging would immediately require formal recession from visible common institutions and would mean reintroducing a national currency. Credibility is thus achieved by imposing a large political cost of withdrawal early on. In contrast, all gradual strategies leave many options to withdraw at a low cost; they therefore have the disadvantage that the public may not believe in the governments' commitment to EEMU because the penalty for abandoning this goal is not perceived to be sufficiently large. As a result, the public may refuse to take bets on EEMU: Interest rates will continue to embed risk premiums for realignments, and wage setters will write wage contracts embedding higher expected inflation rates than warranted if there was no withdrawal (e.g., Giovannini 1990b). This creates market distortions that make EEMU look less attractive and thereby raises the likelihood of a withdrawal.

The Delors strategy and Giovannini's proposal seek to overcome this problem by using exchange-rate policies as a signal of the governments' commitment to EEMU. The *Delors Report* calls for full EMS membership of all EC countries (para. 39). However, as the discussion in Chapters 4 and 5 has shown, EMS membership adds little credibility as long as realignments are possible. Recognizing this weakness, Giovannini in his proposal rules out realignments and adds that a final monetary reform must be undertaken immediately in case of foreign-exchange or money-market turmoil. Ruling out realignments would surely enhance the value of EMS membership as a commitment signal, but Giovannini (1990a, 9) notes that "ostensibly fixed exchange rates have been changed before." As long as national interests count more than EC interest, the probability of realignments will remain.

Giovannini's proposal to speed up the final reform for EEMU rests on the view that destabilizing speculation is the main threat to the EMS in the transition phase. A credible commitment to swift monetary reform in response to speculative capital flows would lower expected speculative profits and thereby prevent speculation from destabilizing the system. Yet this view avoids the more fundamental issue of what determines the expectations behind speculative capital flows. In the absence of convincing empirical evidence that speculation is mainly driven by animal spirits or sunspots, expectations most likely combine information about economic fundamentals with beliefs about the authorities' objectives.[3] Our discussion in Chapter 5 implies that the likelihood of a realignment increases with the size of country-specific shocks and if national authorities have a strong inclination to pursue domestic goals inconsistent with the fixed exchange rate. But in an environment of dominant idiosyncratic shocks and national interests, the threat to speed up the final reform to EEMU in response to speculative attacks lacks credibility itself.

More generally, our view is that fixing exchange rates during the transition phase does not enhance per se the credibility of the commitment to EEMU. The use of fixed exchange rates as a symbol of policy convergence rests on the hope that the power of such a symbol will overcome the underlying economic disparities. This wishful thinking will come true only if the main policy problem today is that European governments are too weak to commit themselves independently to low-inflation policies, and if symmetric shocks to the economies dominate idiosyncratic shocks, so that the need for exchange-rate adjustment to relative shifts in demand and supply conditions between countries is small.

Imposing fixed exchange rates prematurely during the transition to EEMU may even lower credibility. As long as inflation rates have not fully converged, the fixed exchange rate implies a continuous change in real exchange rates and, consequently, in competitive market conditions. Those countries with higher inflation rates will experience increasing competitive disadvantages. But if the public believes that governments will not tolerate such disadvantages for long periods of time, and yet governments do not reduce inflation, then the perceived likelihood of realignments rises, and the credibility of the fixed rate vanishes over time. Private sector contracts and interest rates would embed the likelihood of a realignment and thus add to the failure of inflation and interest rates to converge. This phenomenon is clearly visible in the high ex post real interest rates in French and Dutch money markets compared to the German money market in the late 1980s, which persisted, although realignments did not take place. Eventually, governments may still feel compelled to use the realignment option to reduce the pressures on competitiveness.

At the heart of the credibility problem lies the temptation to use monetary policy in the pursuit of goals other than price stability. Because EEMU is generally deemed desirable only if it entails price stability, removing this temptation would raise the credibility of the commitment to EEMU. The temptation can indeed be reduced by making the central banks in the individual EMS member countries independent of their government and the immediate electoral process and by giving the banks a reward structure favoring price stability.[4] Independent central bankers have no incentive to abuse monetary policy for short-sighted goals and are therefore able to commit credibly to price stability. Central bank independence, on the other hand, is preferable to a rigid monetary rule, because the bank keeps enough policy discretion to respond flexibly to real economic shocks. [5]

This leaves two options to ensure credibility on the road to EEMU: the radical approach of creating an ECB in one step, or a gradual approach in which the national central banks would first be vested with independence and the ECB would later emerge from their fusion. Although setting up independent central banks first may seem like a step backward from the EMS, it would in fact place the transition to EEMU under the control of national monetary authorities credibly committed to price stability and EEMU.

Flexibility

In the transition to EEMU, the monetary authorities in the EC will face greater uncertainty as integration of money and capital markets cause changes in the behavior of money demand and financial institutions and monetary control becomes more difficult. Moreover, the occurrence of severe economic shocks to the Community in the transition phase cannot be ruled out. This suggests that monetary policy should remain flexible enough during the transition to allow for appropriate policy responses though the critical question is what the relative magnitude of the shocks will be. To the extent that idiosyncratic shocks reflect changes in national economic policies relative to the rest of the EC, including regulation of goods and financial markets and income redistribution, the process leading to EU will increase their importance. Once EU is established, however, free mobility of goods and production factors will severely limit the scope and incentives for uncoordinated policy intervention in individual countries, resulting in diminished importance of idiosyncratic shocks. This suggests that nominal exchange-rate flexibility is more valuable during the integration process than after EU has been gained. This contradicts the principle of parallelism advocated by the Delors Commission: The optimal sequence is to achieve EU while retaining exchange-rate flexibility and move on to MU later.

Is there a conflict between credibility and flexibility in the choice of a strategy for EEMU, as suggested, for example, by Giovannini (1990a)? The answer depends entirely on the symbolic value assigned to the exchange rate in the transition phase. The wish to use fixed rates as a signal of commitment to EEMU obviously reduces the scope for flexibility and results in a trade-off between the two criteria. However, no conflict between the two exists at all if the sources of the credibility problem are properly addressed—namely by entrusting the commitment to EEMU to independent central banks.

Effective Institution Building

In view of the uncertainty about monetary control conditions in the future EEMU, the Delors committee concluded that the ECB should be granted a learning phase (*Delors Report* 1989, para. 55): "Stage two must be seen as a period of transition to the final stage and would thus primarily constitute a training process leading to collective decision making, while the ultimate responsibility for policy decisions at this stage would remain with national authorities." The ECB would have time for "learning by doing" to minimize the cost of potential errors of economic policy and acquire the skills necessary in stage three. Indeed, there are important arguments for a learning phase. First, even if the ECB was firmly committed to price stability, there would still be doubt, early on, about whether EEMU is indeed an optimal arrangement. Consequently, countries will want to maintain the option of seceding from the EEMU. Because the economic and political costs of secession are lower early on, it is important to assure that the EEMU functions particularly well in its early phase to minimize the probability of this option being exercised. Poor performance of the ECB, caused by inexperience, would endanger EEMU for inappropriate reasons.

Second, leaping into EEMU with inadequate experience may cost the ECB credibility of its commitment to price stability. Suppose there is a surge in inflation solely because of an error in the ECB monetary control procedure. The public might be unable to differentiate between a control error of an ECB truly committed to price stability and a deliberate monetary surprise. Without previous opportunity to establish its credibility, the ECB would find it difficult to convince the private sector of the true source of inflation.

Despite its desirability, however, there are strong reasons to suspect that a learning process as envisioned in the Delors proposal would not achieve its goal. First, learning by doing assumes *doing*. But the ECB in stage two would have only limited responsibilities and vaguely defined functions. The same criticism applies to the learning processes in Giovannini's proposal and to the HECU proposal. Second, the ECB would face very different policy incentives and constraints during the learning phases than an ESCB controlling a European currency: Currency competition implies competitive central banks; EEMU implies a monopolistic central bank. It is not obvious that a monopolistic ECB can gain much experience in an environment of competing currencies.

A third constraint to a training phase is that the ECB will find it difficult to attract qualified people willing to invest in an institution of little importance and reputation (Bofinger 1989). The Council of Economic Advisors to the German Minister of Economics (1989) warns that a weak institution with vague responsibilities would specialize in activities like coalition building, logrolling, and infighting that prevent the creation of a politically independent Community monetary authority. In the absence of clearly defined functions, members of the ECB may seek control over other aspects of economic policy and pervert the character of the institution (Bank of England 1990a). Furthermore, the coexistence of central and decentralized decisionmaking in stage two of the Delors proposal will create conflict between the institutions, which, in the absence of rules to resolve it, makes room for political discretion in the conduct of monetary policy. Eichengreen's (1991) account of the early history of the U.S. Federal Reserve System provides ample evidence for the adverse effects of uncertain allocation of monetary policy authority on central bank performance. Without clear provisions regarding the sterilization of ERSA foreign exchange interventions and the effective authority of the board over ERSA, Giovannini's proposal shares the same weaknesses. The result is additional uncertainty and a predisposition for decision-making processes and outcomes that reflect political opportunism rather than economic rationale. In sum, a flawed learning phase poses the risk of resulting in adverse performance of the EEMU.

The End-Game Problem

End games arise in the transition from one institutional arrangement to another, when the decisionmakers know the current arrangement terminates at a certain time, and perceive they can influence their relative wealth or income positions in the new arrangement by taking final actions before the old regime expires. An illustrative example comes from the round of wage negotiations between labor and management after German monetary union that took place in the old, formerly socialist companies. Under normal circumstances, the survival of the firm puts a limit on unions' wage demands and management's wage concessions. However, when both sides agree that the firm will go bankrupt anyway, an end game arises. Labor will demand excessive wages to secure generous benefit levels if, as in Germany, unemployment benefits are tied to exit wages. Management has no reason to object, but may have good reasons to concede. Managers who were appointed for political merits under the socialist regime are more interested in building a reputation of concern for workers for future jobs in the union sector than in preserving the firm's viability. The end game predicts exactly what happened during 1990: high wage increases despite falling production, high unemployment, and small productivity gains.

The end-game problem is that incentives change dramatically during an institutional transition—and in ways that are detrimental to both the old and new regime. The same may happen when the EEMU is introduced. Confronted with the announcement of a new currency or permanently fixed exchange rates to be introduced at a certain date, governments have an incentive to enter the new regime with a depreciated currency and a lower real value of government debt. If the announcement specifies a date and a final parity, governments would postpone disinflations to shortly before joining the union. Labor unions, on the other hand, would push for wage hikes shortly before the monetary union begins so as to attain a relatively high level of purchasing power of their wages in the union.

Another type of end game may result from the prospective rules of seignorage distribution in the monetary union (see Chapter 8). For example, if the distribution of seignorage in the new regime depends on the relative sizes of the national monetary bases, governments have an incentive to increase monetary base growth to secure a larger seignorage share for themselves. If seignorage distribution depends on the fiscal stance of national governments, with fiscally weak, highly indebted governments granted a larger share of seignorage, there is an incentive for them to raise budget deficits to increase debt levels shortly before they enter the union; the result is pressures on interest and exchange rates.[6]

The important point is that in the transition phase, governments and the public have incentives to engage in policies aimed at manipulating their position in the new regime rather than assuring sound monetary and fiscal conditions. Optimal end-game strategies will depend on governments' previous fiscal stances, the level of debt outstanding, and the relative size of export industries. They are likely to work against the convergence of economic performance required for the introduction of EEMU.

Theoretically, end games can be mitigated by keeping the conditions and the timing of the transition sufficiently uncertain to the relevant decisionmakers. But in the present case, this is not an option. On the one hand, the transition is necessarily the subject of international agreements and treaties that require time and specificity to pass the national legislative and administrative channels. On the other hand, such uncertainty would require that the timing and conditions are set by an authority other than the participating governments, which, again, is politically unfeasible. Alternatively, end games could be avoided if those parameters of the monetary union that determine the distribution of wealth and income and the competitiveness of the members are tied to empirical criteria determined before the announcement of the final transition to EEMU. For example, the distribution of seignorage might depend on the fiscal stance of national governments in the year (or years) before the announcement. Because the final parities represent one set of critical parameters, this would require that the transition to EEMU be announced only after the convergence of economic conditions and inflation rates is already complete. The same purpose could be achieved by defining entry conditions prospective EEMU members would have to meet for a certain period of time. Such conditions, as currently discussed in the EC, would include maximum inflation rates and upper limits on government deficits.

Finally, critical factors in the relevance of end games will be the extent to which monetary policy in the transition phase depends on government policies and the extent to which governments can change their debt positions significantly in the short run. This suggests that before announcement of the final decision, government power over monetary policy should be curtailed by increasing central bank independence in all participating countries.

9.5 Adjustment to Central Bank Dominance

We argued in Chapter 8 that the private sector would benefit from the central bank regaining full independence vis-à-vis the fiscal authorities. We now give operational content to this concept within the context of EEMU.

Consider a (relatively) high-inflation, high-debt country like Italy wanting to join a monetary union in an environment with a high degree of financial and goods market integration—that is, the situation prevailing today. To simplify the analysis, let the rest of the EEMU exert price leadership over Italy, meaning that prices and interest rates in the rest of the union are given for the Italian economy. Italy has a demand for monetary base

$$(9.1) \qquad\qquad m_t - p_t = at - R_t,$$

where m is the log of the monetary base, p the log of the Italian price level, a the growth rate of Italian output, t time, and R the market rate of interest in Italy. Italy is financially integrated with Germany. If debt is growing faster (slower) than real output in Italy, lira-denominated assets suffer (enjoy) a risk premium:

$$(9.2) \qquad\qquad R_t = R_t^* + E_t s_{t+1} - s_t + \eta_t,$$

where R^* is the interest rate in the rest of the union, E the expectation operator, s the log of the exchange rate (the lira price of one DM), and η the risk premium. There are several possible sources of such a risk premium. Governments can resort to direct capital levies, to debt consolidation (Italy in the 1920s and the 1930s), to administrative constraints on the banking system (Italy in the 1970s and the early 1980s), or to debt repudiation (see Alesina 1988; Fratianni and Spinelli 1991). The risk premium evolves according to

$$(9.3) \qquad\qquad \eta_t = \delta(\alpha - a),$$

where δ is a coefficient and α the growth rate of Italian real debt. Equation (9.3) reflects the intertemporal budget constraint of the Italian government. Debt growth cannot exceed real output growth permanently without at some future time requiring an increase in taxes or a surprise monetary expansion to monetize part of the debt. The risk premium compensates buyers of Italian debt for the capital loss incurred if this would happen. The Italian price level adjusts to the MU price level and a stochastic real exchange rate, $\tilde{q}$,

$$(9.4) \qquad\qquad p_t = p^*_t + s_t + \tilde{q}_t.$$

The monetary base is created by monetizing part of the debt:

$$(9.5) \qquad\qquad m_t = \mu_0 + \mu_1 t + \tilde{\gamma}_t,$$

where μ_1 is the monetization parameter and $\tilde{\gamma}$ a stochastic term.

In the MU, realignments are ruled out and the expected change in the exchange rate is zero. With union price leadership, the monetary base in Italy must adjust so as to maintain the fixed exchange rate. More formally, with $E_t s_{t+1} - s_t = 0$,

$$(9.6) \qquad\qquad R_t = R^*_t + \delta(\alpha - a)$$
and
$$(9.7) \qquad \mu_0 + \mu_1 t + \tilde{\gamma}_t = p^*_t + s_t + \tilde{q}_t + at - c[R^*_t + \delta(\alpha - a)].$$

We set $p^*_t = s_t = 0$ for analytical convenience and solve for the monetary base:

$$(9.8) \qquad\qquad \mu_0 = - c(R^*_t + \delta(\alpha - a)), \ \tilde{\gamma}_t = \tilde{q}_t, \ \mu_1 = a.$$

According to this solution, the monetary base responds positively to output growth and negatively to an increase in the union interest rate R^*

and the risk premium. The more real debt growth exceeds real output growth, the more restrictive Italian money policy must be to prevent a continuous shift into DM-denominated assets. This is the market discipline that ultimately constrains fiscal authorities—and about which the *Delors Report* is very skeptical.

To see the implications of this on Italy's fiscal policy, we begin by defining the budget deficit

$$(9.9) \qquad \text{Def}/Y + R[(1 - \tau)b_y = m_y\,(\dot{M}/M) + b_y(\dot{B}/B),$$

where Def = the primary budget deficit, Y = nominal GNP, τ = tax rate on interest income, B = nominal value of debt, b_y = the ratio of debt to GNP, and m_y = the ratio of the monetary base to GNP. In long-run equilibrium, Italian real government debt cannot grow faster than real GNP, so that the debt/GNP ratio must be constant. The steady-state solution of the debt to GNP, $\overline{b}_y$, is

$$(9.10) \qquad \overline{b}_y = [\text{Def}/Y - m_y(\dot{M}/M)]/[a - R(1 - \tau)].$$

Monetary dominance means that in the monetary union, the fiscal authority has to accept the growth rate of the monetary base as given. Therefore, the money growth rate μ_1 = a implies that the budget deficit must adjust as follows:

$$(9.11) \qquad \text{Def}/Y = \overline{b}_y[a - (R^* + \delta(\alpha - a))(1 - \tau)] + m_y a.$$

Note that an increase in the domestic interest rate forces the fiscal authority to reduce its deficit. Now suppose that the Italian Treasury chooses a debt growth rate that exceeds the growth rate of real GNP. From equations (9.8), the central bank will respond by reducing the monetary base so as to raise the domestic interest rate and prevent continuous capital outflows. In turn, the ensuing rise in the domestic interest rate induces the treasury to reduce its deficit. In this sense, monetary dominance, coupled with the risk premium, exerts discipline on fiscal policy.

According to equation (9.6), the risk premium is proportional to the difference between the growth of real debt and the growth of output. The solutions in equations (9.8) say that the discipline of a noninflationary monetary union translates into a money rule that sets the growth rate of the monetary base equal to the growth of output. Figure 9.1 plots the average value of this difference for the period 1984-1988 for nine countries of the Community. The graph can be interpreted either as an index of country risk or as a measure of the deviation from steady-state equi-

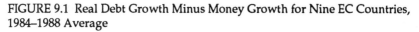

FIGURE 9.1 Real Debt Growth Minus Money Growth for Nine EC Countries, 1984–1988 Average

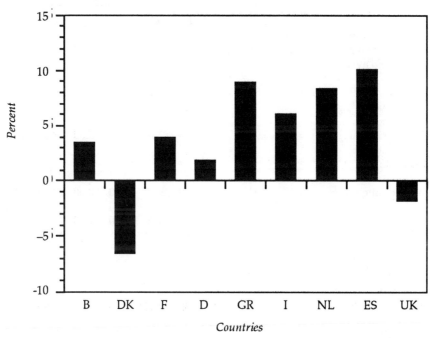

librium. Systematic differences between real debt and output growth are not sustainable.

Table 9.2 explores the budgetary implications of an independent and dominant monetary policy. The question we try to answer is this: Suppose the monetary authorities followed a money rule consistent with the average of the output growth for the period 1984-1988 and wanted to stabilize the debt-to-output ratio at the 1990 value; how would the fiscal authorities have to adjust? This endogenous adjustment is called the required primary deficit in Table 9.2. The last row of the table shows the size of the adjustment from the actual to the required primary deficit using the 1989 values of m_y and τ. Belgium, Greece, Italy, and the Netherlands have been the high-debt countries of the Community. Belgium, Denmark, France, and the United Kingdom had a primary surplus in 1990, an indication of rather conservative fiscal policies in the mid-1980s. Italy has reduced its primary deficit since 1985, whereas Greece continues to be fiscally profligate. Germany, the Netherlands, and Spain show modest levels of primary deficits. Greece, Italy, and Spain have high values of m_y, in part reflecting high reserve requirements.

TABLE 9.2 Required Primary Deficit to Stabilize the Debt Ratio at 1990 Values (percent)

	B	DK	D	F	GR	I	NL	ES	UK
Money rule = a (1984–1988 average)	2.28	2.11	2.52	2.14	2.00	2.96	2.34	3.50	3.40
Net debt/GNP 1990 value	119.60	23.50	23.60	24.70	82.40	97.20	60.00	30.50	30.70
Short-term real rate of interest 1990 value	4.89	5.96	5.13	6.45	–2.10	6.38	5.89	8.06	4.90
Withholding tax	25.00	0.00	0.00	27.00	25.00	12.50	0.00	20.00	25.00
Money base/GNP 1989 value	7.18	4.72	10.50	6.00	20.00	15.60	9.60	22.40	4.30
Required primary deficit/GNP	–1.50	–0.80	–0.35	–0.51	3.35	–2.09	–1.91	–0.12	0.06
Primary deficit /GNP 1990 value surplus = –	–4.00	–2.60	0.90	–1.00	7.60	0.30	0.60	0.90	–2.20
Required adjustment	–2.50	–1.80	1.25	–0.49	4.25	2.39	2.51	1.02	–2.26

Note: B = Belgium, DK = Denmark, D = Germany, F = France, GR = Greece, I = Italy, NL = Netherlands, ES = Spain, and UK = United Kingdom. Primary deficit refers to general government.

Sources: OECD, Economic Outlook N. 45, N. 48 data diskettes; IMF, International Financial Statistics.

Greece, the Netherlands, and Italy would have to make the largest adjustments in their primary deficits. Greece would have to achieve and maintain permanently a primary budget deficit of 3.35 percent of GNP against an actual deficit of 7.6 percent of GNP. For Italy the stabilization of b_y requires a permanent primary surplus of 2.1 percent of GNP; for the Netherlands a primary surplus of 1.9 percent; for Germany a surplus of 0.35 percent; and for Spain almost a balanced primary budget. On the other hand, Belgium, Denmark, France, and the United Kingdom would have to continue the policies already implemented. The positive message of Table 9.2 is that fiscal adjustment is within reach and limited to a small group of the EC countries.[7]

One peculiar feature of Table 9.2 is that Greece, a high-debt and -deficit country, can stabilize the debt-to-income ratio by running a primary deficit instead of a surplus. This results from the negative Greek expost real rate of interest, which in turn reflects the importance of controls on exchange rates and capital flows that insulate Greece from the rest of the world. Once these controls are removed, Greek real rates of interests would have to rise to the Community level, and the Greek government would have to achieve a primary surplus to stabilize the debt-to-income ratio. To see what a competitive cost of borrowing means for fiscal adjustment, assume that Greece liberalized its capital flows and that, as a consequence, real interest rates in Greece rose to the level of real interest rates in Italy. If everything else remains the same, the Greek government would have to run a primary surplus of 1 percent of GNP instead of a deficit of 3.3 percent of GNP to stabilize b_y at the 1990 value. Consequently, the fiscal adjustment of Greece, under a regime of monetary dominance, would be on the order of 8.6 percent of GNP. Italy, on the other hand, no longer relies on strong exchange and capital controls and faces a competitive cost of borrowing. For Italy, the fiscal adjustment to a regime of monetary dominance requires a permanent surplus.

Table 9.3 explores what EMS countries would gain if, as a result of monetary dominance and a commitment of the treasuries to this regime, differences in risk premiums among the Community members disappeared. Table 9.3 assumes that R is equal to 5 percent.[8] Not surprisingly, the gains would be significant for high-debt countries. Italy could run a primary surplus of 0.9 percent of GNP instead of 2.1 percent. The Netherlands could gain more than 50 basis points.

9.6 How Long Should the Transition Period Be?

As the Community prepared for the December 1991 intergovernmental monetary conference to revise the Treaty of Rome, a controversy emerged over the length of stage two. For example, Peter Norman in the *Financial Times* of September 17, 1990, stated:

Mr. Pöhl, influenced by Germany's difficult experience with monetary union, voiced his concern about early institutional changes to Europe's monetary system in a speech in Munich [given at the Mont Pelerin Society General Meeting on September 3] before the Rome meeting. Spain put forward an alternative to Mr. Delors' fast track plan in Rome, that envisages moving to stage two at the beginning of 1994. Stage two would then last for

TABLE 9.3 Required Primary Deficit to Stabilize the Debt Ratio in Absence of Risk Premium (percent)

	B	DK	D	F	GR	I	NL	ES	UK
Money rule = a (1984–1988 average)	2.28	2.11	2.52	2.14	2.00	2.96	2.34	3.50	3.40
Net debt/GNP 1990 value	119.60	23.50	23.60	24.70	82.40	97.20	60.00	30.50	30.70
Short-term real interest rates no risk premia	5.00	5.00	5.00	5.00	5.00	5.00	5.00	5.00	5.00
Withholding tax	25.00	0.00	0.00	27.00	25.00	12.50	0.00	20.00	25.00
Money base/GNP 1989 value	7.18	4.72	10.50	6.00	20.00	15.60	9.60	22.40	4.30
Required primary deficit/GNP	–1.59	–0.58	–0.32	–0.24	–1.04	–0.91	–1.37	0.63	0.04
Primary deficit /GNP 1990 value surplus = –	–4.00	–2.60	0.90	–1.00	7.60	0.30	0.60	0.90	–2.20
Adjustment	–2.41	–2.02	1.22	–0.76	8.64	1.21	1.97	0.27	–2.24

Note: B = Belgium, DK = Denmark, D = Germany, F = France, GR = Greece, I = Italy, NL = Netherlands, ES = Spain, and UK = United Kingdom. The value of the ratio of government claims to money base for Italy comes from 1987, that for the United Kingdom from 1986. Primary deficit refers to general government.

Sources: OECD, *Economic Outlook* N. 45, N. 48 data diskettes; IMF, *International Financial Statistics*.

an extended period of five or six years to enable EC economies to converge before EMU's third and final stage.

Andrew Fisher in the *Financial Times* of September 21, 1990, reported the conditions the Bundesbank considers "indispensable" before moving to the last stage suggested in the Delors committee's document: convergence of inflation rates, harmonization of central bank statutes, rules on budgetary discipline, and full implementation of the single-market program. Given the strength of these conditions, it is fair to conclude that the Bundesbank wants a very long stage two. Its position is consistent with the bank's historical antipathy toward fixed exchange-rate arrangements. Its preconditions are the same as those the "economists" referred to in Chapter 2 stated in the 1970s. The views of the Bundesbank are close to those of the British government, expressed first by Margaret Thatcher and subsequently by John Major, who value EU much higher than MU. The French and Italian governments, in contrast, push for a rapid move to stage three of the Delors proposal.

For political reasons, the German government is more likely to side with the French and Italian governments than with the Bundesbank on the issue of implementing EEMU. The German-Franco-Italian government alliance can use three arguments to justify a rapid move from stage one to stage three. The first is the credibility of the exchange-rate commitment and the commitment to EEMU, as discussed earlier in this chapter. A second reason to favor an early implementation of stage three can be found in the empirical results of Chapter 5, where we showed that France and Italy are underrepresented in the monetary policy making process of the current EMS. By forming a common central bank, these two countries may hope to gain more power in the European monetary policy process than they currently perceive they have. A final reason is predicated on the hypothesis that an early implementation of stage three would facilitate economic and eventually political integration. Furthermore, countries with large public debts, such as Italy, may gain from an early implementation of EMU by counting on the increasing solidarity among the member countries. As we discussed in Chapter 8, such solidarity transforms country risks into Community risk and provides insurance to the fiscally weak members against severe financial crisis.

Articles in the press (e.g., *The Economist*, 1991) suggest that Europe's political leaders have opted for speedy implementation of EEMU: The European Council will be empowered to set the date for the beginning of the third stage of EEMU when it judges that the majority of the member states satisfy five basic "entry" conditions: inflation convergence, long-term interest rate convergence, soundness of fiscal policies, central bank independence, and exchange-rate stability. Although these conditions are numerically quantified, the council will most likely consider a country's movement toward the thresholds over time more important than the strict satisfaction of the convergence targets. Countries that do not meet the convergence criteria when the council sets a date for stage three, will be placed on a "waiting list," and their position will be reassessed at some fixed interval.

In essence, EEMU will be reached at different speeds. The first group of countries—those first to satisfy the convergence criteria—will form its core; the others will have to adjust and converge to the core countries before being granted entry. Obviously, this scheme, would represent a victory for those who insist on EMU as the "coronation" of a long process of economic integration and convergence. However, with the large degree of convergence already achieved among the members of the most likely core group—France, Denmark, Germany, Belgium, Luxembourg, and the Netherlands—this victory does not involve an important setback for the early advocates of EEMU as an instrument to achieve convergence, most notably the French and the Belgian governments and monetary institutions.

For the political economy of EEMU, the agreement to adopt a multispeed approach has two important implications. One is the agreement of the United Kingdom not to veto the EEMU, which will allow the remaining countries to move forward despite the British opposition to a single European currency. The other is the southern EC members' loss of bargaining power in the process, because the multispeed approach allows the core countries to refuse the southern countries' demand for increased financial aid and protective social legislation as a precondition for EEMU.

9.7 Conclusions

Just as there are many ways to Rome, there are many ways to introduce an economic and monetary union in Europe. In this chapter, we have reviewed the main criteria for choosing a particular strategy. On the way to EEMU, institutions and policies should be designed to assure the credibility of the governments' commitment to the final goal, to preserve enough flexibility to react to unforeseen events, to build an efficient European central bank, and to mitigate adverse incentive effects in the transition phase.

The *Delors Report* presented a strategy that relies on four principles: parallelism, gradualism, the EMS as a basis for EEMU, and restrictions on national fiscal policies in the monetary union. Our assessment is that this strategy is not a very promising approach: it favors centralized decision-making, regulatory market interventions, a disruptive transition phase, and the emergence of a monetary authority prone to national political interests rather to credible pursuit of price stability. These deficiencies of the Delors strategy are the price for preserving the influence of the national monetary authorities and for reducing the perceived threat of fiscal dominance.

Our discussion of the strategic alternatives emphasizes what principles ought to be followed in the construction of EEMU. At all stages of the transition phase, EC monetary policy should evolve in an environment in which institutions have clear-cut responsibilities. Central bank independence should be strengthened in the individual EMS countries to mitigate the credibility problem and yet preserve enough policy flexibility. Entry conditions regarding inflation rates and budgetary policies during the transition phase could be used to deal with the end-game problem.

Notes

1. It is noteworthy that the HECU might even have been counterproductive in the 1980s. During this period, the lira and the peseta often fluctuated at the lower end of the exchange-rate band in the ERM. An arrangement like the HECU would have forced the Bundesbank to buy DM for lira and pesetas, leading Germany to deflate further relative to Italy and Spain and promoting policy divergence rather than convergence.

2. We emphasize that our interpretation is built on the assumption that central bankers predominantly reason along the lines of the Mundell-Fleming framework of analysis. The fact that this approach represents the intellectual core of most empirical models designed for studying questions of national policy and international policy coordination gives empirical concreteness to our assumption.

3. Indeed, Giovannini (1990a) contends that irrational speculation is empirically significant. He speaks of "speculative pressures that were not dictated by fundamentals (i.e., self-fulfilling speculation)" and "nonfundamental speculation" by which "speculators provoke exchange-rate turbulence for their own profit" (p. 5).

4. The central bank independence can be regarded in the context of a principal-agent relationship between the electorate (the principal), which agrees on the long-run desirability of price stability but succumbs to the temptation of reneging on the price stability commitment in the short run, and the central bank (the agent), which expects no gain from reneging (O'Flaherty 1990; Fratianni et al. 1991).

5. Bade and Parkin (1987) provide a useful classification to determine the degree of independence of a central bank. In their 1987 study, they conclude that for Switzerland and Germany there is a significant statistical relationship between central bank independence and inflation performance. For a critique and summary of a number of studies in this area see Burdekin and Willett (1991). For a discussion of the strategic aspects of central bank independence, see Neumann (1991) and Fratianni et al. (1991). For a discussion of the Bundesbank example, see Neumann and von Hagen (1992).

6. The end game here resembles the behavior of individual firms in a cartel when cartel profits are distributed according to relative capacities.

7. Similar considerations can be read in *European Economy* (1990, 174).

8. Five percent is approximately the real rate of interest prevailing in Belgium, Germany, and the United Kingdom.

10

Conclusions:
A Strategy for the Transition to EMU

We have come to the end of our analysis of the EMS and European monetary unification. It is now time to underscore the main conclusions. We will not summarize once more the issues but rather highlight the most important points. To conclude, we present a proposal for reform of the EMS that would transform it into a more flexible structure well-suited to achieving the ultimate objective of monetary union.

The purpose of this book was to explain how the EMS came into being, how it works, and how it may develop into a full-fledged monetary union. The overriding explanation for the EMS and its future cause is the desire of policymakers on the European continent to use monetary integration to achieve political union. Germany, the largest country in the Community and the country where the vision of a political union in Western Europe has had the strongest tradition since World War II, has not dominated the EMS in a strategic sense. This assessment runs against the popular wisdom that sees Germany as the hegemon of the EMS, playing a similar role as the United Kingdom played during the period of the Classical Gold Standard and the United States performed in the Bretton Woods system. Yet the theoretical underpinning of the popular view—the idea that countries can "borrow credibility" from a stability-oriented Bundesbank—is frail, and empirical evidence clearly rejects it. In contrast, the Bundesbank did enjoy long-run policy independence in the EMS. Such independence must not be confused with dominance, however, because dominance implies that other countries "submit" themselves to German hegemony, whereas Bundesbank independence merely implies that other countries' policies have no lasting influence on German policy.

Disinflation was a general phenomenon of the 1980s in the industrialized world. In the EMS countries, it turned out to be less successful than in other countries inside and outside the region that did not belong to the system. This means that the success of the EMS cannot be found in its impact on the members' inflation trends, as the popular view claims. Significant success of the exchange-rate system can be found, instead, in the reduction of exchange-rate and inflation uncertainty, in the achievement of greater symmetry of inflation shocks originating in the region, and in a weaker impact of shocks originating outside the region. Monetary policy cooperation in the EMS has paid off by distributing the effects of adverse economic shocks more evenly among the members and by reducing uncertainty in the system. Furthermore, policy cooperation has contributed to the elimination of country-specific shocks rooted in uncoordinated aggregate demand management in the participating countries. Policy cooperation, not an ostensible discipline imposed by an alleged hegemon, is the successful aspect of the EMS.

There is no categorical reason to prefer a monetary union to a regime of flexible exchange rates. The choice between these two approaches depends critically on the nature of the shocks that affect the economies. Flexible exchange rates do better than monetary unions when the economies suffer mainly from idiosyncratic shocks and policymakers hold very different views about economic policies and the best long-run inflation rate; monetary unions do better than flexible exchange rates when the economies suffer mainly from common shocks and there is widespread agreement on policies and the importance of price stability. It is not obvious that significant country-specific shocks can be excluded in the future or that the EC governments have reached a sufficient degree of agreement. Therefore, the EC would do well to preserve a degree of exchange-rate flexibility large enough to cope with unforeseen tensions on the way to an economic and monetary union. In contrast, the EMS has become an artificially rigid system in which some members believe that fixed exchange rates can serve as a credible signal of their commitment to monetary union. But the symbolic power of the fixed exchange rate must remain in doubt as long as policies and institutions that are compatible with the ultimate goal of monetary union have not been put in place. A too-rigid EMS risks not being a credible strategy for EMU and, thus, endangers the success of the EMS becoming a complete monetary union.

We find it appropriate to end our book with a proposal for a strategy that would improve the current EMS as a basis for EMU by making it more flexible and combining it with a gradual institutional reform process. Our strategy consists of five basic elements.

1. The ERM is transformed into a two-tier system. Participating currencies adhere to bands of ±6 percent around the central parities. Compulsory interventions backed with the current financing mechanism of the EMS will be undertaken to defend these bands. Within this wide band, participating

monetary authorities declare voluntary narrow bands, initially of ±2.25 percent as a policy commitment. Interventions to defend the narrow bands are not compulsory and are not eligible for the financing mechanisms provided by the EMS.

Each monetary authority in the two-tier EMS has the option to adhere to narrow bands or to choose the wider band. Governments are free to signal their commitment to price stability and EMU by adhering to narrow bands vis-à-vis the most stable currencies in the EMS and, over time, by reducing their size. The system is not exposed to speculative attacks as exchange rates approach the limits of the narrow bands, because interventions are not compulsory, and consequently, speculators bear the risk of capital losses even at the margins of the narrow bands. Therefore, the two-tier EMS does not need the possibility of imposing capital and exchange controls. The voluntary nature of the narrow-band interventions means that hard-currency central banks in the system cannot be forced to soften their monetary discipline in support of weaker currencies. This fosters the convergence of inflation rates at a low level. The system will tend to be asymmetric between high- and low-inflation members in the sense that the former will be entirely responsible for maintaining the narrow bands they wish to adopt. But this asymmetry is limited to the narrow bands; the following provisions assure symmetry by allowing countries to choose to maintain the inflation differentials they wish.

The specific width of 12 percent of the large band conforms with current EMS practice and hence minimizes formal changes in the current setup. Obviously, if all monetary authorities were to honor a commitment to a narrow band—say, around the DM—the wide band would lose practical importance. During the transition phase to EMU, the wide band functions as a barrier to speculative bubbles and ensures against the exchange-rate effects of very large and sudden asymmetric shocks, such as a banking crisis in a participating country.

2. The council of EMS central bank governors meets at least ten times a year to discuss monetary policy in the EMS and make policy recommendations. Until EMU has been achieved, authority over monetary policy rests entirely with the national institutions. If individual exchange rates move outside the narrow band for more than, say, five consecutive days, the council must meet and discuss the situation. If individual rates move outside the band for more than, say, ten consecutive days, the council must reach and issue a formal decision to realign or to maintain the relevant central parities.

The institution of regular policy meetings of the council resembles existing procedures of national central bank councils. The council of governors would formulate joint monetary targets or other forms of consistent monetary strategies in the EC. This would build experience and provide the information necessary for increasingly closer policy coordination and, eventually, a common monetary policy. On the other hand, our proposal avoids the institutional ambiguity created by a gradual transfer of policy authority from the national to the Community level.

Making realignment decisions regular and formal events would reduce, first, the symbolic and political content of these decisions. This would destroy the current, unfortunate perception in some EMS countries of a trade-off between political commitment to EMU and desirable exchange-rate flexibility.[1] The requirement of a formal realignment decision, on the other hand, would encourage the monetary authorities to state the reasons for the realignment. There is no reason why the private sector would interpret a realignment caused by country-specific shocks as evidence of a weak commitment to EMU. Central bank credibility is earned by the practice of delivering low rates of inflation. Therefore, the two-tier EMS combines credibility with a large degree of exchange-rate flexibility to respond to asymmetric shocks.

Finally, the two-tier EMS creates an early-warning system that assures realignments will be small in the sense that the new central parity will most likely fall within the outer band. In this way, realignments contribute little to nominal and real exchange-rate variability, and the danger of speculative attacks is further reduced.

> 3. All participating governments commit to gradually reducing their influence on monetary policy. The council of EMS central bank governors issues an annual statement on the state of central bank independence to assess how far this commitment has been honored.

The institutional reform thus embedded in the proposal lays the foundation for the creation of an independent European central bank. It forces the participating governments to give up their power over monetary policy before EMU is reached and thereby induces them to adopt budgetary policies compatible with central bank independence on the way to EMU. Furthermore, national central bankers would have much less incentive to manipulate the competitiveness of national industries or the real value of government debt by their policies during the final transition. Note that the criterion applied during the process is the judgment of the council rather than formal legislative criteria. Thus, central bank independence can be achieved de facto and does not require laborious institutional reforms in the individual member countries.

4. The transition to EMU will be marked by both increasing independence of the monetary authorities and a stepwise narrowing of the inner band in the exchange-rate mechanism, features reflecting the growing convergence of the economies and the commitment of the national authorities to fixed exchange rates.

The gradual tightening of the inner band of the EMS can proceed as asymmetric shocks peter out and as the commitment of all members to EMU grows over time. There is no reason, in contrast, to change the width of the outer band.

5. EMU, including the creation of an ECB with full responsibility for European monetary policy, can be announced following a decision by the European Council, but no earlier than, say, three years without a realignment decision, and after the level of independence of the national monetary authorities has been judged comparable to the level desired for the European central bank.

This provision recognizes the political prerogative in making the final decision about EMU. But our provision gives the council of EMS central bank governors a veto power, because it would judge central bank independence and make realignment decisions. The requirement that three years pass without a realignment *decision* rather than a realignment means that for some time before the inception of EMU, exchange rates will not have left the narrow bands for more than nine consecutive days. This would demonstrate a large degree of political and economic convergence as a basis for EMU and put a limit on the importance of end games in the transition phase.

In sum, the two-tier EMS would overcome the main weaknesses of the existing proposals for achievement of EMU. It would be easy to implement and it would foster convergence and policy coordination at the speed chosen by the member governments. Therefore, it would also be a credible and practicable strategy for EMU.

Notes

1. That such a change in political and symbolic value of a monetary policy variable is possible without much difficulty is exemplified by the German discount rate. Up until the mid-1970s, changes in the discount rate received much public attention because they were generally regarded as an indication of future policy intentions. Since then, this role has been taken by other Bundesbank instruments, and discount rate changes go widely unnoticed in Germany. See, for example, Neumann and von Hagen (1992).

Bibliography

Abrams, Burton A., and Dougan, William R. (1986). "The Effects of Constitutional Restraints on Governmental Spending." *Public Choice* 49: 101-116.

ACIR (Advisory Commission on Intergovernmental Relations) (1976). *Significant Features of Fiscal Federalism.* Washington, D.C.: U.S. Government Printing Office.

_____ (1987a). *Significant Features of Fiscal Federalism.* Washington, D.C.: U.S. Government Printing Office.

_____ (1987b). *Fiscal Discipline in the Federal System: National Reform and the Experience of the States.* Washington, D.C.: U.S. Government Printing Office.

Aizenman, Joshua, and Frenkel, Jacob A. (1985). "Optimal Wage Indexation, Foreign Exchange Intervention, and Monetary Policy." *American Economic Review* 75: 402-423.

Alesina, Alberto (1988). "The End of Large Public Debts." In Francesco Giavazzi and Luigi Spaventa (eds.), *High Public Debt: The Italian Experience.* Cambridge: Cambridge University Press.

Allen, Polly A. (1989). "The Ecu and Monetary Management in Europe." In Paul de Grauwe and Theo Peeters (eds.), *The Ecu and European Monetary Integration.* London: Macmillan.

All Saints' Day Manifesto for European Monetary Union (1975). *Economist,* November 1. Reprinted in Michele Fratianni and Theo Peeters (eds.), *One Money for Europe.* London: Macmillan, 1978.

Artis, Michael J. (1987). "The European Monetary System: An Evaluation." *Journal of Policy Modeling* 9(1): 175-198.

_____ (1989). "Roads to EMU." University of Manchester. Mimeograph.

Artis, Michael P., and Taylor, Mark J. (1988). "What Has the European Monetary System Achieved?" In Francesco Giavazzi, Stefano Micossi, and Marcus Miller (eds.), *The European Monetary System.* Cambridge: Cambridge University Press.

Artus, Patrick (1988). "The European Monetary System, Exchange Rate Expectations, and the Reputation of the Authorities." Paper presented at the Conference on International Economic Policy Coordination, Aix en Provence, June 24-25.

Atkeson, Andrew, and Bayoumi, Tamim (1991). "Do Private Capital Markets Insure Against Risk in a Common Currency Area? Evidence From the United States." Working paper, University of Chicago and International Monetary Fund.

Bade, Robin, and Parkin, Michael (1987). "Central Bank Laws and Monetary Policy." University of Western Ontario. Mimeograph.

Baer, Gunter D., and Padoa-Schioppa, Tommaso (1989). "The Werner Report Revisited." In Committee for the Study of Economic and Monetary Union (ed.), *Report on Economic and Monetary Union in the European Community.* Luxembourg: European Community.

Baffi, Paolo (1989). "Il Negoziato sullo SME." *Bancaria* (January): 67-70.

Banca d'Italia (1973). *Relatione Annuale.* Roma: Banca d'Italia.

Bank for International Settlements (1990). *60th Annual Report.* Basle.

Bank of England (1990a). "Central Banking in Europe." Bank of England *Quarterly Bulletin* 30 (February): 59-67.

_____ (1990b). "The United Kingdom's Proposals for Economic and Monetary Union." Bank of England *Quarterly Bulletin* 30 (August): 347-351.

Barro, Robert (1983). " Inflationary Finance Under Discretion and Rules." *Canadian Journal of Economics* 16:1-16.

Barro, Robert, and Gordon, David (1983). "Rules, Discretion, and Reputation in a Model of Monetary Policy." *Journal of Monetary Economics* 12: 101-121.

Basevi, Giorgio; Kind, P.; and Poli, G. (1988). "Economic Cooperation and Confrontation Between Europe and the USA: A Game-Theoretic Approach to the Analysis of International Monetary and Trade Policies." In R. E. Baldwin, C. B. Hamilton, and A. Sapir (eds.), *Issues in US-EC Trade Relations.* Chicago: University of Chicago Press.

Batten, Dallas; Blackwell, Michael; Kim, In-Su; Nocera, Simon E.; and Ozeki, Yuruzu (1990). *The Conduct of Monetary Policy in the Major Industrial Countries: Instruments and Operating Procedures.* IMF Occasional Paper N. 70. Washington: D.C.: International Monetary Fund.

Bean, Charles; Malinvaud, Edmund; Bernholz, Peter; Giavazzi, Francesco; and Wyplosz, Charles (1990). *Policies for 1992: the Transition and After.* CEPS Paper N. 42. Brussels: Centre for European Policy Studies.

Begg, David, and Wyplosz, Charles (1987). "Why the Ems? Dynamic Games and the Equilibrium Policy Regime." In R. C. Bryant and R. Portes (eds.), *Global Macroeconomics.* London: Macmillan.

Bini-Smaghi, Lorenzo (1990). "Issues in the Process of European Monetary Unification." Banca d'Italia. Rome. Mimeograph.

Bofinger, Peter (1988). "Das Europäische Währungssystem und die geldpolitische Kooperation in Europa." *Kredit und Kapital* 21: 317-345.

_____ (1989). "Zum Bericht zur Wirtschafts- und Währungsunion in der Europäischen Gemeinschaft des Ausschusses zur Prüfung der Wirtschafts - und Währungsunion - Delors Bericht." *Kredit und Kapital* 22: 429-447.

Boyer, Russell S. (1978). "Optimal Foreign Exchange Market Intervention." *Journal of Political Economy* 86: 1054-1065.

Branson, William H. (1989). "Financial Market Integration and Monetary Policy." Mimeograph.

Bredenkamp, Hugh, and Deppler, Michael (1990). "Fiscal Constraints of a Hard Currency Regime." Mimeograph.

Brittan, Samuel (1979). "European Monetary System: A Compromise That Could Be Worse Than Either Extreme." *World Economy* 2: 1-30.

Burdekin, Richard C. K., and Willett, Thomas D. (1991). "Central Bank Reform: The Federal Reserve in International Perspective." *Public Budgeting and Financial Management* 3: 619-649.

Caesar, Rold, and Dickertmann, Dietrich (1979). "Einige kritische Anmerkungen zum Europäischen Währungssystem." *Kredit und Kapital* 12(3): 279-312.

Camen, Ulrich (1986). "FRG Monetary Policy Under External Constraints, 1979-1984." CEPS Paper N. 21. Brussels: Centre for European Policy Studies.

Canzoneri, Matthew B. (1982). "Exchange Intervention Policy in a Multiple Country World." *Journal of International Economics* 13: 267-289.

Canzoneri, Matthew, and Gray, Jo A. (1985). "Monetary Policy Games and the Consequences of Non-Cooperative Behavior." *International Economic Review* 26: 547-564.

Canzoneri, Matthew B., and Henderson, Dale W. (1988). "Is Sovereign Policymaking Bad?" *Carnegie-Rochester Conference Series on Public Policy* 28: 93-140.

_____ (1991). *Monetary Policy in Interdependent Economies.* Cambridge, MA.: MIT Press.

Canzoneri, Matthew B., and Rogers, Carol A. (1990). "Is the European Community an Optimal Currency Area? Optimal Tax Smoothing Versus the Cost of Multiple Currencies." *American Economic Review* 80: 419-433.

Casella, Alessandra, and Feinstein, Jonathan (1989). "Management of a Common Currency." In Marcello de Cecco and Alberto Giovannini (eds.), *A European Central Bank.* Cambridge: Cambridge University Press.

CEPR (1989). *The EMS in Transition,* London, Center for European Policy Research.

Chouraqui, Jean C., and Price, R.W.R. (1984). "Medium-term Financial Strategy: The Co-ordination of Fiscal and Monetary Policies." *OECD Economic Studies* 2: 7-49.

Christie, Herbert, and Fratianni, Michele (1978). "EMU: Rehabilitation of a Case and Some Thoughts for Strategy." In Michele Fratianni and Theo Peeters (eds.), *One Money for Europe.* London: Macmillan.

Cohen, Benjamin J. (1981). "The European Monetary System: An Outsider's View." *Essays in International Finance* N. 142. Princeton, NJ: Princeton University Press.

Cohen, Daniel, and Wyplosz, Charles (1989). "The European Monetary Union: An Agnostic Evaluation." In Ralph C. Bryant et al. (eds.), *Macroeconomic Policies in an Interdependent World.* Washington, D.C.: Brookings Institution, Centre for European Policy Research, and International Monetary Fund.

Collins, Susan (1988). "Inflation and the European Monetary System." In Francesco Giavazzi, Stefano Micossi, and Marcus Miller (eds.), *The European Monetary System.* Cambridge: Cambridge University Press.

Commission of the European Communities (1975). "Report of the Study Group Economic and Monetary Union 1980." [Marjolin Report.] Brussels.

_____ (1977). "Report of the Study Group on the Role of Public Finance in European Integration." [MacDougall Report.] Vols. 1 and 2. Brussels.

_____ (1979). "The European Monetary System." *European Economy* 3 (July): 65-111.

_____ (1982). "The European Monetary System." *European Economy* 12 (July): 13-128.

_____ (1984). "Annual Economic Report 1984-1985." *European Economy* 22 (November): 5-53.

_____ (1990). "One Market, One Money." *European Economy* 44: 5-347.

Commission on the Role of Gold in the Domestic and International Monetary System (1982). *Report*. Washington, D.C.: Government Printing Office.

Cooley, Thomas F., and LeRoy, Steven F. (1985). "Atheoretical Macro-economics: A Critique." *Journal of Monetary Economics* 16: 283-308.

Council of Economic Advisors to the German Minister of Economics (1989). *Europäische Währungsordnung*. Bonn.

Council of the European Communities (1970). *Interim Report on the Establishing by Stages of Economic and Monetary Union*. Supplement to Bulletin 11-1970 of the European Communities, the Werner Group, under the chairmanship of Pierre Werner. Luxembourg: Office for Official Publications of the European Communities.

Cukierman, Alex, and Meltzer, Allan H. (1986). "A Theory of Ambiguity, Credibility, and Inflation Under Discretion and Asymmetric Information." *Econometrica* 54: 1099-1128.

Dale, Reginald (1987). "Bonn's EMS Partners Seek Larger Economic Say-So." *International Herald Tribune*, September 28.

Danmarks Nationalbank (1985, 1986). Annual Reports.

De Grauwe, Paul (1985). "Memorandum." In House of Commons, Treasury and Civil Service Committee, Committee on the Financial and Economic Consequences of UK Membership of the European Communities (eds.), London: *Memoranda on the European Monetary System* 5-11.

_____ (1988). "Is the European Monetary System a DM-Zone?" CEPR Discussion Paper N. 297. London: Centre for Economic Policy Research.

_____ (1990). "The Cost of Disinflation and the European Monetary System." *Open Economies Review* 1:147-173.

_____ (1992). *The Economics of Monetary Integration*. Oxford: Oxford University Press.

De Grauwe, Paul, and Verfaille, Guy (1987). "Exchange Rate Variability, Misalignment, and the European Monetary System." Katholieke Universiteit te Leuven. Mimeograph.

Delors Report (1989). Committee for the Study of Economic and Monetary Union, *Report on Economic and Monetary Union in the European Community*. Luxembourg: Office for Official Publications of the EC.

Diebold, F. X. (1988). *Empirical Modeling of Exchange Rate Dynamics*. Berlin: Springer Verlag.

Diebold, F. X., and Pauly, P. (1985). "The Time Series Properties of the Pre-EMS and EMS Exchange Rates." Philadelphia: University of Pennsylvania. Mimeograph.

Dominguez, Kathryn M. (1990). "Market Responses to Coordinated Central Bank Intervention." *Carnegie-Rochester Conference Series on Public Policy* 32: 121-164.

Dornbusch, Rudiger (1980). *Open Economy Macro-economics*. New York: Basic Books.

_____ (1988). "The European Monetary System, the Dollar, and the Yen." In Francesco Giavazzi, Stefano Micossi, and Marcus Miller (eds.), *The European Monetary System*. Cambridge: Cambridge University Press.

_____ (1989). "Credibility, Debt, and Unemployment: Ireland's Failed Stabilization." *Economic Policy* 5: 174-208.

Dowd, Kevin (1988). *Private Money: The Path to Monetary Stability*. Hobart Paper N. 112. London: Institute of Economic Affairs.

Doyle, Maurice F. (1989). "Regional Policy and European Economic Integration." In Committee for the Study of Economic and Monetary Union (ed.), *Report on Economic and Monetary Union in the European Community* (Delors Report). Luxembourg: Office for Official Publications of the EC.

Dreze, Jacques; Wypslosz, Charles; Bean, Charles; Giavazzi, Francesco; and Giersch, Herbert (1987). "The Two-Handed Growth Strategy for Europe: Autonomy Through Flexible Cooperation." Economic Paper N. 60. Brussels: Commission of the European Communities, October.

The Economist (1987). "No Parity of Power in the EMS," September 19.

_____ (1991a). "A German Idea for Europe," July 27.

_____ (1991b). "Memo to Maastricht," November 30.

Eggerstädt, Harald, and Sinn, Stefan (1987). "The EMS 1979-1986: The Economics of Muddling Through." *Geld und Währung-Monetary Affairs* 3: 5-23.

Eichengreen, Barry (1989). "Hegemonic Stability Theories of the International Monetary System." In Richard N. Cooper, Barry Eichengreen, C. Randall Henning, Gerald Holtham, and Robert D. Putnam (eds.), *Can Nations Agree?* Washington, D.C.: Brookings Institution.

_____ (1990). "One Money for Europe? Lessons from the U.S. Currency Union." *Economic Policy* 10 (April): 119-186.

_____ (1991). "Designing a Central Bank for Europe: A Cautionary Tale from the Early Years of the Federal Reserve System." University of California, Berkeley. Mimeograph.

Engle, R. F. (1982). "Autoregressive Conditional Heteroskedasticity with Estimates of the Variance of U.K. Inflation." *Econometrica* 50: 987-1007.

European Council (1990). "Presidency Conclusions." Document SN 424/1/90 Rev 1. Rome; December 14 and 15.

European Economy (1990). "Budgetary Policies in Stage I of EMU." N. 45, December.

Fischer, Andrew (1990). "Bundesbank Adds a Voice to Bonn's Go-Slow Chorus on EMU." *Financial Times*, September 21.

Fischer, Stanley (1987). "International Macroeconomic Policy Coordination." NBER Working Paper N. 2244. Cambridge, MA.: National Bureau of Economic Research.

Fratianni, Michele (1980). "The European Monetary System: A Return to an Adjustable-Peg Arrangement." *Carnegie-Rochester Conference Series on Public Policy* 13: 139-172.

_____ (1988). "The European Monetary System: How Well Has it Worked?" *Cato Journal* 8: 477-501.

_____ (1992). "Dominant and Dependent Currencies." *The New Palgrave of Money and Finance*. London: Macmillan.

Fratianni, Michele, and Salvatore, Dominick (eds.) (1992). *A Handbook of Monetary Policy*. Westport, CT: Greenwood.

Fratianni, Michele, and Spinelli, Franco (1991). *La storia monetaria d'Italia: 1860-1980*. Milano: Mondadori.

Fratianni, Michele, and von Hagen, Jürgen (1990a). "German Dominance in the EMS: the Empirical Evidence." *Open Economies Review* 1:67-87.

_____ (1990b). "Asymmetries and Realignments in the EMS." In Paul de Grauwe and Lucas Papdemos (eds.), *The European Monetary System in the 1990s*. London: Longman.

_____ (1990c). "The European Monetary System Ten Years After." *Carnegie-Rochester Conference Series on Public Policy* 32:173-241.

_____ (1990d). "Credibility and Asymmetries in the EMS." In Paul de Grauwe and Victor Argy (eds.), *Exchange Rate Policies in Selected Industrial Countries*. Washington, D.C.: International Monetary Fund.

_____ (1990e). "Public Choice Aspects of European Monetary Unification," *The Cato Journal* 10:389.

_____ (1991). "European Monetary Union and Central Bank Independence." Indiana University. Mimeograph.

Fratianni, Michele; von Hagen, Jürgen; and Christopher Waller (1991). "From EMS to EMU." Paper prepared for the CEPR and Paolo Baffi Centre for Monetary and Financial Economics Conference *Monetary Policy in Stage Two of EMU*, Milano, September 27-28, 1991.

Frenkel, Jacob, and Aizenman, Joshua (1982). "Aspects of the Optimal Management of Exchange Rates." *Journal of International Economics* 13:231-256.

Frenkel, Jacob, and Razin, Assaf (1987). "The Mundel-Fleming Model a Quarter Century Later: A Unified Exposition." *International Monetary Fund Staff Papers* 34, N. 4, 567-620.

Funabashi, Yoichi (1988). *Managing the Dollar: From the Plaza to the Louvre*. Washington, D.C.: Institute for International Economics.

Giavazzi, Francesco (1989). "The Exchange Rate Question in Europe." In Ralph C. Bryant et al. (eds.), *Macroeconomic Policies in an Interdependent World*. Washington, D.C.: Brookings Institution.

Giavazzi, Francesco, and Giovannini, Alberto (1987). "Models of the EMS: Is Europe a Greater Deutschmark Area?" In R. C. Bryant and R. Portes (eds.), *Global Macroeconomics*. New York: St. Martin's.

_____ (1988). "The Role of the Exchange-Rate Regime in a Disinflation: Empirical Evidence on the European Monetary System." In Francesco Giavazzi, Stefano Micossi, and Marcus Miller (eds.), *The European Monetary System*. Cambridge: Cambridge University Press.

_____ (1989). *Limiting Exchange Rate Flexibility: The European Monetary System*. Cambridge, MA: MIT Press.

Giavazzi, Francesco, and Pagano, Marco (1985). "Capital Controls and the European Monetary System." In *Capital Controls and Foreign Exchange Legislation*, Euromobiliare, Occasional Paper 1, June.

_____ (1988). "The Advantage of Tying One's Hands: EMS Discipline and Central Bank Credibility." *European Economic Review* 32:1055-1082.

Giavazzi, Francesco, and Spaventa, Luigi (1989). "Italy: The Real Effects of Inflation and Disinflation." *Economic Policy* 5:133-171.

_____ (1990). "The New EMS." In Paul de Grauwe and Lucas Papdemos (eds.), *The European Monetary System in the 1990s*. London: Longman.

Giovannini, Alberto (1990a). *The Transition to European Monetary Union*. Essays in International Finance N. 178. Princeton, N.J.: Princeton University Press.

_____ (1990b). "European Monetary Reform: Progress and Prospects." *Brookings Papers on Economic Activity* 2, 217-291.

Glick, Reuven, and Wihlborg, Clas (1990). "Real Exchange Rate Effects of Monetary Shocks Under Fixed and Flexible Exchange Rates." *Journal of International Economics* 28:267-290.

Goodhart, Charles (1986). "Has the Time Come for the UK to Join the EMS?" *Banker* N. 720 (February): 26-28.

_____ (1989). "The Delors Report: Was Lawson's Reaction Justifiable?" London School of Economics. Mimeograph.

Gressani, D.; Guiso, L.; and Visco, I. (1988). "Disinflation in Italy: An Analysis with the Econometric Model of the Banca d'Italia." *Journal of Policy Modeling* 10:163-203.

Gros, Daniel (1990). "Seigniorage and EMS Discipline." In Paul de Grauwe and Lucas Papdemos (eds.), *The European Monetary System in the 1990s*. London: Longman.

Gros, Daniel, and Thygesen, Niels (1988). "Le SME: Performances and Perspectives." *Observations et Diagnostics Economiques (Banque de France)* 24:55-80.

_____ (1990a). "Concrete Steps Towards Monetary Union." In *Governing Europe*, CEPS Paper N. 44. Brussels: Centre for European Policy Studies.

_____ (1990b). "The Institutional Approach to Monetary Union in Europe." Brussels: Mimeograph.

Harris Bank (various issues). *Weekly Review*. Chicago.

Heins, James A. (1963). *Constitutional Restrictions Against State Debt*. Madison: University of Wisconsin Press.

Hirshman, Albert O. (1970). *Exit, Voice, and Loyalty*. Cambridge, MA: Harvard University Press.

HM Treasury (1989). "An Evolutionary Approach to Economic and Monetary Union." London: Mimeograph. November.

Holtfrerich, Carl-Ludwig (1989). "The Monetary Unification Process in Nineteenth-Century Germany: Relevance and Lessons for Europe Today." In Marcello de Cecco and Alberto Giovannini (eds.), *A European Central Bank? Perspectives on Monetary Unification After Ten Years of the EMS*. Cambridge: Cambridge University Press, 1989.

Hughes-Hallett, A. J., and Minford, Patrick (1989). "The European Monetary System: Does It Achieve Its Aims?" Paper presented at the Konstanz Seminar on Monetary Theory and Policy, Konstanz, Germany.

_____ (1990). "Target Zones and Exchange Rate Management: A Stability Analysis of the European Monetary System." *Open Economies Review* 1: 175-200.

International Monetary Fund (various issues). *International Financial Statistics*. Washington, D.C.

Isard, Peter (1989). "The Relevance of Fiscal Conditions for the Success of European Monetary Integration." IMF Working paper WP/89/6. Washington, D.C.

Jenkins, Roy (1978). "European Monetary Union." *Lloyds Bank Review* N. 127 (January): 1-14.

Jozzo, Alfonso (1989). "The Use of the Ecu as an Invoicing Currency." In Paul de Grauwe and Theo Peeters (eds.), *The Ecu and European Monetary Integration.* London: Macmillan.

Katseli, Louka T. (1987). "Macroeconomic Policy Coordination and the Domestic Base of National Economic Policies in Major European Countries." Paper presented at the conference on the Political Economy of International Macroeconomic Policy Coordination, Andover, MA, November 5-7.

Kenen, Peter B. (1969). "The Theory of Optimal Currency Areas: An Eclectic View." In Robert A. Mundell and A. K. Swoboda (eds.), *Monetary Problems of the International Economy.* Chicago: University of Chicago Press.

Keohane, Robert O. (1984). *After Hegemony: Cooperation and Discord in the World Political Economy.* Princeton, NJ: Princeton University Press.

Key, Sidney J. (1989). "A Financial Integration in the European Community." International Finance Discussion Paper N. 349. Washington, D.C.: Board of Governors of the Federal Reserve System.

Kindleberger, Charles P. (1973). *The World in Depression, 1929-1939.* Berkeley and Los Angeles: University of California Press.

Kirchgässner, Gebhard, and Wolters, Jürgen (1991). "Interest Rate Linkages in Europe Before and After the Introduction of the European Monetary System." University of Osnabrück. Mimeograph.

Klein, Benjamin (1978). "Competing Monies, European Monetary Union, and the Dollar." In Michele Fratianni and Theo Peeters (eds.), *One Money for Europe.* London: Macmillan.

Kneeshaw, J. T., and van den Bergh, P. (1989). "Changes in Central Bank Money Market Operating Procedures in the 1980s." BIS Economic Papers N. 23. Basle: Bank of International Settlements.

Korteweg, Pieter (1980). "The European Monetary System: Will It Really Bring More Monetary Stability to Europe?" *De Economist* 128:15-49.

Kremers, Jeroen J. M. (1990). "Gaining Policy Credibility for a Disinflation: Ireland's Experience in the EMS." *International Monetary Fund Staff Papers* 37:116-145.

Krugman, Paul (1987). "Slow Growth in Europe: Conceptual Issues." In Robert Z. Lawrence and Charles Schultze (eds.), *Barriers to European Growth: A Transatlantic View.* Washington, D.C.: Brookings Institution.

Laffer, Arthur B. (1973). "Two Arguments for Fixed Rates." In Harry G. Johnson and Alexander K. Swoboda (eds.), *The Economics of Common Currencies.* London: George Allen and Unwin.

Lamfalussy, Alexandre (1989). "Macro-coordination of Fiscal Policies in an Economic and Monetary Union in Europe." In Commission for the Study of Economic and Monetary Union (ed.), *Report on Economic and Monetary Union in Europe.* Luxembourg: European Commission.

Laskar, Daniel (1986). "International Coordination and Exchange Rate Stabilization." *Journal of International Economics* 21:151-164.

Lawrence, Robert Z., and Schultze, Charles (1987). "Overview." In Robert Z. Lawrence and Charles Schultze (eds.), *Barriers to European Growth: A Transatlantic View.* Washington, D.C.: Brookings Institution.

Lohmann, Suzanne (1992). "Optimal Commitment in Monetary Policy: Credibility Versus Flexibility." *American Economic Review* 82:273-286.

Lomax, David F. (1983). "Prospects for the EMS." National Westminister Bank *Quarterly Review* (May): 33-50.

_____ (1989). "The Ecu as an Investment Currency." In Paul de Grauwe and Theo Peeters (eds.), *The Ecu and European Monetary Integration*. London: Macmillan.

Lucas, Robert E. (1976). "Econometric Policy Evaluation: A Critique." *Carnegie-Rochester Conference Series on Public Policy* 1:19-46.

Ludlow, Peter (1982). *The Making of the European Monetary System*. London: Butterworths.

_____ (1989). "Beyond 1992: Europe and Its Western Partners." CEPS Paper N. 38. Brussels: Centre for European Policy Studies.

Mankiw, Gregory N. (1987). "The Optimal Collection of Seigniorage: Theory and Evidence." *Journal of Monetary Economics* 20:327-341.

Marston, Richard C. (1985). "Financial Disturbances and the Effects of an Exchange Rate Union." In Jagdeep Bhandari (ed.), *Exchange Rate Management Under Uncertainty*. Cambridge, MA: MIT Press.

Masera, Rainer (1987). *L'unificazione monetaria europea*. Bologna: il Mulino.

Masson, Paul R., and Mélitz, Jacques (1991). "Fiscal Policy Independence in a European Monetary Union." *Open Economies Review* 2:113–136.

Masson, Paul R., and Taylor, Mark (1991). "Common Currency Areas and Currency Unions." Working paper. Washington, D.C.: International Monetary Fund.

Mastropasqua, Cristina; Micossi, Stefano; and Rinaldi, Roberto (1988). "Interventions, Sterilization, and Monetary Policy in the EMS Countries (1979-1987)." In Francesco Giavazzi, Stefano Micossi, and Marcus Miller (eds.), *The European Monetary System*. Cambridge: Cambridge University Press.

McKinnon, Ronald (1963). "Optimum Currency Areas." *American Economic Review* 53:717-725.

Mélitz, Jacques (1985). "The Welfare Case for the European Monetary System." *Journal of International Money and Finance* 4:485-506.

_____ (1988). "Monetary Discipline, Germany, and the European Monetary System: A Synthesis." In Francesco Giavazzi, Stefano Micossi, and Marcus Miller (eds.), *The European Monetary System*. Cambridge: Cambridge University Press.

Meltzer, Allan H. (1986). "Size, Persistence, and Interrelation of Nominal and Real Shocks." *Journal of Monetary Economics* 17:161-194.

_____ (1990). "Some Empirical Findings on Differences Between EMS and non-EMS Regimes: Implications for Currency Blocks." *Cato Journal* 10:455-484.

Micossi, Stefano (1985). "The Intervention and Financial Mechanisms of the EMS and the Role of the ECU." Banca Nazionale del Lavoro *Quarterly Review* N. 155:327-345.

Minford, Patrick (1988). "Das EWS—Eine kritische Betrachtung." In Christian Dräger and Lothar Späth (eds.), *Internationales Währungssystem und Weltwirtschaftliche Entwicklung*. Baden-Baden: Nomos.

Minford, Patrick; Rastogi, Anupam; and Hughes-Hallett, Andrew (1991). "The Price of EMU." Paper presented at the 1991 Konstanz Seminar on Monetary Theory and Monetary Policy, Konstanz, June.

Mortensen, Jorgen (1990). "Federalism vs. Co-ordination: Macroeconomic Policy in the European Community." CEPS Paper N. 47. Brussels: Centre for European Policy Studies.

Mundell, Robert A. (1961). "A Theory of Optimal Currency Areas." *American Economic Review* 51:657-665.

Mussa, Michael (1986). "Nominal Exchange Rate Regimes and the Behavior of Real Exchange Rates: Evidence and Implications." *Carnegie-Rochester Conference Series on Public Policy* 25:117-214.

Neumann, Manfred (1991). "Precommitment by Central Bank Independence." *Open Economies Review* 2:95-112.

Neumann, Manfred, and von Hagen, Jürgen (1992). "Monetary Policy in Germany." In Michele Fratianni and Dominick Salvatore (eds.), *Handbook of Monetary Policy in Industrial Countries*. Westport, CT: Greenwood.

Norman, Peter (1990). "Confusion Reigns on the Road to EMU." *Financial Times*, September 17.

Oates, Wallace E. (1977). *The Political Economy of Fiscal Federalism*. Lexington, MA: D. C. Heath.

OECD (Organization for Economic Cooperation and Development) (1987). *Economic Outlook* N. 41 and N. 48 data diskettes. Paris.

_____ (1988). *Why Economic Policies Change Course: Eleven Case Studies*. Paris.

O'Flaherty, Brendan (1990). "The Care and Handling of Monetary Authority." *Economics and Politics* 2:25-44.

Padoa-Schioppa, Tommaso (1985a). "Policy Coordination and the EMS Experience." In W. Buiter and R. Marston (eds.), *International Policy Coordination*, Cambridge: Cambridge University Press.

_____ (1985b). *Wirtschafts- und Währungspolitische Probleme der Europäischen Integration*. Luxembourg: Publications Office of the European Communities.

_____ (1988). "The EMS: A Long-term View." In Francesco Giavazzi, Stefano Micossi, and Marcus Miller (eds.), *The European Monetary System*. Cambridge: Cambridge University Press.

Papadia, Francesco (1976). "L'unita' di conto europea tipo paniere e i suoi usi nel sistema di cambio intracomunitario." *Moneta e Credito*, March.

Pöhl, Karl Otto (1989). "The Further Development of the European Monetary System." In Commission for the Study of Economic and Monetary Union (ed.), *Report on Economic and Monetary Union in the European Community*. Luxembourg: European Commission.

Radaelli, Giorgio (1989). "Stabilita' dello SME, Controlli sui Movimenti di Capitale e Interventi sui Mercati di Cambi." *CEEP Economia* 1:1-36.

Rogoff, Kenneth (1985a). "The Optimal Degree of Commitment to an Intermediate Monetary Target." *Quarterly Journal of Economics* 100:1169-1189.

_____ (1985b). "Can Exchange Rate Predictability Be Achieved Without Monetary Convergence?" *European Economic Review* 28:93-115.

_____ (1985c). "Can International Monetary Policy Cooperation Be Counterproductive?" *Journal of International Economics* 8:199-217.

Roubini, Nouriel (1988). "Sterilization Policies, Offsetting Capital Movements, and Exchange Rate Intervention Policies in the EMS." Ch. 4, Ph.D. dissertation, Harvard University.

Roubini, Nouriel, and Sachs, Jeffrey (1989). "Government Spending Deficits in the Industrial Countries." NBER Working Paper N. 2919, April. Cambridge, MA: National Bureau of Economic Research.

Russo, Massimo, and Tullio, Giuseppe (1988). "Monetary Policy Coordination Within the European Monetary System: Is There a Rule?" In Francesco Giavazzi, Stefano Micossi, and Marcus Miller (eds.), *The European Monetary System*. Cambridge: Cambridge University Press.

Sachs, Jeffrey, and Sala-i-Martin, Xavier (1989). "Optimum Fiscal Policy and Optimum Currency Areas." Harvard University. Mimeograph.

Sachs, Jeffrey, and Wyplosz, Charles (1986). "The Economic Consequences of President Mitterrand." *Economic Policy* 2:262-322.

Sannucci, Valeria (1989). "The Establishment of a Central Bank: Italy in the Nineteenth Century." In Marcello de Cecco and Alberto Giovannini (eds.), *A European Central Bank? Perspectives on Monetary Unification After Ten Years of the EMS*. Cambridge: Cambridge University Press, 1989.

San Paolo (1987). *Ecu Newsletter*. Torino, January.

Sarcinelli, Mario (1986). "The EMS and the International Monetary System: Towards Greater Stability." Banca Nazionale del Lavoro *Quarterly Review* N. 156:57-83.

Schmidt, Helmut (1990a). "Die Bürokraten ausgetrickst." *Die Zeit*, August 24.

_____ (1990b). "Kampf gegen die Nationalisten." *Die Zeit*, August 31.

Schröder, Wolfgang (1979). "Struktur, Funktionsweise und Ziele des Europäischen Währungssystems." *Konjunkturpolitik* 25(4):225-250.

Snidal, Duncan (1985). "The Limits of Hegemonic Stability Theory." *International Organization* 39:579-614.

Stulz, René M. (1984). "Currency Preferences, Purchasing Power Risks, and the Determination of Exchange Rates in an Optimizing Model." *Journal of Money, Credit, and Banking* 16:302–316.

Tabellini, Guido (1988). "Monetary and Fiscal Policy Coordination with a High Public Debt." In Francesco Giavazzi and Luigi Spaventa (eds.), *High Public Debt: The Italian Experience*. Cambridge: Cambridge University Press.

Tanzi, Vito, and Ter-Minassian, Teresa (1987). "The European Monetary System and Fiscal Policies." In Sijbren Cnossen (ed.), *Tax Coordination in the EC*. Deventer: Kluwer.

Taylor, John B. (1988). "The Current Account and Macroeconomic Policy: An Econometric Analysis." In Albert E. Burger (ed.), *The U.S. Trade Deficit: Causes, Consequences, and Cures*. Boston: Kluwer Academic Press.

Thompson, Earl A. (1981). "Who Should Control the Money Supply?" *American Economic Review* Papers and Proceedings 71:356-361.

Todd, Douglas (1984). "Some Aspects of Industrial Productive Performance in the European Community: An Appraisal." *European Economy* N. 20 (July): 9-27.

Triffin, Robert (1960). *Gold and the Dollar Crisis*. New Haven, CT: Yale University Press.

Tsoukalis, Loukas (1977). *The Politics and Economics of European Monetary Integration*. London: George Allen and Unwin.

Tyrie, Andrew (1990). "A Political Economy of Economic and Monetary Union." Working paper, mimeograph.

Ungerer, Horst (1990). "The EMS, 1979-1990: Policies Evolution Outlook." *Konjunkturpolitik* 36:329-362.

Ungerer, Horst; Evans, Owen; and Nyberg, Peter (1983). *The European Monetary System: The Experience, 1979-1982*. Occasional Paper 19. Washington D.C.: International Monetary Fund.

Ungerer, Horst; Evans, Owens; Mayer, Thomas; and Young, Philip (1986). *The European Monetary System: Recent Developments*. Washington, D.C.: International Monetary Fund.

van Ypersele, Jacques (1979). "Operating Principles and Procedures of the EMS." In Philip H. Trezise (ed.), *The EMS: Its Promise and Prospects*. Washington, D.C.: Brookings Institution.

van Ypersele, Jacques, and Koeune, Jean-Claude (1985). *The European Monetary System: Origin, Operation, Outlook*. Brussels: Commission of the European Communities.

Vaubel, Roland (1978). "Why the EMS May Make Inflation Worse." *Euromoney* December, 139-142.

_____ (1980). "The Return to the New EMS." *Carnegie-Rochester Conference Series on Public Policy* 13:173-221.

_____ (1989a). "A Public-choice Interpretation of the Delors Report." Statement at the Conference on the Political Economy of International Organizations, Claremont, California, November 10-11.

_____ (1989b). "Currency Unification, Currency Competition, and the Private ECU: Second Thoughts." University of Mannheim. Mimeograph.

Vegh, Carlos A., and Guidotti, Pablo E. (1989). "Optimal Taxation Policies in the EMS: A Two-Country Model of Public Finance." IMF Working Paper WP/89/40. Washington, D.C.: International Monetary Fund.

von Hagen, Jürgen (1989a). "Monetary Policy Delegation and Fixed Exchange Rates: Credibility, Reputation, and Inflation in the EMS." Working paper, Indiana University School of Business.

_____ (1989b). "Monetary Targeting with Exchange Rate Constraints: The Bundesbank in the 1980s." *Federal Reserve Bank of St. Louis Review* 71, N. 5:53-69.

_____ (1990). "Policy Effectiveness in an Open Multi-Market Economy with Risk Neutral Exchange Rate Speculation." *Journal of International Money and Finance* 9:110-122.

_____ (1991a). "A Note on the Empirical Effectiveness of Formal Fiscal Restraints." *Journal of Public Economics* 44:199-210.

_____ (1991b). "Fiscal Arrangements in a Monetary Union: Evidence from the U.S." In Don Fair and Christian de Boissieux (eds.), *Fiscal Policy, Taxes, and the Financial System in an Increasingly Integrated Europe*. Deventer: Kluwer.

_____ (1992). "Monetary Policy Coordination in the European Monetary System." In Michele Fratianni and Dominick Salvatore (eds.), *Handbook of Monetary Policy*. Westport, CT: Greenwood.

von Hagen, Jürgen, and Fratianni, Michele (1990). "German Dominance in the EMS: Evidence from Interest Rates." *Journal of International Money and Finance* 9:358-375.

_____ (1991)."Policy Coordination in the EMS with Stochastic Asymmetries." In Clas Wihlborg; Michele Fratianni; and Thomas D. Willett (eds.), *Financial Regulation and Monetary Arrangements After 1992*. Amsterdam: North-Holland.

von Hagen, Jürgen, and Neumann, Manfred J.M. (1990). "Relative Price Risk in an Open Economy." *Open Economies Review* 1:269-289.

Walters, Alan (1986). *Britain's Economic Renaissance: Margaret Thatcher's Reforms 1979-1984*. New York: Oxford University Press.

_____ (1990). "Monetary Constitutions for Europe." Paper presented at the Mont Pelerin Society General Meeting 1990; Munich, September 2-8.

Weber, Axel (1990). "European Economic and Monetary Union and Asymmetries and Adjustment Problems in the EMS: Some Empirical Evidence." Discussion Paper 9-90, University of Siegen.

Weiss, Andrew A. (1986). "Asymptotic Theory for ARCH Models: Estimation and Testing." *Econometric Theory* 2:107-131.

Wihlborg, Clas, and Willett, Thomas D. (1991). "Optimum Currency Area Revisited on the Transition Path to a Currency Union." In Clas Wihlborg; Michele Fratianni; and Thomas D. Willett (eds.), *Financial Regulation and Monetary Arrangements After 1992*. Amsterdam: North-Holland.

Willett, Thomas D. (1988). "National Macroeconomic Policy Preferences and International Coordination Issues." *Journal of Public Policy* 8:235-263.

Williamson, John. (1983). *The Exchange Rate System*. Washington, D.C.: Institute of International Economics.

_____ (1990). "Britain's Role in EMU." London. Mimeograph.

Wyplosz, Charles (1986). "Capital Controls and Balance of Payments Crises." *Journal of International Money and Finance* 5:167-179.

_____ (1988). "Monetary Policy in France: Monetarism or Darwinism?" *Finanzmarkt und Portfolio Management* 2:56-67.

Zellner, Arnold, and Palm, Franz (1974), "Time Series Analysis and Simultaneous Equation Econometric Models," *Journal of Econometrics* 2:17-54.

About the Book and the Authors

When the European Monetary System (EMS) was created in 1978, economists on both sides of the Atlantic predicted its inevitable and early failure. But today EMS is alive and well, continuing to defy conventional economic wisdom.

Professors Fratianni and von Hagen address three questions raised by the success of EMS: how it was created, how it works, and how it may evolve into a full-fledged monetary union. They answer these questions in the context of international economics, explaining why countries with very different rates of inflation might be willing to link their currencies and exploring the choice between a currency union, in which several countries adopt the same money, and an exchange-rate union. They also seek to understand whether members of the European Community should all adopt the same currency and, if so, what kind of adjustment process would be best—a gradual transition or a fast one?

Their presentation is always clear and evenhanded, a model of empirical research and theoretical sophistication. This is an essential book for scholars of European integration in particular and of international political economy in general.

Michele Fratianni and **Jürgen von Hagen** are professors at the School of Business at Indiana University and the University of Mannheim, respectively.

Index